THE DISPUTATION OF SERGIUS THE STYLITE AGAINST A JEW

CORPUS
SCRIPTORUM CHRISTIANORUM ORIENTALIUM
EDITUM CONSILIO
UNIVERSITATIS CATHOLICAE AMERICAE
ET UNIVERSITATIS CATHOLICAE LOVANIENSIS

Vol. 339

SCRIPTORES SYRI
TOMUS 153

THE DISPUTATION OF SERGIUS THE STYLITE AGAINST A JEW

TRANSLATED
BY
A.P. HAYMAN

LOUVAIN
Secrétariat du CorpusSCO
Waversebaan, 49
1973

Imprimerie Orientaliste, s.p.r.l., Louvain (Belgique)

D/1973/0602/9

PREFACE

The Disputation of Sergius the Stylite is an important addition to the Syriac corpus of anti-Jewish literature. Its literary form — a dialogue — is unique in this corpus, though it stands in a long tradition of earlier Greek and Latin dialogues. No Syriac anti-Jewish literature has survived from the period between the sixth and the twelfth century A.D. except for Sergius's Disputation. Consequently the work is of historical importance in that it witnesses to the fact that the earlier anti-Jewish polemic was by and large unsuccessful, not only in converting Jews to Christianity, but even in preventing Christians from being attracted to many aspects of Judaism. The necessity for the Jacobite Church in the thirteenth century to promulgate canons aimed at preventing not only lay people but also clergy from attending synagogue services shows that the Syriac-speaking church never overcame this problem.

From the angle of the history of the tradition of anti-Jewish testimony texts the Disputation is extremely interesting, for it shows how firmly rooted this tradition was, so that even as late as the eight century apocryphal quotations which have never formed part of the manuscript tradition of the Bible, could be quoted and regarded as absolutely authoritative. We can be sure that they were regarded as authoritative because they made explicit what, in the opinion of Christians, the prophets really meant to say. The Disputation also throws light on the way in which the vast mass of testimony material was continually reshaped and adapted throughout the centuries, and, in particular, it witnesses to the existence of a biography of Jesus in Old Testament prophecies which we can detect being used by other anti-Jewish writers also. Towards the end of the work the author introduces several extracts from Josephus's *War of the Jews* and so confirms what earlier scholars have suspected, namely, that at one time a complete Syriac version of Josephus's work existed besides the version of the sixth book preserved in the Codex Ambrosianus B.21 Inf.

In the opinion of many scholars Christian anti-Jewish dialogues do not solely represent a literary activity, but also presuppose the existence of real discussions between Christians and Jews. Sergius's Disputation is no exception. Although it has been subjected to a considerable amount of literary editing, signs that it was based on real experience of discussion with Jews can be detected. In the relative inability of both sides to comprehend the other's position, certainly in the stubborn reluctance of each participant to concede that the other has a point, and in the inconclusiveness of its result, the Disputation enables us to understand a little more of the relations between Jews and Christians at the time when the work was written.

The text has been edited and translated from the sole surviving manuscript of the work, BM Add.17, 199, which may be dated to the late eighth or early ninth century A.D. Square brackets indicate conjectural restorations, and round brackets words which, though they have no basis in the text of the manuscript, are necessary to bring out the sense implied by the Syriac. The notes to the Translation include detailed cross references to the other Syriac anti-Jewish literature in an effort to indicate where the author is dependent upon tradition and where his arguments may be original. Occasional references to non-Syriac works are an attempt to show his relation to the anti-Jewish polemic of the wider church.

I wish to express my deepest gratitude to Dr. K.H. Kuhn of the School of Oriental Studies, Durham, for the constant help and wise advice given to me in the production of this edition, particularly in its earlier stage as a Doctoral thesis for Durham University. I wish also to thank Professor Draguet, the general secretary of CSCO, for his detailed help with preparing the work for publication in the Corpus.

New College,
Edinburgh,
August 1971

A.P.H.

BIBLIOGRAPHY AND ABBREVIATIONS

AB = *Analecta Bollandiana*. Brussels.

Acts of Pilate = *Acta Pilati*, ed. C. Tischendorf, *Ea*, pp. 210-332.

Aphraates, *Demonstrations* = *Aphraatis Sapientis Persae Demonstrationes*, ed. J. Parisot, PS, I-II, Paris, 1894-1907.

Ascension of Isaiah = *The Ascension of Isaiah*, ed. R.H. Charles, London, 1900.

Assemani, *Bibliotheca Orientalis* = Assemani, J.S., *Bibliotheca Orientalis*, 3 vols., Rome, 1719-28.

Athanasius, *De Incarnatione* = *Athanasius, De Incarnatione*, ed. F.L. Cross, London, 1957.

b. = *The Babylonian Talmud*, tr. by I. Epstein, *The Babylonian Talmud in English*, London, 1935-53.

Bardesanes, *Book of the Laws of Countries* = Bardesanes, *Liber Legum Regionum*, ed. F. Nau, PS, II, 490-658, Paris, 1907.

Bardy, *Dialog* = Bardy, G., *Dialog, Reallexicon für Antike und Christentum*, vol. 3,928-55, ed. Th. Klauser, Stuttgart, 1957.

Bar Hebraeus, *Chronicle* = Bar Hebraeus, *Chronicon Syriacum*, ed. P. Bedjan, Paris, 1890.

Bar Hebraeus, *Commentary* = Grīghōr (*Abu al-Faraj*), *called Bar-Hebraeus, Commentary on the Gospels*, tr. and ed. W.E.W. Carr, London, 1925.

Barnabas = *The Epistle of Barnabas*, ed. K. Lake, *The Apostolic Fathers*, vol. I, pp. 337-409, Loeb Classical Library, London, 1965.

Baumstark, *Geschichte* = Baumstark, A., *Geschichte der syrischen Literatur mit Ausschluss der christlich-palästinensischen Texte*, Bonn, 1922.

Bedjan, *Homiliae Jacobi Sarugensis* = *Homiliae Selectae Mar-Jacobi Sarugensis*, ed. P. Bedjan, 5 vols., Paris, 1905-10.

Bethune-Baker, *Nestorius and his Teaching* = Bethune-Baker, J.F., *Nestorius and his Teaching*, Cambridge, 1908.

B.J. = Josephus, *Bellum Judaicum*, ed. Niese, *Josephi Opera*, vol. VI.

Blumenkranz, *Juifs et Chrétiens* = Blumenkranz, B., *Juifs et Chrétiens dans le monde occidental*, Paris, 1960.

BM = British Museum manuscript.

BR = Brockelmann, C., *Lexicon Syriacum*, 2nd ed., Halle, 1928.

Burkitt, *Evangelion* = *Evangelion Da-Mepharreshe*, ed. F.C. Burkitt, 2 vols., Cambridge, 1904.

BZAW = *Beihefte zur Zeitschrift für die Alttestamentliche Wissenschaft*. Berlin.

Cedrenus, *Compendium* = *George Cedrenus, Compendium Historiarum*, PG, cxxi, 521-540, Paris, 1864.

Chronica Minora = *Chronica Minora*, ed. I. Guidi, E.W. Brooks, J.B. Chabot, CSCO, Scriptores Syri, III.4, Paris, 1903-5.

Chronicon ad 1234 = *Anonymi auctoris Chronicon ad annum Christi 1234 Pertinens*, tx. vols. I-II, ed. J.B. Chabot, CSCO, Scriptores Syri, III.14-15 (81/Syr. 36 and 82/Syr. 37), tr. vol.I, by J.B. Chabot in CSCO, 109/Syr.56, Paris-Louvain, 1916-52.

CHRYSOSTOM, *Eight Homilies* = JOHN CHRYSOSTOM, *Eight Homilies Against the Jews*, PG, xlviii, 844-942, Paris, 1863.

Codex Ambrosianus = *Translatio Syra Pescitto Veteris Testamenti ex codice Ambrosiano sec.fere vi Photolithographice Edita*, ed. A.M. CERIANI, Milan, 1876-1883.

COMBEFIS, *Illustrium Martyrum* = COMBEFIS, F., *Illustrium Martyrum Lecti Triumphi*, Paris, 1660.

CONYBEARE, *Dialogues* = *The Dialogues of Athanasius and Zacchaeus and of Timothy and Aquila*, ed. F.C. CONYBEARE, *Anecdota Oxoniensia*, Classical Series, part VII, Oxford, 1898.

CSCO = *Corpus Scriptorum Christianorum Orientalium.* Paris-Louvain.

CSEL = *Corpus Scriptorum Ecclesiasticorum Latinorum.* Wien.

CURETON, *Ancient Syriac Documents* = CURETON, W., *Ancient Syriac Documents*, London, 1864 (reprinted, Amsterdam, 1967).

CYPRIAN, *Against the Jews* = S. THASCI CAECILI CYPRIANI, *Testimoniorum Libri Tres ad Quirinum*, ed. G. HARTEL, CSEL, III.1, pp. 33-184, Wien, 1868.

DANIÉLOU, *Études* = DANIÉLOU, J., *Études d'exégèse judéo-chrétienne*, Paris, 1966.

DANIÉLOU, *Theology* = DANIÉLOU, J., *The Theology of Jewish Christianity*, London, 1964.

DbS, *Against the Jews* = *Dionysius bar Salibhi Against the Jews*, ed. J. de ZWAAN, Leiden, 1906.

DbS, *Commentaries* = DIONYSIUS BAR SALIBHI, *Commentarii in Evangelia*, 2 vols. (in 3), tx. vol.1, ed. I. SEDLACEK and J.B. CHABOT, CSCO, Scriptores Syri II.98, 2.1 ed. A. VASCHALDE in CSCO, 95 Syr.47, 2.2, CSCO, 113 Syr. II.99. Tr. vol. I by I. SEDLACEK, adiuvante J.B. CHABOT, in CSCO, Scr. Syr.II.98,2.1 tr. by A. VASCHALDE in CSCO, 98/Syr. 49, 2.2, CSCO, 114/Syr. II.99. Paris-Louvain, 1906-53.

DELEHAYE, *Les saints stylites* = DELHAYE, H., *Les saints stylites*, Brussels, 1923.

Descensus Christi ad Inferos = *Descensus Christi ad Inferos*, ed. C. TISCHENDORF, *Ea*, pp. 417-432.

Dialogue of Athanasius and Zacchaeus = *The Dialogue of Athanasius and Zacchaeus*, ed. F.C. CONYBEARE, *Dialogues*, pp. 1-64.

Didascalia = *Didascalia Apostolorum Syriace*, ed. P. de LAGARDE, Osnabrück-Wiesbaden, 1967 reprint of 1854 edition. English translation by R.H. CONNOLLY, *Didascalia Apostolorum : the Syriac version translated and accompanied by the Verona Latin Fragments*, Oxford, 1929.

DIETTRICH, *Pešitto zum Propheten Jesaia* = DIETTRICH, G., *Ein Apparatus criticus zur Pešitto zum Propheten Jesaia*, BZAW, VIII, 1905.

DOBSCHÜTZ, *Das Decretum Gelasianum* = *Das Decretum Gelasianum de Libris Recipendis et non Recipiendis*, ed. E. von DOBSCHÜTZ, TU, 38.4, Leipzig, 1912.

DODD, *According to the Scriptures* = DODD, C.H., *According to the Scriptures*, London, 1953.

DOWNEY, *A History of Antioch* = DOWNEY, G., *A History of Antioch in Syria*, Princeton, 1961.

DTC = *Dictionnaire de théologie catholique.* Paris, 1903-50.

DUVAL, *La littérature syriaque* = DUVAL, R., *La littérature syriaque*, Paris, 1907.

EISLER, *The Messiah Jesus* = EISLER, R., *The Messiah Jesus and John the Baptist*, London, 1931.

EMERAU, *Iconoclasme* = EMERAU, C., *Iconoclasme*, DTC, VII, 575-95.

EPHRAEM, *Commentary (Armenian)* = *S. Éphrem, Commentaire de l'evangile concordant, version arménienne*, tr. L. LELOIR, CSCO, 145/Arm.2, Louvain, 1954.

EPHRAEM, *Commentary on Genesis and Exodus* = *Sancti Ephraem Syri in Genesim et in Exodum commentarii*, ed. R.M. TONNEAU, tx. in CSCO, 153/Syr.72, tr. in CSCO, 152/ Syr.71, Louvain, 1955.

EPHRAEM, *Commentary (Syriac)* = *Saint Éphrem, Commentaire de l'evangile concordant, texte syriaque (manuscrit Chester Beatty 709)*, ed. and tr. L. LELOIR, Chester Beatty Monographs, 8, Dublin, 1963.

EPHRAEM, *Hymns on Unleavened Bread* = *Des heiligen Ephraem des Syrers, Paschahymnen (De azymis, de crucifixione, de resurrectione)*, ed. E. BECK, tx. in CSCO, 248/Syr.108, tr. in CSCO, 249/Syr.109, Louvain, 1964.

EPHRAEM, *Madrasha on the sons of Shamuni* = *Sancti Ephraemi Syri hymni et sermones*, ed. T.J. LAMY, III, pp. 686-695, Mechliniae, 1882-1902.

EPHRAEM, *Opera Omnia* = *Sancti Patris Nostri Ephraem Syri, Opera Omnia*, ed. J.S. ASSEMANI, S.E. ASSEMANI, and P. MOBARREK, 6 vols., Rome, 1732-43.

EPHRAEM, *Sermon c. Jews* = *Sancti Patris Nostri Ephraem Syri Adversus Judaeos Sermo, Opera Omnia*, III, 209-224.

EPHRAEM, *Sermones de Fide* = *Des heiligen Ephraem des Syrers, Sermones de Fide*, ed. E. BECK, tx. in CSCO, 212/Syr.88, tr. in CSCO, 213/Syr.89, Louvain, 1961.

EUSEBIUS, *Chronicle* = *Die Chronik des Hieronymus* ed. R. HELM, GCS, *Eusebius Werke*, Band 7, Berlin, 1956.

EUSEBIUS, *Ecclesiastical History* = *The Ecclesiastical History of Eusebius*, ed. K. LAKE and J.E.L. OULTON, 2 vols., Loeb Classical Library, London, 1926-32.

EUSEBIUS, *Ecclesiastical History in Syriac* = *The Ecclesiastical History of Eusebius in Syriac*, ed. W. WRIGHT and N. MCLEAN, Cambridge, 1898.

GAVIN, *Aphraates and the Jews* = GAVIN, F., *Aphraates and the Jews*, JSOR, vii(1923,) pp. 95-166.

GCS = *Die griechischen christlichen Schriftsteller*. Berlin.

HAGE, *Die syrisch-jakobitische Kirche* = HAGE, W., *Die syrisch-jakobitische Kirche in frühislamischer Zeit*, Wiesbaden, 1966.

HARRIS, *Ephraem* = HARRIS, J. RENDEL, *Ephraem on the Gospel*, London, 1895.

HARRIS, *Testimonies* = HARRIS, J. RENDEL, and BURCH, V., *Testimonies*, 2 vols., Cambridge, 1916-20.

HARRIS and MINGANA, *Odes* = *The Odes and Psalms of Solomon*, ed. J. RENDEL HARRIS and A. MINGANA, 2 vols., Manchester, 1916-20

HAYMAN, *Sergius* = HAYMAN, A.P., *An Unpublished Christian-Jewish Disputation Attributed to Sergius the Stylite Edited from a Syriac Manuscript in the British Museum (BM Add. 17, 199) with Translation and Commentary*, Doctoral Dissertation of the University of Durham, 1968.

HERFORD, *Christianity in Talmud* = HERFORD, R.T., *Christianity in Talmud and Midrash* London, 1903.

ISHO'DAD, *Commentaries* = *The Commentaries of Isho'dad of Merv*, ed. M.D. GIBSON, *Horae Semiticae*, V-VII,X-XI, Cambridge, 1911-13.

ISIDORE, *Against the Jews* = ISIDORE OF SEVILLE, *De Fide Catholica Contra Judaeos*, PL, lxxxiii, 449-538, Paris, 1850.

ISTRIN, *La prise* = *La prise de Jérusalem*, ed. V. ISTRIN, 2 vols., Paris, 1934-8.

JACOB OF SARUG, *Against the Jews* = *Three Homilies Against the Jews by Jacob of Sarug*, ed. I.K. COSGROVE, Doctoral Dissertation of London University, 1931.

JAMES, *Ezra* = JAMES, M.R., and BENSLEY, R.L., *The Fourth Book of Ezra, Texts and Studies*, III, Cambridge, 1895.

JAMES, *Lost Apocrypha* = JAMES, M.R., *The Lost Apocrypha of the Old Testament*, London, 1920.

JBL = *Journal of Biblical Literature*. Boston - New Haven.

Jewish Encyclopaedia = *The Jewish Encyclopaedia*, New York, 1901-6.

JSOR = *Journal of the Society for Oriental Research*. Toronto.

JSS = *Journal of Semitic Studies*. Manchester.

JTS = *Journal of Theological Studies*. Oxford.

JUSTER, *Les Juifs* = JUSTER, J., *Les Juifs dans l'empire Romain*, 2 vols., Paris, 1914.

JUSTIN, *Trypho* = JUSTIN MARTYR, *The Dialogue with Trypho the Jew*, PG, vi, 471-800, Paris, 1857.

KAHLE, *Cairo Geniza* = KAHLE, P., *The Cairo Geniza*, 2nd ed., Oxford, 1959.

KAWERAU, *Die jakobitische Kirche* = KAWERAU, P., *Die jakobitische Kirche im Zeitalter der syrischen Renaissance*, Berlin, 1960.

KAZAN, *Isaac of Antioch's Homily* = KAZAN, S., *Isaac of Antioch's Homily against the Jews*, OC, 45 (1961), pp. 30-53, 46 (1962), pp. 87-98, 47 (1963), pp. 89-97, 49(1965), pp. 57-78.

KESELING, *Chronik des Eusebius* = KESELING, P., *Die Chronik des Eusebius in der syrischen Überlieferung*, OC. 1 (1927), pp. 23-48, 223-241, 2(1927), pp. 33-56.

KLAUSNER, *Jesus of Nazareth* = KLAUSNER, J., *Jesus of Nazareth*, London, 1928.

KOTTEK, *Bellum Judaicum* = *Das sechste Buch des Bellum Judaicum*, ed. H. KOTTEK, Berlin, 1886.

KRAFT, *Barnabas' Isaiah Text* = KRAFT, R.A., *Barnabas' Isaiah Text and the "Testimony Book" Hypothesis*, JBL, 79 (1960), pp. 336-350.

LACTANTIUS, *Divine Institutes* = LACTANTIUS, *Divinarum Institutionum*, ed. S. BRANDT, CSEL, XIX.1, Wien, 1890.

LINDARS, *New Testament Apologetic* = LINDARS, B., *New Testament Apologetic*, London 1961.

List of Old Testament Peshitta Manuscripts = *List of Old Testament Peshitta Manuscripts*, ed. The Peshitta Institute, Leiden University, 1961.

LXX = The Septuagint, ed. A.E. BROOKE and N. McLEAN, *The Old Testament in Greek*, Cambridge, 1906-. *Septuaginta, Vetus Testamentum Graece*, Societas Litterarum Gottingensis, Gottingen, 1931-.

McGIFFERT, *Dialogue* = *Dialogue between a Christian and a Jew*, ed. A.C. McGIFFERT, New York, 1889.

MANSON, *The Argument from Prophecy* = MANSON, T.W., *The argument from Prophecy*, JTS, 46 (1945), pp. 129-136.

MELITO, *On the Pascha* = *Die Passa-Homilie des Bischofs Meliton von Sardes*, ed. B. LOHSE *Textus Minores*, xxiv, *Leiden*, 1958.

MICHAEL THE SYRIAN, *Chronicle* = *Chronique de Michel le Syrien*, ed. J.B. CHABOT, 4 vols., Paris, 1899-1924.

MICHEL and BAUERNFEIND, *De Bello Judaico* = *Flavius Josephus : De Bello Judaico*, ed. O. MICHEL and O. BAUERNFEIND, 3 vols., Munich-Hamburg, 1960-69.

Mishnah = *The Mishnah*, tr. H. DANBY, Oxford, 1933.

MOMBRITIUS, *Sanctuarium* = MOMBRITIUS, B., *Sanctuarium seu Vitae Sanctorum*, 2 vols., Paris, 1910.

MOORE, *Judaism* = MOORE, G.F., *Judaism in the First Centuries of the Christian Era*, 3 vols., Harvard, 1927-30.

MS = Manuscript.

MT = The Massoretic Text, ed. R. Kittel, *Biblia Hebraica*, 3rd ed., Württemburg, 1962.

Nestle, *Kirchengeschichte des Eusebius* = Nestle, E., *Die Kirchengeschichte des Eusebius aus dem Syrischen übersetz*, TU, xxi, Leipzig, 1901.

Neusner, *Aphrahat and Judaism* = Neusner, J., *Aphrahat and Judaism, Studia Post-Biblica*, 19, Leiden, 1971.

Niese, *Josephi Opera* = *Flavii Josephi Opera*, ed. B. Niese, 7 vols., Berolini, 1885-95.

Nöldeke, *Kottek* = Nöldeke, Th., review of Kottek's *Bellum Judaicum* in *Literarisches Centralblatt*, 26(1886), 882-4, Leipzig.

Nöldeke, *S.G.* = Nöldeke, Th., *Kurzgefasste Syrische Grammatik*, Leipzig, 1898 (reprint, Darmstadt, 1966). English tr. by J.A. Crichton, *A Compendious Syriac Grammar*, London, 1904.

Novatian, *De cibis Iudaicis* = Novatian, *De cibis Iudaicis*, PL, iii, 953-964, Paris, 1844.

OC = *Oriens Christianus*. Leipzig-Wiesbaden.

or. scr. = original scribe.

P = The Peshitta Version of the Bible. For the Old Testament : *Codex Abrosianus*. Trinitarian Bible Society Edition, London, 1954 (reprint of the American Bible Society Edition, Urmia, 1852). *Pentateuchus Syriace*, ed. W.E. Barnes, London, 1914. *The Peshitta Psalter*, ed. W.E. Barnes, Cambridge, 1904. For the New Testament : *The New Testament in Syriac*, British and Foreign Bible Society, London, 1962. *Tetra Evangelion Sanctum, Simplex Syrorum Versio*, ed. G.H. Gwilliam, Oxford, 1901.

Parkes, *Conflict* = Parkes, J., *The Conflict of the Church and the Synagogue*, London, 1934.

Peters, *Jacques de Saroug* = Peters, P., *Jacques de Saroug appartient-il à la secte monophysite ?*, AB, 66 (1949), pp. 134-198.

Petersen, *Treatise* = Petersen, R.H., *Treatise of Dionysius Bar Salibhi against the Jews* Doctoral Dissertation of Duke University, U.S.A., 1964.

PG = *Patrologia Graeca*, ed. J.P. Migne, Paris.

Philoxenus, *Discourses* = *The Discourses of Philoxenus*, ed. E.A. Wallis Budge, London, 1894.

PL = *Patrologia Latina*, ed. J.P. Migne, Paris.

PS = *Patrologia Syriaca, ed.* R. Graffin, 3 vols., Paris, 1894-1926.

PS, *Thes.* = Smith, R. Payne, *Thesaurus Syriacus*, 2 vols., Oxford, 1897-1901.

Psalms Midrash = *The Midrash to the Psalms, tr. from the Hebrew and Aramaic*, by W.G. Braude, 2 vols., *Yale Judaica Series*, 13, New Haven, 1959.

Pseudo-Dionysius, *Chronicon* = *Incerti auctoris chronicon pseudo-Dionysianum vulgo dictum*, 2 vols., tx. of vols. 1-2 ed. J.B. Chabot in CSCO, Scriptores Syri, III.1 (104/Syr.53), tr. of vol.I by J.B. Chabot in CSCO, 121/Syr.66, Paris-Louvain, 1927-52.

Pseudo-Matthaean Infancy Gospel = *Pseudo-Matthaei evangelium*, ed. C. Tischendorf, *Ea*, pp. 51-112.

Resch, *Agrapha* = Resch, A., *Agrapha*, TU, XV.3/4, Leipzig, 1906.

Rosenblatt, *Interpretation of the Bible in the Mishnah* = Rosenblatt, S., *The Interpretation of the Bible in the Mishnah*, Baltimore, 1935.

Rubenstein, *Observations* = Rubenstein, A., *Observations on the Old Russian Version of Josephus' Wars*, JSS, 2 (1957), pp. 329-348.

S^c = The Curetonian Syriac version of the Gospels, ed. F.C. Burkitt, *Evangelion*.

Silvester, *Discussion* = *The Discussion of St. Silvester with the Jews*, Syriac text, ed. E.W. Brooks in Zacharias Rhetor, *Historia Eccl.*, vol.I, pp. 69-93.

SIMON, *Recherches* = SIMON, M., *Recherches d'histoire judéo-chrétenne*, Paris, 1962.

SIMON, *Verus Israel* = SIMON, M., *Verus Israel, Étude sur les relations entre Chrétiens et Juifs dans l'empire Romain (135-425)*, 2nd ed., Paris, 1964.

S.scr. = Serṭā scribe (cf. Introduction to text vol., p.xf.).

TERTULIAN, *Against the Jews* = Q.S.F. TERTULLIANUS, *Adversus Judaeos*, Pl, ii, 595-642, Paris, 1844.

THACKERAY, *Josephus* = *Josephus*, *Works*, tx. and tr. by H.St.J. THACKERAY, R. MARCUS A. WIKGREN, and L.H. FELDMAN, Loeb Classical Library, 9 vols., London, 1926-65.

TISCHENDORF, *Ea* = *Evangelia Apocrypha*, ed. C. TISCHENDORF, Leipzig, 1876.

tr. = translation.

TU = *Texte und Untersuchungen*. Leipzig-Berlin.

tx. = text.

URBINA, *Patrologia* = URBINA, ortiz de, *Patrologia Syriaca*, *Rome*, 1958.

WILLIAMS, *Adversus Judaeos* = WILLIAMS, A.L., *Adversus Judaeos : A Bird's-eye View of Christian Apologiae until the Renaissance*, Cambridge, 1935.

WILLIAMS, *Justin* = WILLIAMS, A.L., *Justin Martyr : the Dialogue with Trypho*, London, 1930.

WRIGHT, *Catalogue* = WRIGHT, W., *Catalogue of Syriac Manuscripts in the British Museum*, 3 vols., London, 1870-2.

ZACHARIAS RHETOR, *Historia Eccl.* = *Historia Ecclesiastica Zachariae Rhetori Vulgo Adscripta*, 2 vols., ed. E.W. BROOKS in CSCO, Scriptores Syri, III.5-6, Paris, 1919-24.

Manuscripts

H = BM Add. 17, 161, folios 31v-43v (Jacob of Sarug's Homilies 1-5 Against the Jews).

J = Paris, Bibliothèque Nationale, Syriac MS 196, folios 202v-205r (Jacob of Sarug's Homily 6 Against the Jews).

S = BM Add. 12, 174, folios 200v-205r (The Acts of Silvester).

INTRODUCTION

CHAPTER I

THE AUTHORSHIP AND DATE OF THE DISPUTATION

For information about the authorship and date of the Disputation of Sergius the Stylite we are entirely dependent upon the sole surviving manuscript of the work (BM.Add.17, 199) [1]. The heading of the manuscript is as follows :—

'The letter (or treatise) of the Blessed Sergius the Stylite of Gousit, which was composed by him against a Jew, who contended that God has no son, and (that) God has not begotten.' (Ch.i.1).

The colophon [2] is clearly dependent upon this heading.

Three references in the body of the work appear to date it fairly precisely :—

(1). 'Behold, your eyes are darkened today, seven hundred years without prophet, without king, without priest, without temple, without city, without altar, and without the putting on the ephod, as Hosea prophesied.' (Ch.viii.5).

(2). 'But now that you worship God, as you assert, and do not reverence idols, and observe circumcision and sabbath, why has this wrath been laid upon you for seven hundred years, and (why) has he not sent to you even one consolation, or prophet, or worthless dream ?' (Ch.viii.6)

(3). 'And (why) are you not ashamed that, behold, for seven hundred years no man has been found among all your people who prays either for a dead or a sick man, and is heard ?' (Ch.xiv.5).

Sergius the Stylite and his Disputation are briefly mentioned by Baumstark [3]. He regards Sergius as a writer of the mid-sixth century, who came perhaps from the region of Emesa. Urbina [4] gives the same information. S. Kazan, in the course of a review of the Syriac anti-

[1] See the Introduction to the Text Volume, pp. IX-X.

[2] Chapter xxii. 19.

[3] *Geschichte*, p. 180.

[4] *Patrologia*, p. 103.

Jewish polemical literature [5], also mentions Sergius and his Disputation and gives the date of his death as A.D.547. As their authority for these statements, Urbina and Kazan refer to Baumstark's *Geschichte* and to the manuscript BM.Add.17, 199; Baumstark refers only to the manuscript. We are driven, therefore, to conclude that none of these authors has actually read the manuscript, and that they are all dependent upon William Wright's description of it [6]. The grounds upon which Baumstark has dated Sergius in the sixth century cannot be ascertained, for Sergius and his Disputation seem to be entirely ignored in the extant Syriac literature [7].

We are thus thrown back upon our manuscript, which must be investigated more closely for the information which it suplies about the author of the Disputation. That Sergius was a stylite is confirmed by the following speech made by the Jew :—

'But I, as one who loves the truth, have drawn near to you, although nothing but my (own) intentions has compelled me, because I marvel at your (adopting an) ascetic way of life on this column, by which action you have devoted yourself to the restraint of an ascetic way of life like this.' (Ch.xviii. 15).

Whether Sergius was orthodox or monophysite is difficult to tell from the Disputation itself; he was certainly not a Nestorian. His one brief excursus into Christology is capable of either an orthodox or a monophysite interpretation :—

'But to the faithful and discerning it is known that the Godhead is three persons, one nature. And one of these three persons — that is to say, the Word — united our nature to himself by means of the God-bearing holy Mary, without confusion and without division.' (Ch.ii.8).

Since Sergius mentions only one ܟܝܢܐ (nature) — that of the humanity of Christ, and one ܩܢܘܡܐ (person) — that of the second person of the Trinity, and since his use of the word ܟܝܢܐ (nature) in the trinitarian formula prevents it from being equated with ܩܢܘܡܐ (person), his language could well be monophysite. On the other hand, it could be perfectly orthodox as the ܕܠܐ ܚܘܠܛܢܐ ܘܠܐ ܦܘܠܓܐ (with-

[5] *Isaac of Antioch's Homily*, OC,46, p. 88.

[6] *Catalogue*, no.DCCXV, vol.II, p. 612f. See the Introduction to the Text Volume, p. IX.

[7] DELEHAYE, *Les saints stylites*, p. cxviiiff, lists all the known stylites; Sergius the Stylite of Gousit is not among them.

out confusion and without division) implies [8]. The doctrinal difference between the monophysite and the orthodox Christians was in reality so small that they can only be easily distinguished by their attitude to the Council of Chalcedon, Pope Leo's Tome, and to the representative theologians of each party, such as Flavian or Severus. Sergius does not make any reference to these in his Disputation.

The date as given in the Disputation needs examining more closely. A comparison with other Christian anti-Jewish works shows that their authors have a tendency to stress the length of the period during which Jerusalem has lain destroyed, and the Jews have been dispersed 'without prophet, priest, or king'. Of the Syriac writers Aphraates [9], Jacob of Sarug [10], and Dionysius bar Salibhi [11], date their works by this method. In non-Syriac anti-Jewish literature this practice is found in *The Dialogue of Papiscus and Philo* [12], *The Dissertation against the Jews Attributed to Anastasius of Sinai* [13], and *The Letter of Rabbi Samuel* [14]. The *terminus a quo* in Sergius's Disputation could be either the destruction of Jerusalem in A.D.70 or the crucifixion of Christ. The former seems to be implied in the text, but we must note that Dionysius bar Salibhi says that the Jews have been dispersed for 1140 years [15], or more significantly that prophets and priests have ceased for 1142 years [16]. If we calculate from the Fall of Jerusalem this gives as the date for Dionysius's work A.D.1210-1212. However Dionysius died in 1171 and the elaborate calculations of ch.viii.7 of his work show that he wrote in 1166 so that the figure 1140 (or 1142) must be calculated from approximately the time of Christ's crucifixion [17]. In view of this it is best to set the date of Sergius's Disputation within the wide limits A.D.730-770.

We note then, that the date implied in the Disputation is widely at variance with that suggested by Baumstark. It is, of course, possible that a scribe has altered ܫܒܥܡܐܐ (seven hundred) in the manuscript from ܚܡܫܡܐܐ (five hundred), but if so, it is difficult to see

[8] See the Translation, ch.ii, n. 18.

[9] *Demonstrations*, I, 944.

[10] H, fol. 43r-v.

[11] *Against the Jews*, i.12, iii.21, iv.3.

[12] §§10,16, McGIFFERT, *Dialogue*, pp. 65,78.

[13] WILLIAMS, *Adversus Judaeos*, p. 175.

[14] WILLIAMS, *Adversus Judaeos*, p. 228, n. 4

[15] *Against the Jews*, i. 12.

[16] *Against the Jews*, iv. 3.

[17] For the problems of Bar Salibhi's chronology cf. PETERSEN, *Treatise*, pp. 260-268.

why he did this. Besides, a date in the eigth century is confirmed by the fact that a large part of the work is taken up with discussion of images of the cross, and pictures and icons of the saints, subjects relevant to the eighth century when the iconoclastic controversy was raging, but less relevant to the sixth century. Moreover, the fact that Sergius makes use of the Syriac version of Eusebius's Chronicle, or Syriac chronographers who drew upon this version [18], argues against a date in the sixth century, since this version was probably made only at the beginning of the seventh century [19]. We may, therefore, accept with reasonable confidence the date in the eighth century which the Disputation itself supplies.

The heading to the manuscript provides two pieces of information which could not have been derived from the work itself. One, the description of the work as a letter (ܐܓܪܬܐ), is dealt with in n.1 to ch.i of the Translation. The other, that Sergius lived in, or came from, Gousit, merits further examination. W. Wright suggests that Gousit was near Ḥomṣ [20] (Emesa), a suggestion which is confirmed by the *Chronicon Anonymum ad 819 Pertinens* which mentions a town Beʿeltan near Gousit, in the region of Ḥomṣ [21].

Michael the Syrian mentions Gousit in connection with a very interesting story [22]. He tells us that in the year A.D. 635, the Byzantine Emperor Heraclius ordered Theodoricus, his brother, to assemble an army and march against the Arabs. When the army arrived at 'a town called Gousit, in the region of Antioch' they came across a stylite on his column, whom Michael describes as a Chalcedonian. The stylite prophesies victory for Theodoricus so long as he, on his part, promises to wipe out the monophysite adherents of Severus of Antioch. The interchange between the stylite and Theodoricus is overheard by a soldier (described by Michael as orthodox [23]) who later, when the Arabs defeat the Romans, mocks Theodoricus for having trusted the prophecy of the stylite.

This story is recounted, no doubt directly from Michael's work, by

[18] See p. 48ff.

[19] Cf. Keseling, *Chronik des Eusebius*, OC, 1(1927), p. 27, 2(1927), p. 54f.

[20] *Catalogue*, vol. II, p. 612f.

[21] *Chronica Minora*, Pars Tertia, tx. p. 245.

[22] *Chronicle*, vol. IV, p. 414f.

[23] i.e. monophysite, since Michael was the Jacobite Patriarch of Antioch and tells the story in order to discredit the Chalcedonian stylite.

Bar Hebraeus [24], and the *Chronicon ad Annum Christi 1234 Pertinens* [25], which also locates Gousit in the region of Emesa.

We must first note that Michael and Bar Hebraeus say that Gousit was in the region of Antioch. This does not conflict with the information contained in the *Chronicon Anonymum ad 819 Pertinens* and the *Chronicon ad Annum Christi 1234 Pertinens*, for the expression 'the region of Antioch' could well include that of Emesa. Gousit, then, was situated somewhere near Emesa, and this fact makes it more likely that Sergius was a monophysite Christian belonging to the Jacobite church. However, the most interesting aspect of this story is that it presents us with an anonymous stylite living in Gousit in A.D.635. Is the coincidence with the heading of our manuscript so strong that we must identify the two stylites?

We have seen above that there are strong arguments for rejecting the opinion that Sergius lived and wrote his Disputation in the sixth century. There are no arguments in favour of a date in the seventh century except the fact that we know that a stylite lived in Gousit in A.D. 635. The statement that this stylite was a Chalcedonian is of no help, since we have seen that Sergius's language can be interpreted as either Chalcedonian or monophysite. The stylite in Michael's story is an ardent supporter of Chalcedonian orthodoxy, whereas in his Disputation Sergius shows no sign of being interested in Christological controversy. But neither of these observations is of much value, since, on the one hand Michael tells his story with a very pronounced anti-Chalcedonian bias which should make us wary of accepting all the details of the story, while on the other hand, there is no reason why Sergius's Disputation, concerned as it is with anti-Jewish polemic, should mention the internal doctrinal disputes of the Christian church.

Supposing, however, that we make the identification of the two stylites, how are we to account for the threefold occurrence in the text of the Disputation of ܫܢ̈ܝܐ ܫܒܥܡܐܐ (seven hundred years)? If it only occurred once, it would be possible to regard it as a scribal error, but its threefold occurrence rules out this possibility. If ܫܬܡܐܐ (six hundred) was originally present in the text, it is extremely difficult to see why a scribe should deliberately alter it to ܫܒܥܡܐܐ (seven hundred). If we are dealing with an eighth century work falsely attri-

[24] *Chronicle*, p. 100.

[25] *Chronicon ad 1234*, tx.vol.I, p. 242ff.

buted to a seventh century author, the real author must be convicted of gross incompetence at providing a convincing pseudonym. In fact, any attempt at identifying these two stylites founders on the internal dating of the work in our manuscript. Besides, it is still relevant to recall that the Disputation seems more at home in the century of the iconoclastic controversy than in any earlier period. We must conclude, therefore, that Michael's story is of little value for our purposes. However, the existence of two stylites in Gousit, separated by more than a century, does suggest that a colony of stylites had established itself there [26]. Probably several generations of stylites took over columns left vacant by the deaths of their previous occupants. It is, of course, even possible that there was only one column in Gousit, and that we are presented with two successive occupants of the same column. Either way, Michael's story increases our confidence in the historicity of Sergius the Stylite.

We have, therefore, to be content with the meagre facts that the Disputation was written by an otherwise unknown stylite, named Sergius, probably a member of the Syrian monophysite church, who composed it either around A.D.730 or 770 in a town called Gousit, situated somewhere near Emesa in Syria. Whether Sergius actually wrote the Disputation as it now stands, or whether his conversation with a Jew has been expanded into the present work by another hand, will have to be considered in a later chapter [27].

CHAPTER II

THE LITERARY SOURCES OF THE DISPUTATION

A. The Bible

In any discussion between a Christian and a Jew the Bible was bound to play a principal part, for it was common ground to them both. In fact, most Christian/Jewish dialogues are little more than extended series of arguments about the proper interpretation of the Old Testament. Sergius's Disputation is no exception; almost the whole of the work is devoted to the discussion of the interpretation of a large number of Old Testament texts, something like 300 in all. The New Testament

[26] Cf. Delehaye, *Les saints stylites*, who describes how colonies of ascetics grew up around famous stylites.

[27] See pp. 67ff below.

is used less frequently being quoted about 40 times (except for the cases where it provides the text of Old Testament quotations). The situation with regard to the text of these biblical quotations is exceedingly complex. Sometimes the Peshitta version of both the Old and the New Testaments is quoted. Sometimes the disputants quote from memory. Frequently, where an Old Testament text is cited in the New Testament, it is reproduced in the Disputation in its New Testament form. Often the author reshapes Old Testament texts to make them conform more easily to the Christian interpretation which he wishes to give them, or he even interpolates this interpretation into the quotation itself. On one or two occasions we can observe reminiscences of the Old Syriac versions of the New Testament. Most important of all, there is a clearly defined block of quotations, which have no basis in the biblical text as we know it but belong to the class of agrapha. The whole situation is, however, further complicated by the fact that, since we possess only one manuscript of Sergius's Disputation, we cannot tell to what extent the scribe of this manuscript has rendered the biblical quotations faithfully or has inserted the text with which he was most familiar. This proviso must be continually born in mind.

The biblical quotations [1] can be arranged into the following four groups :—

1. *Quotations from the Peshitta version of the Bible*

Excluding for the moment those texts which belong to group 2, about 130 of the Disputation's biblical quotations exactly reproduce the Peshitta text. Some of them, for example the quotation of Is.66.16-22 (ch.xx.6), are so long that it seems unlikely, though not impossible, that they are the result of quotation from memory. Two of these quotations provide good examples of Sergius's method of biblical interpretation. In his quotation of Ps.146.7f (ch.i.13) he interpolates into the text references to its New Testament fulfillment. In his quotation of Ps.82. 2-5 (ch.xv.20) he interpolates explanatory additions and omits other phrases, all of which serves the purpose of bringing out the interpretation he requires. As we shall see, however, Sergius is quite capable of substantially altering the biblical text itself in order to make it serve his purpose.

[1] The agrapha, and those quotations which exhibit peculiar texts having no basis in the extant ancient versions of the Bible, will be dealt with in a separate section ; see below, pp. 9ff.

2. *Old Testament quotations following or influenced by the text of the New Testament*

This group of 14 quotations consists mainly of well known *testimony texts*, that is, biblical texts commonly used by early Christian writers as evidence for the foreshadowing of Christ and the Church in the Old Testament, and for the rejection of the Jews as God's chosen people. A typical example is the quotation of Jer.31.15 in ch.i.7 where the author follows the text of Mt.2.18. Many of these quotations exhibit mixed texts; for example, Is.61.1f. (ch.i.12), where the word ܡܩܒܠܬܐ (acceptable) comes from Lk.4.19.

3. *Quotations from memory*

This group, consisting of approximately 75 quotations, gives us a better idea than any other of the way in which Sergius treats the Bible. Although many of the variations from the Peshitta may be no more than accidental (and some, of course, may be due to scribal error), some alterations are clearly deliberate. In Sergius's mind text and interpretation become fused together into an inseparable whole; his practice is not unlike that of the Jews and Jewish Christians who regarded text and interpretation as equally authoritative [2]. For example, his treatment of Dan.9.24 (ch.i.15) carries much further a process begun in the Peshitta itself — the Christianization of an Old Testament text. In ch. xi.15 Sergius has turned Ps.47.9 into a prophecy by reading ܢܬܦܢܘܢ (they shall turn) for the ܐܬܦܢܘ (they turned) of the Peshitta. And in ch.ii.5 he has added ܘܡܠܬܗ (and his Word) to the Peshitta text of Is.48.16, in order to find a reference to all three Persons of the Trinity. There are many other examples like these.

4. *New Testament quotations influenced by the Old Syriac versions*

Four quotations or allusions seem to reflect knowledge of Old Syriac readings : Jn.1.14 (ch.vii.2), Jn.4.6 (ch.vii.4), Mt.3.17,17.5 (ch.ix.13), and Lk.23.48 (ch.xxi.1).

This brief survey of Sergius's handling of the biblical text [3] reveals the the striking flexibility of his approach. He feels by no means bound by the actual 'letter' of the text, but regards both 'letter' and 'spirit' as equally authoritative [4]. This is made easier for him by his habitual

[2] Cf. Daniélou, *Études*, passim, and n.4 below.

[3] For a more detailed survey see Hayman, *Sergius*, pp. 14-25.

[4] 'Accurate reproduction of the traditional wording of the Divine oracles took second

practice of quoting from memory, for we may be certain that in many cases the quotations in the Disputation have been harmonised to the Peshitta; the notes to the Syriac Text reveal that the Serṭā corrector frequently corrects the manuscript along these lines, no doubt continuing an already existing process. Of course, there will be many occasions where Sergius manages to quote the Peshitta accurately from memory. Nonetheless, the overriding impression we get from this work is that of a very firmly established tradition of exegesis, strong enough to invade and remould the text of the Bible.

B. The Testimony Book

1. *Biblical quotations and Agrapha*

There is in the Disputation a series of biblical quotations and agrapha which merit special attention, since there is good reason to believe that Sergius derived these, not from the Bible, but from a special collection of *testimony texts* specifically designed for use in anti-Jewish polemic. The relevant texts, taken in the order of their appearance in the Disputation, are as follows :—

a) *Zech.3.1f* (*Ch.i.11*).

A comparison of the form of this quotation as it appears in the Disputation with that found in the *Discussion of St. Silvester with the Jews* [5] reveals the following interesting facts :—

a) Sergius's Disputation and the *Discussion of St. Silvester* agree together against P, MT, LXX, by reading ܚܙܝܬ (I saw) in v.1 instead of ܚܘܝܢܝ (he showed me).
b) Also in v.1 they agree against P, MT, LXX, in omitting ܩܕܡ ܡܠܐܟܗ ܕܡܪܝܐ (before the angel of the Lord).
c) They agree in omitting the subject of v.2; in the case of MT and LXX יהוה, ὁ κυρίος (the Lord), and in the case of P ܡܠܐܟܗ ܕܡܪܝܐ (the angel of the Lord) [6].

place to publication of what was held to be their essential meaning and immediate application', Manson, *The Argument from Prophecy*, JTS, 46(1945), p. 136.

[5] Silvester, *Discussion*, p. 74f. The Greek version of the *Discussion* is edited in Combefis, *Illustrium Martyrum*, pp. 290-336, while an abbreviated account of the story appears in Cedrenus, *Compendium*, 521-540. The Latin version is edited in Mombritus, *Sanctuarium*, vol.II, pp. 517-529. For a detailed discussion of this work see below, pp. 15-22.

[6] S.scr. corrects to P by adding ܡܠܐܟܐ in the margin.

In the rest of v.2 the Disputation diverges from the *Discussion of St. Silvester* and follows the Peshitta more closely.

It is interesting to observe that Justin Martyr, in citing Zech.3.1f [7], agrees with Sergius's Disputation and the *Discussion of St.Silvester* in points b) and c) [8]. He has a further agreement with the latter in reading only once the phrase in v.2 'the Lord rebuke you'. He does, however, cite the normal text of Zech.3.1f elsewhere in the *Dialogue with Trypho*[9].

It can be easily seen that this particular form of Zech.3.1f is another example of the process we have observed earlier in Sergius's handling of the biblical text. The Old Testament text is revised in the light of its supposed fulfilment — Mt.4.1-11, Lk. 4.1-13. Variant (a) may be inserted to emphasize that Zech.3.1f is a prophecy, though it is difficult to be sure of this. Variant (b) removes the 'angel of the Lord' from the scene, and variant (c) allows us to read the text as though Christ, not the Lord or the angel of the Lord, rebukes Satan. It is, moreover, clear that Zech.3.1f was seen as a prophecy of the Temptation by early Christians through the link 'Jesus/Joshua' [10].

b) *An agraphon based probably on Jer.4.3* (*ch.i.16*).

This agraphon also appears in the *Discussion of St.Silvester* [11], and is quoted by Isidore of Seville [12] and Dionysius bar Salibhi [13]. Its form in Sergius's Disputation closely agrees, both in its introductory rubric and its text, with the Greek version of the *Discussion of St.Silvester* [14], the Latin version [15], and with Isidore. Bar Salibhi's text agrees with Sergius's except for the substitution of ܚܛܗ̈ܘܝ (its sins) for ܣܟܠܘ̈ܬܗ (its transgressions). Here the Syriac version of the *Discussion of St. Silvester* agrees with Dionysius, reading ܚܛ̈ܗܝܗܘܢ (its sins), though in the rest of the quotation it has a text peculiar to itself.

Jer.4.3f is used as a *testimony text* by many earlier Christian anti-Jewish polemicists [16], and once again we are presented with an Old

[7] *Trypho*, 79. Cf. also LACTANTIUS, *Divine Institutes*, iv. 14.

[8] He omits the beginning of the verse.

[9] *Trypho*, 115.

[10] Cf. HARRIS, *Testimonies*, II, pp. 54ff.

[11] SILVESTER, *Discussion*,p.75

[12] *Against the Jews*, I. 31.

[13] *Against the Jews*, vi. 9.

[14] COMBEFIS, *Illustrium Martyrum*, p. 300.

[15] MOMBRITUS, *Sanctuarium*, p. 520.

[16] Cf. BARNABAS, ix.5, JUSTIN, *Trypho*, 28.2, CYPRIAN, *Against the Jews*, i.8, TERTUL-

Testament text developed and expanded in the Christian testimony tradition [17]. P. Kahle regards this agraphon as reflecting a midrashic interpretation of the Hebrew text, quoting the Targum : ולא תבעון פרקן בחובין (you shall not seek redemption whilst (you) are in sins). He says that 'the source must have been a Greek translation of Jewish origin, differing entire'y from the Christian "Septuagint", the readings of which were still used by Christian authors in the seventh century and perhaps later' [18]. It is, however, much more likely that the ultimate source of this agraphon is the Jewish Christian midrash on Jeremiah which Daniélou [19] posits as lying behind many Jewish Christian works.

c) *An Ezra Agraphon* (*i.17*)

The same agraphon appears in the *Discussion of St.Silvester* [20], and a variant form of it is found in an eleventh century manuscript of the Spanish recension of 4 Ezra (Codex Mazarinaeus) where it is inserted after 4 Ezra 1.33 [21]. Dionysius bar Salibhi quotes the agraphon [22], and a shorter form of it appears in the *Dialogue of Timothy and Aquila* [23]. It is impossible to reconstruct the original text of the agraphon from these various sources, because we lack critical editions of most of them. But they nearly all show the same fluctuation between the second person singular and plural in the verbs which we find in Sergius's version, though the *Dialogue of Timothy and Aquila* has the verbs in the third person plural. However, we can observe the striking fact that both

LIAN, *Against the Jews*, iii, LACTANTIUS, *Divine Institutes*, iv.3, and HARRIS, *Testimonies*, I, pp.36,79.

17 For other discussions of this agraphon, cf. JAMES, *Ezra*, p. xxxviiiff, and WILLIAMS, *Adversus Judaeos*, p. 342.

18 *Cairo Geniza*, p. 262f.

19 *Theology*, p. 102ff.

20 SILVESTER,*Discussion*,p.75, Greek text in COMBEFIS, *Illustrium Martyrum*,p.300f, Latin text in MOMBRITIUS, *Sanctuarium*,p.520. JAMES, *Ezra*, p.xxxviiif quotes a slightly different Latin text according to a twelfth century manuscript of the *Acts of Silvester* now in the library of Peterhouse, Cambridge.

21 Cf. JAMES, *Ezra*,p.xxxix.

22 *Against the Jews*,vi.5.

23 CONYBEARE, *Dialogues*, p. 71. According to WILLIAMS, *Adversus Judaeos*, pp. 67ff, the *Dialogue of Timothy and Acquila* was composed c.200 A.D. However, not only the heading to the work in the Vatican MS used by Conybeare and the reference to «the king and his angelic bishop' (fol.138r), but also its advanced Christology (fol.93r) and its reference to Origen's Quinta and Sexta (fol.77r), require a fourth or fifth century date for its composition.

in the text and word order of the agraphon Sergius's Disputation invariably agrees with the Greek and Latin versions of the *Discussion of St.Silvester* against the Syriac version.

It is interesting to observe that Justin Martyr [24] and Lactantius [25] also use an Ezra agraphon as a testimony against the Jews. Justin complains to Trypho that the Jews have removed this text 'from the expositions which Ezra gave of the law concerning the Passover'. It was thus clearly attached to Ezra 6.19ff, and seems to have been developed out of such passages as I Cor.5.7, Phil.2.8 etc. Jean Daniélou is of the opinion that it belonged to a Jewish Christian midrash on II Esdras, and quotes another agraphon concerning the cross which he claims came from this same midrash [26]. Now although there are some points of contact between Justin's Ezra agraphon and that found in Sergius's Disputation it is probable that the one has not developed out of the other. This is made particularly clear to us by Dionysius bar Salibhi, who continues thus after citing the agraphon : And by the 'crying' he signifies that which they cried, 'Crucify him, crucify him !' (Lk.23.21, Jn.19.6) and, 'We have no king but Caesar' " (Jn.19.15) [27]. The *Dialogue of Timothy and Aquila* also places the agraphon in this context. Thus our agraphon has been developed out the Passion narrative, and the ܒܝܬ ܕܕܝܢܐ (the seat of the judge) is the *Βῆμα* of Mt.27.19, Jn.19.13 — the judgement seat of Pilate.

Is the connection with 4 Ezra 1 in the Codex Mazarinaeus original or secondary ? 4 Ezra 1.7 lends itself to the kind of development we find in the first half of our agraphon, and its insertion after 4 Ezra 1.32 is certainly understandable. But 4 Ezra 1 and 2 are Christian additions to the original Ezra Apocalypse and are attested only in the Latin version of the work, whereas the earliest and widest attestation of the agraphon comes from the East. It is more probable that the agraphon came to the West through the Latin version of the *Discussion of St.Silvester* and was subsequently interpolated into an appropriate place in the text of 4 Ezra in one Vulgate manuscript.

If the connection with 4 Ezra is secondary, then we could suggest that the agraphon originally belonged to the Jewish Christian midrash

[24] *Trypho*, 72. Cf. Resch, *Agrapha*, p. 304f.

[25] *Divine Institutes*, iv. 18.

[26] *Theology*, p. 101f. Cf. also the Ezra agraphon in DBS, *Against the Jews*, v.5, and the well known agraphon cited in Barnabas, xii.1, from 4 Ezra 5.5.

[27] *Against the Jews*, vi.6.

on II Esdras which Daniélou sees as the source of Justin's agraphon. The principal difficulty with this suggestion is the time lag between this postulated midrash (early second century ?) and the first appearance of our agraphon in the *Dialogue of Timothy and Aquila* (late fourth or early fifth century). Probably our agraphon is one of the results of the continuing process of midrashic reworking of the Ezra literature in the interests of anti-Jewish polemic to which the production of 4 Ezra 1-2 and the numerous Ezra agrapha bear abundant witness. Its contacts with the Passion narrative in the Gospels are such as to preclude an origin as early as the first half of the second century A.D.

d) *Jer.20.7*, *Lam.3.14* (*i.18*)

The text in the Disputation represents a deliberate modification of either Jer.20.7 or Lam.3.14 to make it apply accurately to the crucifixion. The key addition, ܠܥܡܐ ܗܢܐ (to this people), also appears in the *Discussion of Silvester* [28] where, as with agrapha (2) and (3), Sergius' Disputation agrees closely both in the introduction and the text with the Greek and Latin versions rather than with the Syriac version [29]. Dionysius bar Salibhi uses Jer.20.7 as a testimony text [30] but the version he quotes is clearly a garbled rendering of the Peshitta. The modification of Jeremiah or Lamentations in this quotation must be compared with Sergius's method of treating scripture as it has been described above. What we probably have here is a text from Jeremiah or Lamentations being revised in the light of Mt.27.41 and Ps.22.6f. It is unlikely that it goes back to any of the midrashim on Jeremiah, since it is not quoted by anybody earlier than the Discussion of Silvester (early sixth century), nor are these texts used elsewhere for anti-Jewish polemic.

e) *Another Jeremiah Agraphon* (*i.20*)

Once again this agraphon is found in the *Discussion of Silvester* and, as we have by now come to expect, the Greek text agrees exactly with that of Sergius even down to the word order [31]. The Latin text [32] exactly follows that of the Greek, while there are two changes of word order

[28] COMBEFIS, *Illustrium Martyrum*, p. 300.
[29] SILVESTER, *Discussion*, p. 75.
[30] *Against the Jews*, vi. 12.
[31] COMBEFIS, *Illustrium Martyrum*, p. 301.
[32] MOMBRITUS, *Sanctuaruim*, p. 520.

in the Syriac [33]. Dionysius bar Salibhi also quotes this agraphon with a text [34] identical with that of Sergius.

A Jeremiah agraphon similar to, but more extensive than, the one quoted by Sergius was well known in the early church [35]. In his discussion of this agraphon Daniélou [36] assigns it to the Jewish Christian midrash on Jeremiah which we have mentioned above. Its Jewish Christian origin is apparent for it deals with a problem felt acutely in this sector of the church — the fate of the righteous dead of old Israel. But as regards the relation of the two agrapha and the origin of the one cited by Sergius we are confronted with the same problem as we met earlier in connection with the relation of the two Ezra agrapha. Only this time the two quotations are more closely connected. We may solve the problem in one of two ways : either we may say that they are two parallel passages from the same Jeremiah midrash, or we may suggest that the text cited by Sergius is an abbreviated form of the earlier agraphon, so revised as to make it applicable to the wider Gentile church by paring down its Jewish overtones. On the whole, it is best to adopt the latter alternative, and conclude that the shorter form of the agraphon has evolved in the testimony tradition out of the longer form.

f) *Is.66.24* (*iii.4*, *xx.13*)

In the text of this quotation the Disputation agrees with Aphraates [37] in reading ܘܬܦܩܘܢ ܘܬܚܙܘܢ (you shall go forth and see) against the Peshitta's ܘܢܦܩܘܢ ܘܢܚܙܘܢ (they shall go forth and see). The reversal of the words ܬܘܠܥܬܗܘܢ ܠܐ ܬܡܘܬ (their worm shall not die) [38] as against the Peshitta is made under the influence of Mk.9.48. The agreement of Sergius and Aphraates will require further investigation, particularly in view of the fact that they both cite Is.66.16 immediately preceding this quotation, and for the same purpose — as testimonies to the Last Judgement.

33 Silvester, *Discussion*, p. 75.

34 *Against the Jews*, vii. 2.

35 Cf. Justin, *Trypho*, 72.4, Resch, *Agrapha*, p. 320f.

36 *Theology*, p. 102f,233f. Other discussions of the two agrapha can be found in James, *Ezra*, p. xlif, *Lost Apocrypha*, p. 63f, Williams, *Adversus Judaeos*, p. 342, *Justin*, p. 153, n.1.

37 *Demonstrations*, I, 32.

38 Also found in Aphraates, *Demonstrations*, I, 1034, and dbs, *Against the Jews*, viii. 5

2. *The Disputation of Sergius the Stylite and the Discussion of St.Silvester*

It is clear from the foregoing study of the peculiar testimony texts in Sergius's Disputation that its relationship with the *Discussion of St. Silvester* merits further attention. The *Discussion* forms the second part of the apocryphal Acts of Pope Silvester [39]. The exact date and origin of this work is, however, uncertain. It has been studied by Jean Juster [40], who gives an extensive bibliography, A.L. Williams [41], who gives a good summary of the *Discussion*, and the Syriac versions of the Acts have been studied by A. Baumstark [42], Ortiz de Urbina [43], and R. Duval [44]. It seems that the legend of Pope Silvester is of Oriental origin, quite probably from Syria, and that it was created at the end of the fourth century. The original legend concerned only the miraculous deeds of Silvester and his baptism of Constantine, for we possess a Syriac homily attributed to Jacob of Sarug [45] which contains only this part of the legend, although the bishop who baptises Constantine is anonymous. Urbina [46] and P. Peters [47] (following W. Levison [48]) regard this homily as spurious; Baumstark [49], on the other hand, thinks that it may be genuine. There is also a twelfth century Syriac manuscript which contains only this first part of the Acts of Silvester, this time with the bishop (Silvester) who baptises Constantine being named [50]. That the two sections of the Acts were originally separate is confirmed by the fact that in the Greek and Latin editions they are printed separately.

The fuller form of the Acts, with the Discussion added, first appears in Syria in the sixth century, for they are incorporated in the anonymous history compiled by a Syrian Jacobite, which is edited by E.W. Brooks under the title *The Ecclesiastical History of Zacharias Rhetor* [51].

39 For the texts and versions of the *Discussion* see n.5 above to this chapter.

40 *Les Juifs*, vol.I, pp. 66ff.

41 *Adversus Judaeos*, pp. 339-347.

42 *Geschichte*, p. 97.

43 *Patrologia*, pp. 98,190.

44 *La littérature syriaque*, p. 184f.

45 See Baumstark and Urbina, *opera cit.*

46 *Patrologia*, p. 98.

47 *Jacques de Saroug*, pp. 194-196.

48 *Konstantinische Schenkung und Silvesterlegende*, *Studie e Testi*, 38 (1924), pp. 159-247, cited by Peters, *op. cit.*

49 *Geschichte*, p. 97

50 S, fol. 200v-205r.

51 Zacharias rhetor, *Historia Eccl.*

The author of this work has included Zacharias's work, which covers the period 450-491 A.D., as Books 3-6 of his 12 Book work. The whole corpus dates from 569 A.D., as the author tells us in Bk.I,1,3. The Acts of Silvester appear as Bk.I, ch.vii. Juster thinks that the legend came to the West, and received its final redaction probably in Rome, at the end of the fifth century. For the legend is first mentioned in the Pseudo-Gelasian decretal [52], and then the whole of the Acts are described by Gregory of Tours [53] and later Western historians. We have then the definite fact that the fuller form of the Acts of Silvester, including the *Discussion* which interests us, emerged during the first half of the sixth century. In the light of this it seems that the homily attributed to Jacob of Sarug (who lived c.451-521 A.D.) could well be original. If we date Jacob's homily towards the end of the fifth century, we can summarise the probable growth of the legend of St.Silvester as follows : first, at the end of the fourth and the beginning of the fifth century an anonymous legend of the baptism of Constantine grew up in the Orient; towards the end of this century the name of Pope Silvester was added to it; and lastly, about the beginning of the sixth century the final redaction of the Acts took place when the Discussion of Pope Silvester with twelve Jews before Queen Helena and Constantine, was added to the legend.

Greek is clearly the original language in which these Acts were composed, for the author of the Latin version tells us explicitly that he translated his work from the Greek [54], and the Syriac version bears every sign of being a translation, with a very heavy incidence of rare Greek loan words. It is probable that the final redaction — the combination of the legend and the *Discussion* — took place in the Orient, probably Syria, although it may be conceded to Juster that the Latin is the fullest form and the work did, therefore, receive additions when it eventually reached Rome. Juster [55] says that it is difficult to decide whether the Syriac translation is earlier or later than the Latin; it is probable that they are approximately contemporaneous, although we cannot now tell whether the two parts of the Acts ever circulated separately in the West as they did in Syria.

[52] Dobschütz, *Das Decretum Gelasianum*, 4.4.3. This work probably dates from c.500 A.D.

[53] *History of the Franks*, 2. 31, a work which was completed in 591 A.D., cited by Juster *Les Juifs*, vol. I, p. 67, n.2.

[54] Mombritus, *Sanctuarium*, p. 508.

[55] *Les Juifs*, p. 66f.

This digression on the date and origin of the Acts of Silvester was necessary in order to clarify the relation of the work to Sergius's Disputation. We will proceed to investigate this relationship by applying the five criteria which Rendel Harris used in his two volume work *Testimonies* [56] in order to detect the use of an anti-Jewish Book of Testimonies by the New Testament writers [57]. These criteria are :

a) *Peculiar texts* — the recurrence of readings, with the arguments based upon them, unique to Christian anti-Jewish writings.
b) *Recurrent sequences* — recurrent sequences of testimony texts in different anti-Jewish writers.
c) *Erroneous authorship* — the recurrence in such works of identical false ascriptions of authorship to Old Testament texts.
d) *Editors' prefaces, comments, and questions* — the recurrence of identical introductory and explanatory clauses attached to particular testimonies.
e) *Matter for the use of the controversialist* — material which could be used in direct confrontations between Christians and Jews, such as direct challenges and questions following the quotation of testimony texts.

a) *Peculiar texts*

We have seen above that every agraphon which Sergius quotes is exactly paralleled by the *Discussion of Silvester*. It is to be particularly noted that, apart from Bar Salibhi's work and, in one case, the *Dialogue Timothy and Aquila*, these agrapha are confined to the two works, being found nowhere else in precisely the same form. We must, therefore, posit some literary relationship — either borrowing on the part of Sergius or mutual dependence upon some other work. The first alternative is virtually ruled out by the fact that the text of the quotations in Sergius's Disputation invariably agrees with the Greek and Latin versions of the *Discussion* against the Syriac. Since Sergius nowhere shows any knowledge of Greek [58], and since the parallels with the *Discussion* are confined to biblical texts, with no borrowing from the substance of the work, we must opt for the second alternative.

56 Harris, *Testimonies I-II.*

57 *Testimonies*, I, p. 8. For the debate on Harris's thesis, a debate which is by no means concluded, see Daniélou, *Études*, passim, Williams, *Adversus Judaeos*, pp. 3-13, Kraft, *Barnabas' Isaiah Text*, Dodd, *According to the Scriptures*, pp. 28-60, Lindars, *New Testament Apologetic*, pp. 13-31.

58 The equation of ܦܪܗܡܢܐ and ܐܘܢܘܣܐ, and ܦܪܢܝܣܝܐ and ܦܪܘܣܠܝܐ,

b) *Recurrent sequences*

It may have been noted in the discussion of the testimony texts that they all occur in chapter i.16-20 of Sergius's Disputation and on p.74f of the Syriac text of the *Discussion of Silvester*. To illustrate this facet of the relation between the two works, we will set out in columns the sequence of the biblical quotations in the Discussion, with the parallel quotations from the Disputation alongside.

Text	Discussion of Silvester	Disputation of Sergius
Ps.74.22	p.72,1.12 [59]	
Dt.32.39	p.72,1.23	
Ps.33.6	p.73,1.5,74,1.2	ii.5
Ps.2.7	p.73,1.9	i.2
Gen.1.26	p.73,1.13	vi.1
Ps.51.11	p.73,1.28	ii.1
Is.57.16	p.74,1.1	
Lk.2.52	p.74,1.10	vii.2
Is.7.14	p.74,1.20	i.3
Bar.3.35ff	p.74,1.22	i.9
Zech.3.1f	p.74,1.26	i.11
Wis.2.12	p.75,1.2	
Ps.41.9	p.75,1.6	i.16
Ps.22.18	p.75,1.6	i.18,x.5
Ps.27.12	p.75,1.8	i.16
Jeremiah agraphon a)[60]	p.75,1.9	i.16
Ps.69.21	p.75,1.11	i.18,x.5
Lam.3.14,Jer.20.7	p.75,1.13	i.18
Ezra agraphon	p.75,1.15	i.17
Jeremiah agraphon e)[61]	p.75,1.18	i.20
Col.2.9	p.80,1.7	
Jn.3.5	p.80,1.10	
Mt.4.10	p.81,1.10	
Gen.22.18	p.82,1.12,86,1.3	ix.7,xi.5 13

which Sergius makes in iv.5 and xi.11 respectively, requires only a knowledge of what is a loan word, not a knowledge of Greek.

[59] Page numbers of the Syriac version, ZACHARIAS RHETOR, *Historia Eccl.*, I, 69-93.

[60] See p. 10 above.

[61] See p. 13 above.

Text	Discussion of Silvester	Disputation of Sergius
Ps.132.11	p.82 1.12	
Dt.18.15	p.85,1.18	xvii.7, xxii passim
Dan.9.25f	p.85,1.19	i.15,viii.3
Dt.32.8f	p.86,1.4	
Ex.3.15	p.86,1.14	
Dt.32.39	p.90,1.25	

What is immediately striking about this list is that the section from Is.7.14 to Jeremiah agraphon (c) is almost exactly paralleled by Sergius's Disputation, and roughly in the same order, and certainly within the same small compass. Elsewhere the parallels are very scattered, and are in any case not very significant, except for the section on the Trinity on p.73. Now if we look at the subject matter in the parallel sections of the Disputation and the *Discussion*, we find that in each case we are presented with a biography of Jesus Christ in Old Testament quotations. On p.74 of the *Discussion* Godaliah, the third Jew to speak, asks for proof from the Old Testament regarding the whole life of Jesus. Silvester responds with this list of testimony texts. In Sergius's Disputation the whole of the first six folios (chapters i-iii) is devoted to just such a biography. Now Rendel Harris mentions with approval the view that 'a small collection of Old Testament extracts was gathered together in such a way as to be a biography of the Lord in prophecies' [62]. Can we not detect here the common use of such a collection by the author of the *Discussion of Silvester* and by Sergius the Stylite? There is also evidence to suggest that a collection of quotations on the Trinity and the Holy Spirit existed in the testimony tradition [63], and it seems possible that we can detect the use of such a collection on p. 73 of the *Discussion* and in chapter ii of Sergius's Disputation. It looks, therefore, as though the common source of the two works was a book of testimonies, containing at least one and perhaps two of the collections which we have isolated.

c) *Erroneous authorship*

There are no cases of erroneous ascriptions of authorship common to our two works, but we will note later on that Sergius has an error of this sort in common with Aphraates.

62 *Testimonies*, II, p. 36.
63 Harris, *Testimonies*, II, pp. 133ff.

d) *Editor's prefaces, comments, and questions*

There are some interesting agreements between these two works in the manner in which they introduce their testimony texts. We will again set these out side by side for the purpose of comparison.

The Discussion of Silvester	The Disputation of Sergius
Bar.3.35ff. *ὅτι δὲ καὶ ἀνθρώποις συναναστραφήσεται, ἄκουε τοῦ προφήτου Ἰερεμίου* ... [64]	"And (prophesying) that he would live among men, Jeremiah said......"
Ps.41.9 *ὅτι δὲ καὶ παρὰ μαθητοῦ προδοθήσεται, λέγει ὁ ψαλμῳδός* ... [65]	"And concerning (the fact) that he would be betrayed by his disciple, the psalm says......"
Ps.22.18. "And (prophesying) that he would be stripped and his garments shared out, the prophet said......" [66]	"And (concerning the fact) that they shared out his garments, David said......"
Ps.27.12. "And (prophesying) that he would be accused by false witnesses, again the prophet said......" [66]	"And concerning the false witnesses he writes......"

Jeremiah agraphon (b). The introduction to Sergius's quotation exactly reproduces that to the Greek text of the *Discussion*; the Syriac text differs slightly.

Ps.69.21. *ὅτι δὲ καὶ χολὴν τραφήσεται καὶ ὄξος ποτισθήσεται, ὁ προφήτης Δαυὶδ λεγει* ... [67]	"And (concerning the fact) that they gave him vinegar and bitter herbs, David said......"

Lam.3.14,Jer.20.7. Sergius's introduction exactly follows that of the Greek text of the *Discussion*, while again the Syriac text is different.

The Ezra agraphon. Here Sergius seems to have only partly reproduced the heading to the quotation, the Syriac version of the *Discussion* having a fuller form, and the Greek text the fullest form.

[64] CEDRENUS, *Compendium*, 525 A.
[65] CEDRENUS, *Compendium*, 525 B.
[66] My trans. of SILVESTER, *Discussion*, p. 75.
[67] CEDRENUS, *Compendium*, 525 B.

Jeremiah agraphon (e). All the texts agree exactly in the introduction to this quotation.

Here again we have a remarkable series of agreements between our two works, though it does look as though each author or translator occasionally rearranges his material. As with the texts of the agrapha, so with the introductions to them, we observe that Sergius's Disputation almost invariably follows the Greek text of the *Discussion*. The formula for introducing these texts should be noted : in Syriac it is usually ܘܕ followed by a participle, the subject of the quotation, the name of the Old Testament author, and ܐܡܪ. Occasionally it is varied, usually by substituting ܘܡܠܠ for ܘܕ. It is clearly a translation of the Greek ὅτι δε followed by a verb in the future tense [68]. We may conclude, therefore, that the headings are drawn from the Book of Testimonies which we must posit lies behind our two works

e) *Matter for the use of the controversialist*

Of course all these testimony texts are of use in anti-Jewish polemic, but we have no specific examples in common of the sort of direct challenges which Rendel Harris describes. However, we may note that the *Discussion*, though not Sergius's Disputation, contains the archetypal example of this genre — "To whom did he say, 'Let us make man...' " (Gen.1.26) [69]. Independent examples of this practice do occur in Disputation.

Thus by applying Harris's five tests we are inevitably led to the conclusion that both Sergius and the author of the *Discussion of Silvester* used a Book of Testimonies which contained, possibly a section giving the Old Testament evidence for the Trinity, and, at the least, a biography of Jesus Christ in Old Testament prophecies. Since we have concluded that the *Discussion of Silvester* was added to the Acts around the beginning of the sixth century, this Book of Testimonies, in its Greek form, must have been in existence in the fifth century. Now we have seen that it is most unlikely that Sergius borrowed his testimonies form the Syriac version of the *Discussion* (unless more than one Syriac version of the work was in existence), and that it is also unlikely that he drew upon the Greek text. This conclusion will be reinforced when

68 The same formula can be observed in CYPRIAN, *Against the Jews*, and in ISIDORE, *Against the Jews*.

69 SILVESTER, *Discussion*, p. 73. See also DBS, *Against the Jews*, ii. 6ff, JUSTIN, *Trypho*, 72, CONYBEARE, *Dialogues*, p. 67, and HARRIS, *Testimonies*, I, p. 45, II, p. 123.

we come to consider his use of the Syriac version of Josephus's *War of the Jews* [70] and of Eusebius's *Chronicle* [71], for this establishes that it is his practice only to use sources which were available in Syriac. We must, then, surmise that this Testimony Book which we have isolated behind the *Discussion of Silvester* was, at some stage, translated into Syriac, and then used by Sergius, a conclusion which will perhaps account for the fact that although Sergius's quotations follow the Greek text of the *Discussion* more closely than the Syriac, they do not reproduce it exactly. The differences between the texts of the quotations in the *Discussion* and the Disputation, on the one hand, and in Dionysius's treatise *Against the Jews*, on the other hand, may be explained by the fact that Dionysius drew upon this Syriac version of the Testimony Book, the text of which, we may conjecture, had in the course of several centuries been reshaped and simplified.

Before we attempt to trace the Testimony Book back any further in time, we must see if the relation between Dionysius's work and Sergius's Disputation can tell us any more about its contents.

3. *The Disputation of Sergius the Stylite and Dionysius bar Salibhi's Against the Jews* [72]

It is almost impossible to summarize the relation between these two works, for a very large part of Dionysius's treatise finds parallels, both in the texts quoted and in subject matter, with Sergius's Disputation. Rendel Harris makes extensive use of Dionysius's work in reconstructing his hypothetical Book of Testimonies. In discussing the work he says that it "contains many relics of the earlier controversies, and probably whole sections, slightly disguised by their transference into Syriac, of the lost book that we are in quest of". [73] Quoting from a manuscript in his possession [74], he shows that Dionysius actually says that he is using testimonies [75], for in the midst of a list of Old Testament quotations we find the following :—

[70] See below, pp. 32-47.

[71] See below, p. 48ff.

[72] Cf. Petersen, *Treatise*, Baumstark, *Geschichte*, p. 297. Williams, *Adversus Judaeos*, pp. 105-112, Kazan, *Isaac of Antioch's Homily*, OC, 49(1965), pp. 66ff. Bar Salibhi's *Against the Jews* was written 1166/67 A.D. — see above, p. 3.

[73] *Testimonies*, I, p. 7.

[74] J.de Zwaan used this manuscript for his edition of Bar Salibhi's treatise.

[75] *Testimonies*, I, p. 57f.

> 'All these testimonies refer to the three Persons and to the descent and incarnation of God, the Word, one of the Persons, and his first coming...... and the signs which he performed, and his entry into Jerusalem...... and also to his suffering and his crucifixion, and to his disciples who betrayed him, from the prophets' [76].

Here Bar Salibhi gives a very good summary of the first three chapters of Sergius's Disputation. The conclusion is unavoidable that he is summarizing the contents of a collection of testimonies which Sergius also used.

A detailed investigation of the parallels between the two works [77] reveals that, however closely they are related in subject matter, Dionysius never actually quotes Sergius's Disputation. When we refer to the extant Books of Testimonies [78] we find that much of the material which Dionysius and Sergius have in common comes from the headings to the relevant collections of texts, and that they are both drawing upon a stock of arguments well known in the testimony tradition. Thus instead of direct borrowing they are both dependent either upon a Book of Testimonies or an oral (we might say, catechetical) tradition of anti-Jewish polemic.

However, chapters v-vii.7 of Dionysius's treatise seem to be mainly drawn from the biography of Jesus Christ in prophecies which we have isolated above in the *Discussion of Silvester* p.74f, and in Sergius's Disputation, chapters i-iii. Dionysius quotes all but one of the agrapha which have been discussed earlier, besides filling in the gap left in the list of parallels with the *Discussion* where Sergius omits Wis.2.12. The following list gives Dionysius's parallels to the *Discussion of Silvester* :—

The Discussion of Silvester	*Bar Salibhi, Against the Jews*
Is.7.14	iv.14
Bar.3.35ff	v.16
Zech.3.1ff	
Wis.2.12	vi.7
Ps.41.9	

[76] DBS, *Against the Jews*, v. 17f.

[77] Cf. HAYMAN, *Sergius*, 53-60.

[78] Such as CYPRIAN, *Against the Jews*, Bk. I, passim, and ISIDORE, *Against the Jews*, II. 8-13.

Ps.22.18	vi.11
Ps.27.12	vi.8
Jeremiah agraphon (b)	vi.9
Ps.69.21	vi.12
Jer.20.7	vi.12
Ezra agraphon	vi.5
Jeremiah agraphon (e)	vii.7

In this list only two quotations in the two works differ in their order of occurrence — the Ezra agraphon and Ps.22.18; they are both also placed in a different position in Sergius's Disputation. Dionysius places the Ezra agraphon in the context of Jesus's trial, as we have already noted above [79], and its position in the Disputation also really implies the same context. Like Dionysius, Sergius also places Ps.22.18 alongside Ps.69.21, but after, not before it, so we cannot be sure of its exact position in the original collection of testimonies. However, the otherwise striking agreement in the order of the quotations confirms our hypothesis that Dionysius is also a witness to the Book of Testimonies underlying the *Discussion of Silvester* and Sergius's Disputation.

Dionysius, like Sergius, has a much fuller series of texts in this biography, and from the parallels between them we can add the following texts to the contents of our hypothetical Book of Testimonies : Ps. 72.10 f, Job 19.25, Is.40.3, Jer.16.16, Is.53.4, Zech.9.9, Jer.31.31f, Zech.12.10, Is.53.7, Dan.7.13f, Ps.110.1, Ps.50.3, Is.66.24, Ps.24.7 [80]. This does not mean, of course, that all these texts were necessarily part of the collection as it existed in the fifth century. It was the sort of work that easily lent itself to expansion; many of the quotations in Sergius's work are clearly of this nature. The lack of parallels to some of his quotations, besides their bizarre appearance, indicates that he has added them himself to the original collection which formed the basis of his first few folios. Nevertheless, since so many of the texts which we have listed here are used as testimony texts from the earliest times [81], we cannot rule out the possibility that the author of the *Discussion of Silvester* has abstracted only a few quotations from the Book of Testimonies, and not quoted all those which he found in it. The fact that he does not

[79] See p. 12.

[80] The notes to the Translation of the Disputation indicate where these texts occur in Dionysius's treatise.

[81] See Harris, *Testimonies*, passim and the notes to the Translation.

complete the 'dispensation' of Christ with testimonies to the Resurrection, Ascension, Parousia, and the Last Judgement, indicates that this may have been his practice.

We find then, that Dionysius bar Salibhi's treatise *Against the Jews* confirms our hypothesis of a Book of Testimonies, consisting of at least a biography of Jesus in prophecies, which existed in Syria from the fifth century onwards. The wide extent of the parallels between Sergius's work and that of Dionysius suggests that this Book of Testimonies may also have included collections of texts dealing with such subjects as circumcision, the Sabbath, the Old and New Covenants, the Incarnation, and the worship of the cross and saints' bones. However, the evidence that these latter collections were written and not oral is a good deal less conclusive than that for the former.

Before we sum up our study of the Book of Testimonies, we must consider the parallels between Sergius's Disputation and Aphraates *Demonstrations* to see whether or not we can trace this Book back before the fifth century

4. *The Disputation of Sergius the Stylite and the Demonstrations of Aphraates*

When we come to consider the parallels between Sergius's Disputation and Aphraates' *Demonstrations*, it immediately becomes apparent that there is a very wide area of overlapping material. Of course, much of this overlap can be explained by the fact that the primary concern of both works is the Christian as opposed to the Jewish interpretation of the Old Testament [82]. Rendel Harris regards Aphraates like Dionysius as a witness to his hypothetical Testimony Book [83], and indeed, in many places the *Demonstrations* are little more than collected lists of texts on various subjects. For example, Dem.1, sections 6-10, is based on one of the oldest collections of testimony texts — the λίθος group [84], while in Demonstration 16, and 19, sections 3-4, we find very ancient collections of testimony texts on the calling of the Gentiles and the rejection of

[82] See GAVIN, *Aphraates and the Jews*, and for a very positive (perhaps too positive) estimate of Aphraates' originality within the Christian - Jewish debate see NEUSNER, *Aphrahat and Judaism*.

[83] *Testimonies*, II, p. 23, 61.

[84] See CYPRIAN, *Against the Jews*, I. 16ff, which contains most of the texts cited by Aphraates. Of this collection Sergius cites only Is. 28. 16. See also HARRIS, *Testimonies*, I, pp. 18ff, DANIÉLOU, *Études*, p. 8, 133, *Theology*, p. 83, 89.

Israel. Elsewhere Demonstrations 11 (Concerning Circumcision), 13 (Concerning the Sabbath), 17 (Concerning Christ the Son of God), etc., all contain blocks of testimony texts which can be paralleled from anti-Jewish Christian works of all periods. We may safely conclude, therefore, that Aphraates used and reflects the earliest collections of testimony texts, though we cannot tell whether he had a complete Book of Testimonies combining all the various collections, as Harris argues, or whether he had only separate collections, or indeed, whether some of his material was only oral and not written. After studying the parallels between Aphraates and Jacob of Sarug's *Homilies Against the Jews*, I.K. Cosgrove confirms our conclusion by saying that both authors used written collections of testimony texts [85].

But does Aphraates show any knowledge of the Book of Testimonies which we have suggested was used by the author of the *Discussion of St.Silvester*, by Sergius, and by Dionysius bar Salibhi ? We may without hesitation answer this question in the negative, for there is no sign in the *Demonstrations* of the characteristic texts of this work — the agrapha, Bar.3.35ff, Zech.3.1f, Wis.2.12 etc. There are scattered parallels to some of the texts which are common to Sergius and Dionysius [86], but since these are frequently used in the testimony tradition and Christian apologetics in general, we can prove nothing from them. Aphraates' nearest approach to this biography of Jesus is in Demonstration 17, sections 9-10, where Ps.2.7, Is.7.14, Dan.9.25ff, Ps.22.17-19. Is.53, Ps. 16.10, Zech.14.7, and Ps.69.21 are quoted in reply to the Jewish statement that 'the Messiah has not yet come'. But both the motive for the citation of these texts, and the omission of those characteristic of our Testimony Book rule out the possibility that Aphraates is using it here.

Nevertheless, there are one or two interesting parallels between the *Demonstrations* and Sergius's Disputation which are difficult to account for on the hypothesis of oral tradition or common dependence upon the Syriac exegetical tradition :

(1) Both Sergius (i.19) and Aphraates (I,28) wrongly ascribe Am.8.9 to Zechariah. We have here a case of 'erroneous authorship' corresponding

85 Jacob of Sarug, *Against the Jews*, ch. v, p. 7. Neusner, *Aphrahat and Judaism*, does not pronounce on Aphraates' use of testimony collections but from his comments on p. 201 where he appears to align himself with Dodd and Lindars against Rendel Harris's Testimony Book hypothesis, it is probably not too much to deduce that he would deny Aphraates' indebtedness to such collections.

86 See above, p. 24.

to one of the criteria used by Harris for detecting the use of his Book of Testimonies [87]. Harris's explanation for these cases of erroneous ascription of authorship would also account for the error made by Aphraates and Sergius. Am.8.9 and Zech.14.7 may have lain together in a written collection of testimony texts, preceded by an introduction combining elements from both, and 'the error lies in the covering of two passages with a single reference' [88].

The combination of Am.8.9 and Zech.14.7 forms part of one of the oldest collections of testimony texts, witnessing to the darkness at the time of the crucifixion [89]. Aphraates (I,812) uses Zech.14.7 elsewhere for this purpose, and so does Dionysius [90]. The heading to the quotation in Sergius's Disputation contains elements of both texts and was clearly meant to introduce both. Aphraates, on the other hand, clearly means to quote Am.8.9 but ascribes the text to Zechariah instead. It is difficult to resist the temptation to conclude that both authors had a written collection of testimonies in front of them in which both Am.8.9 and Zech.14.7 were part of a section dealing with the darkness at the time of the crucifixion, that the Zechariah quotation came first, and that their eyes slipped from the word Zechariah to the Amos quotation which they proceeded to give. Alternatively, we could draw the same conclusion as Harris does with regard to the attribution by Justin and Irenaeus of Num. 24.17 to Isaiah [91], and say that the error lay in the collection of testimonies before them. A third alternative is to suppose that they were both quoting from memory, and that never having been able to think of the one quotation apart from the other, they quite naturally confused them [92].

The difference between the first two alternatives is not all that important, but in the former we do not have to assume that Sergius and Aphraates were using the same collection of testimonies. The decision between all three alternatives must necessarily be taken on the subjective ground of probability; how far can we stretch the factor of coincidence ? We can be reasonably certain that in ch.i.16-20 Sergius is using

[87] *Testimonies*, I, p. 10f, 21f.

[88] *Testimonies*, I, p. 11.

[89] Cf. DANIÉLOU, *Études*, pp. 68-71.

[90] *Against the Jews*, vi. 10.

[91] *Testimonies*, I, p. 10f.

[92] PETERSEN, *Treatise*, p. 200 lists nine instances of such mistaken attributions in Dionysius bar Salibhi's *Against the Jews*.

a written collection of testimonies, and the introduction which he provides for Am.8.9 certainly looks as though it is literary with its combination of elements from both texts. Dionysius, whom we suspect of using the same collection of testimonies, quotes Zech.14.7 right in the middle of the section in his work where the presence of this collection is most apparent. I think it probable that Sergius had a written collection before him, that he reproduces the introduction to the section on the darkness at the time of the crucifixion, and then quotes only one of the two texts which the section contained; Dionysius omits this one and quotes the other. The decision as to whether or not Aphraates is dependent on the same written source is finely balanced. The scales are just tipped in the direction of quotation from memory and its resultant confusion (the third alternative) by the fact that nowhere else does he seem to be using the biography of Jesus in prophecies which was, if not the whole content, at least the base of Sergius's testimony book.

(2) In citing Is.26.19 both Sergius (i.14) and Aphraates (I,382) insert ܡܪܝܐ (O Lord) after ܡ̈ܝܬܝܟ (your dead). This verse fluctuates in the ancient testimony tradition between two groups — that connected with Christ's raising of the dead, where it is usually combined with Is.53.4 [93], and that connected with the resurrection of the dead, where it is usually combined with the sort of texts which Sergius cites in ch. iii.3 — Ez. 37 and Dan.12.2f [94]. Sergius places it in the first context, Aphraates in the second. It is, therefore, unlikely that the variant common to them both is due to their mutual dependence on the same collection of testimonies. But it is, nevertheless, difficult to see why they make the insertion. Perhaps they wish to make it clear that it is to the Lord's, i.e. Christ's, dead that the text applies, and not to Israel's dead as the context implies. The only other possibility is that Sergius is directly dependent upon Aphraates, but the different way in which they use the text argues against this.

(3) The text of their quotations of Is.66.24 [95]. Sergius and Aphraates combine Is.66.16 and 24 as testimonies to the Last Judgement, while Dionysius [96] quotes v.24 only. It seems that the use of these texts is peculiar to these Syriac works. How are we to explain this unique

[93] Cf. Harris, *Testimonies*, I, p. 9f.

[94] Cf. Daniélou, *Études*, p. 117.

[95] f) in the list of testimony texts on p. 14.

[96] *Against the Jews*, viii. 5.

reading? The clue to one possible explanation is given by Sergius's long quotation of Is.66.16-22 (xx.6). The verses are applied to Christians, and in v.18 Sergius makes the same alteration from third to second person which he makes when citing v.24. Perhaps then, the text of v.24 has been altered to make it clear that this particular verse applies to Jews not Christians — the 'you' is the Jewish opponent to whom the threat is applied, whereas the promises in the text are applied to Christians, following a well known canon of Christian interpretation of the Old Testament. This may explain the origin of the reading, but if we are not to conclude either that Sergius is directly dependent upon Aphraates or that they are both dependent upon a Syriac testimony book, we must fall back again upon the hypothesis of coincidence - they are both making the alteration independently, but for the same reason. However, if the reading belonged to a book of testimonies we would expect it to be more widely known, and specifically, we would expect Dionysius to follow it; he does not. Unless, therefore, there is more evidence that Sergius is using Aphraates' *Demonstrations* or that Aphraates is dependent upon the Book of Testimonies used by Sergius we must be content, for the time being, either with the hypothesis of coincidence or with the surmise that the reading has passed from Aphraates to Sergius by some indirect route which we can no longer trace.

There are many other parallels between our two authors indicated in the notes to the Translation, but these are less specific than the ones which we have been considering and they cover much exegetical material held in common with other Syriac writers. On the whole, it is more likely that Sergius has received this material from an indirect route through the Syriac tradition of biblical exegesis rather than from direct borrowing. The same conclusion also applies to the testimony material which he has in common with Aphraates, for we can find no definite trace of the Testimony Book which he uses any earlier than the eighth century in the Syriac-speaking church, since Sergius himself is our first witness to it. This does not mean, of course, that Aphraates and the earlier Syriac writers did not make use of written collections of testimony texts either for catechetical or polemical purposes. They probably did, and Sergius and Dionysius reflect such collections in their discussions of subjects like the Sabbath, the Trinity, circumcision, and the rejection of the Jews. But these should be seen as part of a fluid testimony tradition, part written, part oral, which evolved and developed to meet changing circumstances. Much of this material is very primitive, going back in some cases to the earliest period of the church, and forming part of the tradition of anti-Jewish polemic common to all sections of the church. The biography of Jesus in prophecies, however, is specifically a written work, which appears at a definite point in time.

5. *The Origins of Sergius's Testimony Book*

From what has been said so far it is clear that we must look for the origins of this Book of Testimonies in the general stream of the testimony tradition to which the earliest anti-Jewish writers bear witness. We have already seen that Justin has the same peculiar text of Zech.3.1f which we find in Sergius's Disputation and the *Discussion of Silvester*; that Jer.4.3 is used as a testimony text by Justin, Cyprian, and Tertullian; that the *Dialogue of Timothy and Aquila* has a shorter form of the Ezra agraphon found in our three witnesses to the Testimony Book, while Justin and Lactantius have a similar Ezra agraphon; that the Jeremiah agraphon on Christ's burial probably developed out of a similar one found in Justin and Irenaeus; and that, besides, nearly all the texts which we have isolated as belonging to our Testimony Book were used by earlier anti-Jewish polemicists. We have also traced some of the agrapha to an early Jewish Christian milieu. The Testimony Book is, then, either a very early compilation, or draws upon very early material. A comparison with the earliest extant Book of Testimonies compiled by Cyprian [97] will show that the second alternative is more likely to be true.

Most early books of testimonies consist of two sections — 'those which are directed against the Ancient Religion, and those which are occupied with the work of the Founder of the New Religion, the Testimonies against the Jews and Testimonies concerning the Christ' [98]. Book II of Cyprian's work falls into the latter category. Reading through the sections in this Book it soon becomes apparent that many of the quotations which make up our Book of Testimonies are scattered at random through Cyprian's work, frequently being applied to different subjects than those to which they are attached in Sergius's Disputation[99]. Cyprian does not construct or reflect a biography of Jesus in prophecies but the materials for constructing one are present in his work. We

97 *Against the Jews.*

98 Harris, *Testimonies*, II, p. 95.

99 For a detailed comparison see Hayman, *Sergius*, p. 69f.

find precisely the same state of affairs in Justin's *Dialogue with Trypho*; no complete biography in prophecies is discernible, but the materials for composing one are. Tertullian too does not construct an elaborate biography, but in chapters ix and x of his *Adversus Judaeos*, dealing respectively with 'the prophecies of the birth and achievements of Christ' and 'the Old Testament predictions of the passion', the beginnings of one can be seen. In the light of this evidence must we not conclude that our biography belongs to a later stratum of the testimony tradition, but has been composed and constructed out of much earlier testimony material? Rendel Harris's observations on the development of the tradition fully support this conclusion, for he says that 'The four great facts of Christ, Birth, Life, Death, and Life again, are not treated in the primary Testimony Book as biographical factors but as explanatory factors...... These matters also would, in the course of time, be divided into detail and labelled in harmony with the actual story of the Gospels. The process is seen going forward in the Cyprianic text, and complete in the Spanish text of Isidore's time'[100].

Without accepting Harris's theory of the existence of only one basic Testimony Book, it looks, nevertheless, as though our Testimony Book is part of the continuing process which he describes : it was built upon the basis of the earlier collections of testimony texts, given its definitive form in Greek sometime in the fifth century, subsequently translated into Syriac (and perhaps Latin [101]), and finally attained the complexity of the biography constructed on its basis by Sergius the Stylite in the eighth century. Whether or not this biography had by Sergius's time been amalgamated with other collections of testimony texts to form a comprehensive Book of Testimonies is difficult to ascertain. Many such works were composed in the early church. However, the differing structure of Sergius's Disputation and Dionysius's treatise *Against the Jews* suggests that they did not use the same comprehensive Book of Testimonies, though, of course, there would have been no necessity for them

[100] *Testimonies*, II, p. 36. The *Dialogue of Timothy and Aquila* also shows signs that the testimony material is in the process of being reshaped into a biography in prophecies; see Conybeare, *Dialogues*, pp. 69ff.

[101] It is difficult to tell whether Isidore of Seville whose *Against the Jews*, Bk. I. v-lxi, consists of a biography of Jesus in prophecies, and who even quotes one of the Jeremiah agrapha (see above, p. 10), is dependent upon a Latin translation of our Book of Testimonies, or draws upon the Latin version of the Acts of Silvester, or even drew the quotation from the general testimony tradition.

to model their works exactly according to their sources. Thus, on the evidence available, we can be reasonably sure that they used the same biography of Jesus in Old Testament prophecies, but the precise extent of the work remains uncertain.

C. Josephus's War of the Jews

One of the main literary sources of Sergius's Disputation is Josephus's *War of the Jews*. In ch.xxi.4 Sergius (perhaps following the example of Eusebius [102]) introduces Josephus as a witness to 'the destruction of Jerusalem after the crucifixion of the Son of Mary'. In the rest of ch.xxi he provides several extracts from what he calls the 'Chronicle of the wise Josephus (concerning) what happened in the reign of Caesars Vespasian and Titus'. These extracts are of some textual interest, since it is probable that they preserve sections of a Syriac version of the *War of the Jews*, the greater part of which has long since perished.

1. *The Syriac Version of the War of the Jews*

The earliest, complete manuscript of the Peshitta version of the Bible, the Codex Ambrosianus B.21 Inf. [103] contains at its end a Syriac version of the sixth book of Josephus's *War of the Jews* under the title : ܡܐܡܪܐ ܕܥܠ ܚܘܪܒܗ ܐܚܪܝܐ ܕܐܘܪܫܠܡ (A Treatise on the Last Destruction of Jerusalem) [104]. It comes after the fourth Book of Maccabees, and the conclusion to the version indicates that it was regarded as the fifth Book of Maccabees [105] : ܫܠܡ ܟܬܒܐ ܕܡܩ̈ܒܝܐ ܐܝܬ ܒܗ ܡܐܡܪ̈ܐ ܚܡܫܐ (The Book of Maccabees, in which there are five volumes is finished) [106]. Whether it was included in the Maccabaean corpus because Josephus was credited with the production of the whole of the corpus, or whether Josephus was credited with the production of the corpus *because* book six of his *War of the Jews* was regarded as the fifth Book of Maccabees, is uncertain, particularly in the light of the following extract from 'Abdisho' bar Berikha's catalogue of Syriac writings :—

102 *Ecclesiastical History*, 3. 5-8.

103 See *List of Old Testament Peshitta Manuscripts*, p. 28f.

104 *Codex Ambrosianus*, fol. 320v.

105 For reasons why it was inserted into the canon of the Syrian church see Kottek, *Bellum Judaicum*, introduction, p. 1f.

106 *Codex Ambrosianus*, fol. 330r.

'Of the writer Josephus, the Fables [107], and the story of the sons of Shamuni, and also the Book of Maccabees, and the story of King Herod, and the Book of the Last Destruction of Jerusalem at the hands of Titus' [108].

Here Josephus is clearly credited with the production of the whole of the Maccabaean corpus, though it looks as though 'Abdisho' refers only to the sixth book of the *War of the Jews* and not to a Syriac version of the whole of the work. However, 'the story of King Herod' is a resonable summary of the earlier part of the *War*, and may indicate the existence of a complete Syriac version; it is not a good summary of the *Antiquities*, though this work does contain 'the story of King Herod'. In any case, that such a complete Syriac version existed must be presupposed in the light, not only of the quotations contained in Sergius's Disputation, but also of those contained in other Syriac works [109]. Although most of these writers are indebted to Eusebius for their knowledge of Josephus, there are sufficient quotations which have no parallel in the *Ecclesiastical History* to necessitate the assumption that a complete version of the *War of the Jews* existed in the Syriac-speaking church. The evidence of 'Abdisho' 's catalogue and of the Ambrosian manuscript suggests that this version circulated in two forms — a complete translation and a separate translation of the sixth book incorporated in the Maccabeen corpus. It is difficult to tell whether the latter is abstracted from the former; some internal evidence is in favour of this. For example, at the beginning of the treatise (the sixth book) the use of the word ܕܝܢ (and) [110] and the phrase ܕܐܡܪܢ ܐܝܟ (as we have said), referring to *B.J.*, V.523, a few lines further on, indicate that something preceded, although an independent translator may have been inept enough to leave these indications in the text. We will, however, be in a better position to give an answer to this question when we have studied the two side by side, and seen whether their general characteristics are similar. R. Eisler states categorically that "anterior to the sixth century is a Syriac translation, of which the sixth book of the 'War' was actually incorporated in the canons of the Syrian and Armenian

[107] i.e. Aesop's Fables; see Baumstark, *Geschichte*, p. 26.

[108] Trans. from the Syriac text in Assemani, *Bibliotheca Orientalis*, III. 1, p. 7.

[109] See Hayman, *Sergius*, p, 96f.

[110] *Codex Ambrosianus*, fol. 320v.

churches" [111], or, more cautiously, that "it is not at all improbable that all seven books of the 'War' once existed in a Syriac translation" [112]

The first editor of the extant Syriac version of the *War*, Heimann Kottek [113], claimed that it represents a Syriac revision of the original Aramaic edition which Josephus mentions in his preface to the work [114]. He regards the Greek text as a modified rendering of the Syriac. Although he notes the many places where the Syriac seems to be dependent upon the Greek text, he thinks that the additions and the alterations found in the Syriac which complicate, not simplify, the Greek, necessitate his conclusion. He appeals also to the fact that the deviations of the Greek from the Syriac heighten the glory of the Romans and and criticize the rebels, and therefore clearly represent a version adapted to suit a Roman audience.

Kottek's theory has been unanimously rejected by later scholars - B. Niese [115], R. Eisler [116], H.St.J. Thackeray [117], and especially Th. Nöldeke [118]. Nöldeke sets out his criticisms in a review of Kottek's book, and all other scholars simply refer to this review as having settled the question once and for all. Nöldeke says that Kottek's error has arisen from his recognition that the Syriac text is far worse than the Greek, from which he has deduced that the Syriac represents the first rough edition, which the second, Greek edition has smoothed out. Nöldeke's explanation for the state of the Syriac text is that it is the work of a most incompetent translator : 'Der syrische Text ist eben die ganz flüchtige und fehlerhafte Arbeit eines Mannes, dessen griechische Kenntnisse auffallend mangelhaft waren und der sich mit Rathen half, wo diese versagten' [119]. His general conclusion is that the Syriac text is derived from a Greek original, and must be used as a witness to that original with very great caution.

Without doubt, Nöldeke's criticism, both of Kottek's theory and

111 *The Messiah Jesus*, p. 31.
112 *The Messiah Jesus*, p. 76.
113 *Bellum Judaicum*, introduction.
114 I.3 in Niese's enumeration.
115 *Josephi Opera*, vol. VI, p. xxif.
116 *The Messiah Jesus*, p. 75f.
117 *Josephus*, vol. II, p. x.
118 *Kottek*, 882-4.
119 *Kottek*, 882.

of his actual edition of the text, is justified [120]. There can indeed be little doubt that the Syriac is derived from a Greek original, and that it is a very bad translation. Frequently it is almost incomprehensible as Syriac, and can only be explained by reference to the Greek text. So, if the excerpts in Sergius's Disputation can be shown to possess similar characteristics, we will have confirmation of the suggestion that there was only one complete Syriac version of the *War*, for in his quotations from the sixth book Sergius is clearly drawing upon the Syriac version found in the Codex Ambrosianus.

The textual affinities of the Syriac version of Josephus's *War of the Jews* have never been closely studied. Niese, in the introduction to his edition of Josephus's works, makes a few comments on this subject, besides repeating Nöldeke's opinion of the origin of the version [121]. In general the Greek manuscripts of the *War* fall into two main groups : the first group, P [122], A [123], (M [124], L [125]), is the best text and is usually regarded as reflecting the later, more polished, editions; the second group, V [126], R [127], (C [128]), is regarded by Niese as inferior, and reflects perhaps the earlier unrevised editions of the work. The manuscripts M, L, and C oscillate between the two groups. A notable difference between the two groups is found in the heading which they give to the work, the first having *Ἰουδαικοῦ πολέμου πρὸς Ῥωμαίους*,, the second *Περὶ ἁλώσεως*.. The Syriac may reflect the latter in the heading to the sixth book, but this is more probably a specific heading to this book alone. After a short discussion of the Syriac translation Niese concludes: 'quo igitur usus est codice similior fuit Ambrosiano quam Parisino consensitque interdum et cum L et cum deterioribus' [129]. He does admit, however, that we would attain a greater degree of certainty if an accurate collation of the whole of the Syriac version were to be made. We might also add that a collation of the Syriac with the Slavonic version

120 A much more accurate edition of the text is provided by BEDJAN in his *Homiliae Jacobi Sarugensis*, vol. I, appendix 2, pp. 770-837.

121 *Josephi Opera*, VI, p. xxif.

122 Codex Parisinus Graecus 1425, cent.x or xi.

123 Codex Ambrosianus D.50 superiore, cent.x or xi.

124 Codex Marcianus (Venetus) Gr.383, cent.xi or xii.

125 Codex Laurentianus, plut.lxix.19, cent.xi or xii.

126 Codex Vaticanus Gr.148, c.cent.xi.

127 Codex Palatinus (Vaticanus) Gr.284, cent.xi or xii.

128 Codex Urbinas (Vaticanus) Gr.84, cent.xi.

129 *Josephi Opera*, VI, p. lxxii.

might throw additional light upon the textual affinities of both versions, if, as Eisler supposes [130], the latter is derived from a Greek manuscript representing the earliest edition of the work.

Before we embark upon a consideration of the text of the quotations from Josephus in Sergius's Disputation, it is necessary to add a word of warning. In the light of Sergius's treatment of the biblical text, we cannot doubt that he is quite capable of shaping his sources to suit his own purposes. We must, therefore, bear this possibility in mind, while also remembering that we have only one manuscript of his work, and also only one manuscript of the Syriac version of the *War*, so that we cannot be certain that we possess the true text, except, of course, when the two exactly coindice.

One other factor which could complicate our investigation is the possibility of the mutual influence upon each other of the Syriac versions of Josephus and Eusebius [131], for the latter makes extensive use of the *War of the Jews* in the *Ecclesiastical History*. Two long quotations from *B.J.*, VI, in Bk. 3 of Eusebius's work enable us to make a close comparison of the Syriac versions of these works. The result of such an investigation is that they appear to be quite independent of each other; only in one place do they agree against their respective exemplars — in *B.J.*, VI.298 (Eusebius 3.8), they read ܠܡܕܝܢܬܐ (city) for the plural (τὰς πόλεις) of the Greek texts. Since the difference between the singular and the plural of this word is a Syriac text is indicated only by a diacritical sign (the s^{e}yāmē), this is insufficient evidence to reverse the overwhelming impression of their mutual independence. Nevertheless, we must bear in mind the possibility that Sergius may have been influenced by this Syriac version of the *Ecclesiastical History*, since there is evidence that he both knew and used the work [132].

We will proceed in our investigation of the text of Sergius's quotations from Josephus by isolating them into two groups : first, quotations from book six of the *War*, for which, therefore, there is a parallel Syriac text; second, quotations from the other books of the *War*, for which no other parallel Syriac text is available.

130 *The Messiah Jesus*, p. 32, 79ff. Eisler's opinion of the Slavonic text has, however, found little favour amongst scholars : cf. RUBENSTEIN, *Observations*, 329-348.

131 *Ecclesiastical History in Syriac.*

132 See below, p. 41f.

2. *Quotations in the Disputation from Book Six of the War*

1. Sergius, *Disputation*, xxi.8, has a summarising allusion to *B.J.*, VI. 201-3, a very well known story, which is recounted by Eusebius [133].
2. Josephus, *B.J.*, VI.217f; Sergius, *Disputation*, xxi.8. *Codex Ambrosianus*, fol.325r :—

ܘܢܥܛܐ ܐܢܫܐ ܐ̈ܟܠܝ ܒܢ̈ܝܗܘܢ ܘܠܐ ܢܫܒܘܩ ܬܚܝܬ
ܫܡܫܐ ܡ̈ܕܝܢܬܐ ܕܐܡ̈ܗܬܐ ܕܐܡ̈ܗܬܐ ܕܐܟܠ ܒܗ̇
ܦܐ̈ܪܐ ܕܟ̈ܪܣܝܗܘܢ. ܘܙܕܩ ܕܝܢ ܕܩܘܡ ܐܡ̈ܗܬܐ ܠܐܒ̈ܗܬܐ
ܕܟܬܪ ܬܘܪܣܝܐ ܗܢܐ ܘܥܫܢܐ ܡܪ̈ܝܪܐ ܕܟܦܢܐ ܡܙܝܢܝܢ
ܒܢ̇ ܡܐܢܝܢ.

...'And he would blot out the men who eat their children, and he would not leave under the sun cities, in which the mothers, the mothers, he eats the fruit of their wombs. Yet it is right for the fathers to stand armed before the mothers after such food and the bitter suffering of hunger' [134].

The Greek text [135] :—

Καλύψειν μέντοι τὸ τῆς τεκνοφαγίας μύσος αὐτῷ τῷ τῆς πατρίδος πτώματι καὶ οὐ καταλείψειν ἐπὶ τῆς οἰκουμένης ἡλίῳ καθορᾶν πόλιν, ἐν ᾗ μητέρες οὕτω τρέφονται. προσήκειν μέντοι πρὸ μητέρων πατράσιν τὴν τοιαύτην τροφήν, οἳ καὶ μετὰ τηλικαῦτα πάθη μένουσιν ἐν τοῖς ὅπλοις.

As a general observation, we may note first of all, that Sergius puts Titus's words into direct speech [136], while the Greek and Syriac versions give them in indirect speech. More specific observations are :—
(i) Sergius has introduced ܐܠܗܐ (God) as the subject of the first sentence so that, while in the Greek and Syriac versions Titus states his determination to efface the city, in Sergius's version he exhorts God to do so [137]. The variant is dogmatic, for it emphasises that the Jews are under the wrath of God; we may safely attribute it to Sergius himself,

133 *Ecclesiastical History*, 3. 6.

134 The quotation is deliberately translated literally to emphasize the abysmal state both of the Syriac translation of the Greek and of the text of the Codex.

135 Niese, *Josephi Opera*, VI, p. 541, l. 11-15.

136 So does the Slavonic version — see Istrin, *La prise*, vol. II, p. 161ff.

137 Or states, or prophesies, that God will do so.

who is clearly treating Josephus in the same way as he treats the Bible.
(ii) The two Syriac versions agree in shortening the first clause by rendering *τὸ τῆς τεκνοφαγίας μύσος* by ܐܢܫܐ ܐ̈ܟܠܝ ܒܢ̈ܝܗܘܢ (the men who eat their children) and by omitting altogether the phrase *αὐτῷ τῷ τῆς πατρίδος πτώματι*.
(iii) The phrase *ἐπὶ τῆς οἰκουμένης ἡλίῳ καθορᾶν* is simply rendered ܬܚܝܬ ܫܡܫܐ (under the sun) by the Syriac versions.
(iv) At the end of the first sentence the text of Codex Ambrosianus is clearly faulty and the Disputation provides a better reading. The second ܕܐܡ̈ܗܬܐ must be omitted [138] and the ܐ̈ܟܠܝ of Sergius's version must be read for the ܕܐܟܠ of the Codex.
(v) The Syriac versions have expanded the *ὄυτω* of the Greek into ܦܐܪܐ ܕܡ̈ܥܝܗܘܢ (the fruit of their wombs), providing an object for the verb *τρέφονται* [139].
(vi) In the last sentence the two Syriac versions diverge. The version in the Codex attempts a literal translation and produces nonsensical Syriac: ܘܙܕܩ ܕܝܢ ܕܩܕܡ ܐܡ̈ܗܬܐ ܠܐܒ̈ܗܬܐ is clearly an attempt to render literally *προσήκειν μεντοι πρὸ μητέρων πατράσιν*; the Greek *πρὸ*, here used in the sense of 'rather than', loses its correct meaning in the Syriac translation. The ܕܒܬܪ of the Codex is misplaced and should come before ܢܫܐ ܡܪ̈ܒܝܢܐ, where Sergius places it. His text is either derived from a manuscript which represents an attempt to clear up the incomprehensible rendering of the Codex, or Sergius has done this himself by omitting the difficult ܐܡ̈ܗܬܐ, but retaining ܕܩܕܡ and adding ܗܡܟܠܐ after it. Even so we have to supply the words 'this food' to connect his version with the meaning of the Greek; it may be a scribal omission in the manuscript of the Disputation.

As a result of this investigation it is clear, first of all, that the Syriac version in the Codex Ambrosianus is derived directly from the Greek, of which it is a very literal translation. The agreements of the two Syriac texts against the Greek make it virtually certain that they belong to the same version, while their divergences are best explained as the result of attempts, either by scribes or Sergius himself, to improve and make sense of the very deficient text found in the Codex. One variant may be explained as a dogmatic alteration made by Sergius.
3. The quotation in *Disputation*, xxi.13, from *B.J.*, VI.420, is drawn

[138] Cf. Bedjan, *Homiliae Jacobi Sarugensis*, I, p. 804, n. 1.
[139] The Slavonic adds: 'their children' — see Istrin, *La prise*, II, p. 163.

only indirectly from Josephus via the medium of Eusebius's *Chronicle*, and will be considered separately at a later stage [140].

4. Josephus, *B.J.*, VI.250; Sergius, *Disputation*, xxi.14. *Codex Ambrosianus*, fol.325v :—

ܡܛܠ ܗܢܐ ܕܝܢ ܐܦ ܟܪܙ ܕܝܢܐ ܕܐܠܗܐ ܕܝܩܕܢܗ
ܕܗܝܟܠܐ ܕܡܢ ܩܕܡ ܘܕܝܢܐ ܐܟܪܙ ܗܘܐ.

'And concerning this also the judgement of God had proclaimed long ago the burning of the temple'.

The Greek text :— [141]

τοῦ δ' ἄρα κατεψήφιστο μὲν τὸ πύρ ὁ θὲος πάλαι.

Sergius is clearly drawing here upon the version in the Codex, though he rearranges the word order; the omission of ܗܘܐ is insignificant. The phrase ܝܩܕܢܗ ܕܗܝܟܠܐ (the burning of the temple) in the Syriac versions is not a genuine variant for *τὸ πῦρ* but becomes necessary when *κατεψήφιστο* is translated somewhat loosely by ܟܪܙ ܕܝܢܐ ܕܐܠܗܐ ܐܟܪܙ [ܗܘܐ].

5. Josephus, *B.J.*, VI.266; Sergius, *Disputation*, xxi.14.

The text of Sergius's quotation exactly agrees with that of the *Codex* (fol.326r), which in turn renders the Greek more or less accurately.

6. Josephus, *B.J.*, VI.285; Sergius, *Disputation*, xxi.14. [142]

Here Sergius summarises rather than quotes, and no conclusion can be drawn from his text.

7. Josephus, *B.J.*, VI.251; Sergius, *Disputation*, xxi.15.

Here again Sergius briefly summarises the purport of the passage. The text of the *Codex* (fol.325v) seems to be disturbed [143], apparently contradicting the Greek, though the general context in that version supports the rendering implied by Sergius's summary.

8. Josephus, *B.J.*, VI.408: Sergius, *Disputation*, xxi.15.

The text of Sergius's quotation is identical with that of the *Codex* (fol.329r), except for one small detail — he reads ܐܝܟ ܐܚܪܢ for the Codex's ܐܝܟ. This variant probably reflects the *ἄλλο* in the adverbial phrase of the Greek *κατ' ἄλλο τι*, so that Sergius preserves here a bet-

140 See below, p. 49.

141 Niese, *Josephi Opera*, VI, p. 545, l. 19f.

142 *Codex Ambrosianus*, fol. 326v.

143 Cf. Bedjan, *Homiliae Jacobi Sarugensis*, I, 808, n. 2.

ter text of the Syriac version. The latter departs from the Greek at this point, considerably simplifying a complex Greek sentence, probably through inability to render it exactly.

9. Josephus, *B.J.*, VI.411; Sergius, *Disputation*, xxi. 15.

Here Sergius summarises the introduction to Titus's exclamation, because all that he is really interested in is the theological implications of this speech. His summary serves to emphasize the point that only God could have overthrown such strong fortifications. His text of Titus's speech exactly follows the version in the *Codex* (fol. 329r), except for one insignificant addition.

10. Josephus, *B.J.*, VI.442; Sergius, *Disputation*, xxi.15. *Codex Ambrosianus*, fol.330r :—

ܐܠܐ ܠܐ ܡܩܕܡܘܬܗ ܘܠܐ ܥܘܬܪܗ ܣܓܝܐܐ. ܘܠܐ
ܫܘܡܗܗ ܕܒܟܠܗ ܒܪܝܬܐ ܘܠܐ ܬܫܒܘܚܬܗ ܪܒܬܐ :
ܘܠܐ ܬܫܡܫܬܗ ܣܦܩܐ ܠܗ ܠܚܘܪܒܐ ܕܩܛܠܗ. ܗܕܐ
ܗܝ ܚܪܬܐ ܕܚܘܪܒܗ ܕܐܘܪܫܠܡ.

'But neither her pre-eminence, nor her very great wealth, nor her fame in all the world, nor her great glory, nor her worship, was able (to prevent) the destruction which came upon her. This is the end of the destruction of Jerusalem'.

The Greek text [144] :—

ἀλλὰ γὰρ οὔθ' ἡ ἀρχαιότης οὔθ' ὁ πλοῦτος ὁ βαθὺς οὔτε τὸ διαπεφοιτηκὸς ὅλης τῆς οἰκουμένης ἔθνος οὔθ' ἡ μεγάλη δόξα τῆς θρησκείας ἤρκεσέ τι πρὸς ἀπώλειαν αὐτῇ. τοιοῦτο μὲν δὴ τὸ τέλος τῆς Ἱεροσολύμων πολιορκίας.

On the whole Sergius follows the version in the Codex, which is here a reasonable translation of the Greek. He does, however, have two major variants — the omission of ܣܓܝܐܐ after ܥܘܬܪܗ, and of ܪܒܬܐ after ܬܫܒܘܚܬܗ, and one, minor, insignificant variant — the Pe'al ܩܛܠܗ for Pa'el ܩܛܠܗ. The Codex follows the Greek, so Sergius's variants have probably arisen in the course of the textual transmission of the Syriac version. That Sergius is dependent upon the version represented in the Codex is proved by his agreement with it in translating (or rather mistranslating) *τὸ διαπεφοιτηκὸς ὅλης τῆς οἰκου-*

144 Niese, *Josephi Opera*, VI, p. 570, l. 1ff.

μένης ἔθνος by ܘܠܐ ܥܘܡܪܗ̇ ܕܟܠܗ̇ ܒܪܝܬܐ, by his agreement in breaking down the genitival relationship *ἡ μεγάλη δόξα τῆς θρησκείας* into the syntactical ܘܠܐ ܬܫܒܘܚܬܗ [ܪܒܬܐ] ܘܠܐ ܬܫܡܫܬܗ̇, by translating the aorist *ἤρκεσέ* by the present participle ܡܣܦܩܐ [145], and by translating *αὐτῇ* by ܡܛܠܗ̇ (ܡܛܠܝܗ̇).

The result of this investigation so far is that Sergius is dependent for his text of Josephus's *War of the Jews* upon the Syriac version represented in the Codex Ambrosianus, at least as far as book six is concerned. This creates the presumption that for his text of the other books he will also be dependent upon a Syriac version rather than directly upon the Greek text. As far as the text of his quotations is concerned, although he does seem on occasions to provide a better text than the Codex, he must be used with great caution as a witness to the Syriac version, for we have observed once again his tendency to mould his sources to suit his own purposes. In these quotations there is no parallel text in Eusebius, so that Sergius's variants cannot be explained as the result of influence from that quarter.

3. *Quotations in the Disputation from the other Books of the War*

1. Josephus, *B.J.*, I.12; Sergius, *Disputation*, xxi.7.
The Greek text :— [146]

Τὰ γοῦν πάντων ἀπ' αἰῶνος ἀτυχήματα πρὸς τὰ Ἰουδαίων ἡττῆσθαι δοκῶ κατὰ σύγκρισιν.

(i) The Syriac connects *πάντων* with *ἀτυχήματα*, while the Greek has it in a genitival relationship — 'the misfortunes of all'.
(ii) The Syriac renders the one Greek word *ἀτυχήματα*, with the two words ܐܘ̈ܠܨܢܐ and ܒܝ̈ܫܬܐ.
(iii) The Syriac adds ܕܟܠܕܫܘ, which is implicit in the Greek.
(iv) The manuscript omits ܠܝܗܘ̈ܕܝܐ, though it is added by the Serṭā corrector, but has ܒܐܘܪܫܠܡ, a variant which has no basis in the Greek text.
(v) The Syriac adds ܣܓܝ.

(i) is the sort of error which we have come to expect from the translator responsible for the version of the *War* found in the Codex Ambro-

145 We may surmise that ܗܘܬ has dropped out at a very early stage.
146 Niese, *Josephi Opera*, VI, p. 5, l. 16ff.

sianus. (ii) is best explained by the Semitic partiality towards pairs of synonyms, a trait which can be observed in the Codex [147]. (iii) adds nothing to the sense of the Greek. (iv) is perhaps a genuine variant, though its absence in the Greek manuscript tradition suggests rather that it is a clarifying addition. (v) strengthens the force of the comparison and has probably been added by Sergius himself.
2. Josephus, *B.J.*, III.354; Sergius, *Disputation*, xxi.7.
The Greek text [148] :—

κἀπειδὴ τὸ Ἰουδαίων, ἔφη [149], φῦλον ὀκλάσει [150] δοκεῖ σοι τῷ κτίσαντι, μετέβη δὲ πρὸς Ῥωμαίους ἡ τύχη πᾶσα ...

(i) The Greek of the first clause is very difficult and has given rise to several variants in the manuscript tradition. The Syriac translator seems to have been unable to make any sense out of it [151]. On the other hand, he could have read it as follows : 'since it seems to you, their creator, that the race of Jews has slackened [152] (their zeal for God), their fortune etc.', hence the reading 'the Jews have sinned'. It seems more probable, however, that the Syriac translator avoided rendering the Greek exactly through inability to do so, a characteristic which we have observed in the version found in the Codex Ambrosianus. Either way, it is difficult in the light of Kottek's theory to see how such a difficult Greek text arose out of such a simple Syriac text.
(ii) The Syriac omits the *πᾶσα* of the Greek for no apparent reason.
3. Josephus, *B.J.*, V.401; Sergius, *Disputation*, xxi.7.

The Syriac is a literal translation of the Greek, so literal, in fact, that as Syriac it reads very clumsily.
4. Josephus, *B.J.*, V.412f; Sergius, *Disputation*, xxi.7.
The Greek text [153] :—

ὥστε ἐγὼ πεφευγέναι μὲν ἐκ τῶν ἁγίων οἶμαι τὸ θεῖον, ἑστάναι δὲ παρ ' οἷς πολεμεῖτε νῦν. ἀλλ' ἀνὴρ μὲν ἀγαθὸς οἰκίαν ἀσελγῆ

[147] For example, in *B.J.* VI., 409, the *Codex* (fol. 329r) renders ἀπεθαύμασεν with the two Syriac words ܬܡܗ ܘܬܗܪ.

[148] Niese, *Josephi Opera*, VI, p. 321, 1.3f.

[149] Josephus is praying.

[150] This is Niese's reading; PAML read κολάσαι; Thackeray, *Josephus*, II, p. 676 reads κλὰσαι following a Leyden MS, and renders ὀκλάσαι by 'that it should sink into the dust'.

[151] The Slavonic translator also had difficulty with it see Istrin, *La prise*, I, p. 233, n.3.

[152] Reading ὀκλάσαι.

[153] Niese, *Josephi Opera*, VI, p. 491, l. 6-9.

φεύξεται καὶ τοὺς ἐν αὐτῇ στυγήσει, τὸν δὲ θεὸν ἔτι πείθεσθε τοῖς οἰκείοις κακοῖς παραμένειν.

(i) For the *τὸ θεῖον* [154] of the Greek the Syriac has the Jewish expression ܫܟܝܢܬܐ ܕܐܠܗܐ. This could be taken as favouring Kottek's hypothesis; it is, however, far more likely that either the Syriac translator or Sergius himself is influenced by Ezech.10.18f, 11.23 [155].
(ii) *ἐκ τῶν ἁγίων* is rendered by ܡܩܘܕܫܐ [156] which means much the same.
(iii) The Syriac recasts the second sentence of the quotation, and particularly the last clause. Since the effect of the change is to heighten the rhetorical effect we shall not go far wrong in suspecting here the hand of Sergius himself.
5. Josephus, *B.J.*, V.442; Sergius, *Disputation*, xxi.7.
With one or two minor variants the Syriac is a reasonable translation of the Greek.
6. Josephus, *B.J.*, V.559; Sergius, *Disputation*, xxi.7.
Again with minor variants the Syriac is a literal translation of the Greek.
7. Josephus, *B.J.*, V.566; Sergius, *Disputation*, xxi.8.
The Syriac version of Eusebius's *Ecclesiastical History*, 3.6.19 [157] :—

ܣܒܪ ܐܢܐ ܕܝܢ ܕܐܠܘ ܪܗܘܡܝܐ ܐܫܬܘܚܪܘ ܗܘܘ
ܕܢܐܬܘܢ ܥܠ ܗܠܝܢ ܡܪܘܕܐ: ܐܘ ܒܗܘܬܐ ܡܬܒܠܥܐ
ܗܘܬ ܐܘ ܒܛܘܦܢܐ ܐܒܕܐ ܗܘܬ ܗܝ ܡܕܝܢܬܐ: ܐܘ
ܢܘܪܐ ܕܣܕܘܡ ܡܫܬܕܪܐ ܗܘܬ ܥܠܝܗ̇. ܝܬܝܪ ܡܢ ܗܢܘܢ ܓܝܪ
ܕܚܫܘ ܒܗܠܝܢ ܣܝܒܪܗ ܐܠܗܐ ܠܗܕܐ ܫܪܒܬܐ ܕܐܝܬܝܗ̇
ܕܠܐ ܐܠܗ.

'Now I think that if the Romans had delayed attacking these rebels, this city would either have been swallowed up in the abyss or perished in a flood, or the fire of Sodom would have been sent against it. For God bore with this generation which is more godless than those who suffered in these (visitations)'.

154 One MS, L, reads *τὸν θεόν*.
155 Michel and Bauerfeind, *De Bello Judaico*, II. 1, p. 266f, suggest that Josephus himself is influenced here by Ez. 11. 23.
156 So the Slavonic — Istrin, *La prise*,II,p.111.
157 *Ecclesiastical History in Syriac*, p. 125.

The Greek text of Josephus [158] :—

οἶμαι Ῥωμαίων βραδυνόντων ἐπὶ τοὺς ἀλιτηρίους ἢ καταποθῆναι ἂν ὑπὸ χάσματος ἢ κατακλυσθῆναι τὴν πόλιν ἢ τοὺς τῆς Σοδομηνῆς μεταλαβεῖν κεραυνούς · πολύ γάρ τῶν ταῦτα παθόντων ἤνεγκε γενέαν ἀθεωτέραν.

(i) Sergius's version simplifies the Greek by omitting *τοὺς ἀλιτηρίους* and by making 'the city' the object of the verb 'delayed' and the subject of the following conditional clauses. This tendency towards simplification is characteristic of the version of Josephus found in the Codex Ambrosianus, so that if we are confronted here with the same version, these changes do not represent genuine variants in the Greek text. The Syriac version of Eusebius follows the Greek more closely.
(ii) Sergius's version gives only the very general ܡܚܘܬܐ for the precise *τοὺς ... κεραυνούς* of the Greek; the Syriac of Eusebius again translates more accurately, though not quite literally.
(iii) Both Syriac versions substantially alter the sense of the Greek in the last sentence of the quotation. Thackeray translates the Greek thus : 'For it produced a generation far more godless than the victims of those visitations' [159]. The Syriac versions, however, have taken *ἤνεγκε* in the sense 'endure, bear with, put up with', and then supplied the necessary subject — God. Now this confirms that the Syriac version used by Sergius is secondary to the Greek, but it does raise the question as to the influence of the Syriac version of Eusebius on either the Syriac version of Josephus or directly on Sergius himself. That the influence would be from the direction of the former version is made probable by the relative dates of the versions — the Syriac Eusebius dates from, at the latest, the beginning of the fifth century and may go back into the fourth century [160]. The fact noted above that elsewhere the text of the Syriac version of the *Ecclesiastical History* does not seem to have influenced the text of the Syriac version of the *War*, suggests that, if we are to accept the hypothesis of textual cross influence, it is more probable that Sergius is directly influenced by Eusebius. This, of course,

[158] Niese, *Josephi Opera*, VI, p. 511, l. 17-20; the Greek text of Eusebius is identical except for one minor detail.

[159] *Josephus*, III, p .375. Cf. Michel and Bauerfeind, *De Bello Judaico*, II. 2, p. 211 (n. 241 to Bk. VI).

[160] Eusebius, *Ecclesiastical History in Syriac*,p.ix, and Nestle, *Kirchengeschichte des Eusebius*, p. v.

involves making the by now not unreasonable assumption that Sergius is using a Syriac version of Josephus only part of which is represented in Codex Ambrosianus. However, it is not impossible that the translators of the two versions, in complete independence of each other, took the Greek in the same way, for in the rest of the quotation they certainly represent independent translations, with the Syriac Eusebius decidedly the more accurate and literal.

8. Josephus, *B.J.*, V.567,569; Sergius, *Disputation*, xxi.7.

This is a paraphrase combining two separate texts. The numbers in the Syriac agree with those in the Greek, except that the latter gives the more precise total of 115,880 for the dead thrown out of the city gate.

9. Josephus, *B.J.*, VII.327f; Sergius, *Disputation*, xxi.12.

The Greek text [161] :—

Τὸ πάλαι φίλον αὐτῷ φῦλον Ἰουδαίων κατέγνωστο · μένων γὰρ εὐμενὴς ἢ μετρίως γοῦν ἀπηχθημένος, οὐκ ἂν τοσούτων μεν ἀνθρώπων περιεῖδεν ὄλεθρον, προήκατο δὲ τὴν ἱερωτάτην αὐτοῦ πόλιν πυρὶ καὶ κατασκαφαῖς πολεμίων .

(1) The Syriac substitutes ܕܐܠܗܐ for *αὐτῷ* and adds ܐܠܗܐ as the subject of the second sentence. This is necessary in order to make clear to whom the *αὐτῷ* refers; it is, of course, perfectly clear from the context in the Greek [162].

(ii) The Syriac (by having ܠܐܒܕܢܐ) confirms the reading of LC and the Latin version which add *ἀπωλείαν* before *κατέγνωστο* [163].

(iii) The Syriac alters the structure of the latter part of the quotation. Instead of including the last sentence in the apodosis of the preceding sentence as does the Greek, it starts a completely new sentence which states the grounds on which the conditional sentence is based. The change has the effect of making God much more directly responsible for the destruction of Jerusalem, so once again we may suspect that Sergius's modifying hand has been at work.

4. *Conclusion*

We may draw the following conclusions from our study of the text of Josephus's *War of the Jews* in relation to the quotations from it found in Sergius's Disputation :

[161] Niese, *Josephi Opera*, VI, p. 612, l. 14ff.

[162] The Slavonic does, however, contain the same additions — Istrin, *La prise*, II, p. 237.

[163] Again the Slavonic follows this reading.

(i) For his quotations from book six of the *War* Sergius is drawing upon the Syriac version found in the Codex Ambrosianus. The source of his quotations from the other books seem to be a Syriac version of which that found in the Codex is only a part. For the characteristics of Sergius's quotations from these other books and those of the text of book six in the Codex are identical: the same sort of errors and additions occur in both versions; we notice the same inability to render the Greek when it is difficult, and we notice the same tendency towards simplification. The fact that the quality of the Syriac in the text of Sergius's quotations is much lower than in the rest of the Disputation is added confirmation that he is using the translation represented in the Codex. Sergius's Disputation is, then, an important witness to the existence in the Syriac-speaking church of a single, complete, Syriac version of Josephus's *War of the Jews*.
(ii) Used with caution, the text of Sergius's quotations from book six of the *War* is a valuable addition to the textual apparatus of the Syriac version.
(iii) Sergius's quotations confirm that the Syriac version of the *War* is translated from the Greek, and, therefore, they further invalidate H. Kottek's theory about its origin.
(iv) As a witness to the Greek text, the Syriac text of the *War* must be used with great caution, despite the fact that Codex Ambrosianus is four centuries earlier than the oldest Greek manuscript. This is especially true of Sergius's quotations, for we have continually observed alterations made for dogmatic reasons. The principle on which he has selected his quotations — any text which ascribes to God direct responsibility for the destruction of Jerusalem and emphasizes the Jews' estrangement from God — has effected the text of the quotations themselves. We should also be aware that the sixth book of the *War* was incorporated into the canon of the Syriac-speaking church for the very same reasons for which Sergius uses Josephus in his Disputation, so that any variants in this version which emphasize these factors must be suspect. Nevertheless, in one place (*B.J.*, VII.327) Sergius's quotation is a valuable witness for an important variant in the Greek manuscript tradition.
(v) The text of B.J., V.566 in the Disputation may be evidence that the Syriac version of Eusebius's *Ecclesiastical History* did influence the text of the Syriac version of the *War of the Jews*. But alternative explanations are equally probable.

(vi) Several interesting agreements between the text of Sergius's quotations and the Slavonic version of Josephus merit further study, and, in particular, a collation of the Slavonic with the whole of the Syriac version. Some important facts about the type of Greek manuscripts upon which these versions were based might emerge from such an investigation.

D. Eusebius's Ecclesiastical History

There are three main reasons for suspecting that in chapter xxi Sergius is drawing upon Eusebius's *Ecclesiastical History* in the Syriac version :—

(i) The first has already been discussed — the text of Sergius's quotation of Josephus, *B.J.*, V.566 [164].

(ii) The second reason is that the general structure of this section in the Disputation parallels that of the *Ecclesiastical History*, 3.5-8. The overriding theme in both works is the same — 'the judgement of God at last overtook them (the Jews) for their crimes against Christ and his apostles, completely blotting out that wicked generation from among men' [165]. The theme is then illustrated by selected quotations from Josephus's *War of the Jews* and from Christ's prophecies of the destruction of Jerusalem. Like Sergius, Eusebius presents his quotations from Josephus as confirmation of the fulfillment of Christ's prophecies [166]. However, Sergius presents a wider selection of quotations from Josephus, since he is concerned, not only to describe the horrors of the final siege, but also to illustrate God's estrangement from the Jews. Moreover, neither the quotations from Josephus found in the two works nor the prophecies of Christ overlap to any great extent, so that the most we can say is that Sergius could be dependent on Eusebius for the general idea of combining Josephus's *War of the Jews* with Christ's prophecies to illustrate a theme which has very deep roots in the tradition of Christian anti-Jewish polemic. [167]

(iii) In chapter xxi.6 Sergius may be more specifically dependent on

164 See above, p. 44f.

165 *Ecclesiastical History*, 3. 5. 3.

166 *Ecclesiastical History*, 3. 7. 6.

167 See below, p. 62.

Eusebius. We may compare this section with the Syriac version of Eusebius, *Ecclesiastical History*, 3.7.8f [168] :—

ܗܠܝܢ ܕܝܢ ܙܕܩ ܕܢܘܣܦ ܠܗܝܢ. ܐܝܠܝܢ ܕܡܚܘܝܢܘܬܐ ܐܝܬܝܗܝܢ
ܕܪܚܡܢܘܬܗ ܘܒܛܝܠܘܬܐ ܕܛܒܘܬܗ : ܕܐܪ̈ܒܥܝܢ-
ܫ̈ܢܝܢ ܐܒܝܕܐ ܡܢ ܒܬܪ ܡܪܚܘܬܗܘܢ ܕܥܠ ܡܫܝܚܐ
ܐܘܚܪ ܡܢ ܐܒܕܢܗܘܢ :..... ܕܡܕܒܪܢܐ ܕܐܠܗܐ ܥܕܡܐ
ܠܗܫܐ ܡܓܪ ܗܘܐ ܠܗܘܢ ܪܘܚܐ : ܕܕܠܡܐ ܒܣܘܦ
ܢܬܬܘܢ ܘܢܬܦܢܘܢ ܥܠ ܡܕܡ ܕܥܒܕܘ : ܘܢܗܘܐ ܠܗܘܢ
ܫܘܒܩܢܐ ܘܚܝ̈ܐ.

'But it is right to add these things, which are demonstrations of his mercy and the concern of his goodness — that for forty whole years after their presumption against Christ he averted their destruction...... The administration of God was hitherto patient with them, that perhaps at last they might repent and turn against the things which they had done, and have forgiveness and salvation'.

Sergius gives a succint summary of what Eusebius says, and we may note that certain key words occur in both works — ܪܚܡܢܘܬܗ (his mercy), and [ܗܘܢ]ܡܪܚܘܬܟܘܢ (your [their] presumption). The period of the opportunity for repentance differs, since in this case Sergius is either drawing directly upon Eusebius's *Chronicle* or indirectly by means of some other Syriac chronicle [169]. The statement made in the Disputation that the Jews occupied the period of grace by persecuting the saints is paralleled in the *Ecclesiastical History*, 3.5.2, where Eusebius describes the Jews' deeds in detail.

There is, therefore, a *prima facie* case for suspecting the influence of the Syriac version of the *Ecclesiastical History* upon Sergius. None of the points suggesting this are decisive in themselves, but taken together their force is sufficient to make such dependence a real possibility.

E. Eusebius's Chronicle

In two places Sergius draws either directly upon Eusebius's *Chronicle* or on some work which is dependent on it. The Syriac version of the

[168] *Ecclesiastical History in Syriac*, p. 130f.
[169] See below, p. 50.

Chronicle, like the original Greek, is no longer extant, but fragments have survived in some manuscripts, and P. Keseling [170] in an extensive study has isolated evidence for the existence of two Syriac versions of the work dating from the seventh century.

(i) In chapter xxi.13 Sergius gives a list of the casualties resulting from the siege of Jerusalem. There are three traditions regarding this list of casualties. The first is that of the text of the *War of the Jews* itself (VI.420), where Josephus gives 97,000 as the number of the prisoners taken, and 1,100,000 as the number of those who perished in the siege [171]. The second tradition stems from Eusebius's *Ecclesiastical History*, 3.7.3, which puts the numbers killed by famine and sword at 1,100,000 and the number taken captive at 90,000 [172]. The anonymous chronicle attributed to Dionysius of Tellmahre [173], Isho'dad of Merv [174], and Dionysius bar Salibhi [175], follow this tradition. The third tradition is that of Eusebius's *Chronicle* which, in Jerome's Latin version, reads as follows :—

Titus Iudea capta et Hierosolymis subuersis sescenta milia virorum interfecit. Josephus vero scribit undecies centena milia fame et gladio perisse et alia centum milia captivorum publice uenundata [176].

The Syriac tradition of the text of the *Chronicle* differs at this point by reading 60,000 for the number killed, not 600,000. It is followed by the *Chronicon ad Annum Domini 846 Pertinens* [177], the *Chronicle of Bar Hebraeus* [178], the *Chronicle of Michael the Syrian* [179], the *Chronicon Miscellaneum ad Annum Domini 724 Pertinens* [180], and the *Chronicon Anonymum ad A.D. 1234 Pertinens* [181]. Sergius is clearly dependent upon this third tradition in its Syriac form so he either knew a Syriac version of the *Chronicle* or some other chronicle dependent upon it.

170 *Chronik des Eusebius.*

171 So the *Codex Ambrosianus*, fol. 329r.

172 *Ecclesiastical History of Eusebius in Syriac*, p. 129.

173 Pseudo-Dionysius, *Chronicon*, tx. Vol. I, p. 113.

174 *Commentaries*, VI, p. ܡܓ.

175 *Commentaries*,II.1,p.41.

176 Eusebius, *Chronicle*, p. 187.

177 *Chronica Minora*, tx. p. 180.

178 p. 50f.

179 Vol. IV, p. 101.

180 *Chronica Minora*, tx. p. 117.

181 tx. Vol. I, p. 130.

(ii) In discussing chapter xxi.6 of the Disputation [182] we observed that the period of 39 years mentioned is ultimately derived from Eusebius's *Chronicle*. Jerome's Latin version gives the period from the beginning of Christ's ministry to the destruction of Jerusalem as 42 years [183]. Elsewhere in the *Chronicle* Eusebius says that Christ preached for three years [184], leaving an interval of exactly 39 years from the crucifixion to the fall of Jerusalem. This information is repeated in the Syriac Chronicles which were so heavily indebted to Eusebius, so we can be sure that once again Sergius is drawing either upon a Syriac version of the *Chronicle* or upon one of these Syriac chronicles.

F. Ephraem's Commentary on the Diatessaron

In his biography of the Lord in prophecies Sergius quotes Mt.2.23, which he attributes to Isaiah, and he appends the following explanation :

"And (prophesying) that he would live in Nazareth, Isaiah said : He shall be called a Nazarene. John the teacher explains and says that in the Hebrew language 'nurba' is called 'naṣor' [185] (ch.i.8)."

Although Sergius quotes a certain 'John the teacher' as his authority for this explanation, it goes back to Ephraem's *Commentary on the Diatessaron* [186], at least as far as the Syriac tradition is concerned [187]. The explanation is used by Isho'dad of Merv [188], no doubt borrowing from Ephraem, although he quotes also from a commentary by a certain Bar Bahriz who, he says, bases his interpretation on the same derivation from Is.11.1. Then it is used by Dionysius bar Salibhi [189], and by Bar Hebraeus [190] who, unlike the two previous expositors explicitly

182 Above, p. 48.

183 Eusebius, *Chronicle*, p. 187.

184 *Chronicle*, p. 175.

185 ܢܘܪܒܐ (a shoot) translates the Hebrew נֵצֶר in Is. 11. 1, a well known testimony text — cf. Aphraates, *Demonstrations*, I, 150, Ephraem, *Opera Omnia*, III. 213, and Daniélou, *Études*, p. 143.

186 Harris, *Ephraem*, pp. 40-42, Ephraem, *Commentary* (*Armenian*) p. 30.

187 Its ultimate origin is probably to be found in the earliest tradition of Jewish-Christian exegesis.

188 *Commentaries*, VI, p. ܠܘ.

189 *Commentaries*, tx. I, p. 124.

190 *Commentary*, text, p. 9.

attributes the explanation to Ephraem. Rendel Harris [186] refers to a marginal note in Cod. Vat., Syr.268 which also quotes Ephraem's explanation. Jacob of Sarug [191] mentions the Nazarene (Christ) and then immediately afterwards refers to the 'shoot of Jesse', so he too probably knew Ephraem's explanation.

The unknown John the Teacher, whom Sergius quotes, was probably, therefore, indebted to Ephraem for his explanation of Mt.2.23, though it does seem to have been current in the theological schools of the Syriac-speaking church from Ephraem to Bar Hebraeus [192]. Other possible contacts between the Disputation and Ephraem's *Commentary* are indicated in the notes to the Translation.

CHAPTER III

THE LITERARY NATURE OF THE DISPUTATION AND THE PURPOSE FOR WHICH IT WAS WRITTEN

Introduction

As we have already seen, the introduction and the colophon to the manuscript claim that the work is a disputation written by Sergius the Stylite against a Jew who had argued with him. The manuscript itself, therefore, makes no claim actually to reproduce a verbatim report of the discussion which is purported to have taken place between Sergius and the Jew. It suggests, rather, that the Disputation was written on the basis of the discussion. It is thus necessary to test these hints, contained in the introduction and the colophon, as to the literary nature of the work, by a thorough examination of the text of the Disputation. In the course of this examination answers to the following questions will be sought. Is the Disputation a literary work or the record of an actual discussion? What portrait of the Jew does it reveal — a real historical person or a literary creation? Does the work show any first hand knowledge of Judaism and is there any historical foundation for its comments on the relations between Christians and Jews during the

[191] *Against the Jews*, I, l. 298ff.

[192] For the exegesis of the text in the Greek patristic tradition cf. HARRIS, *Testimonies*, II, p. 62f.

period in which it was written? And finally, what hints does the text give regarding the purpose for which the work was written?

1. *An Analysis of the Contents of the Disputation*

The first page of the Disputation (i.1-3) is a literary introduction of a type common in Christian anti-Jewish polemical literature. The quotation of Dt.6.4f contrasted with Ps.2.7 serves to state vividly the problem with which the Disputation has to deal — has God a son or not? The *Dialogue of Timothy and Aquila* [1], the *Dialogue of Papiscus and Philo* [2], and Aphraates' Demonstration 17 [3], all begin by posing the subject for discussion in terms of the question: 'Has God a Son?' Besides Dt.6.4f and Ps.2.7, Is.7.14 is cited in the Disputation, ostensibly to prove that Ps.2.7 does not apply to David. Since, as has already been suggested, Sergius made use of *testimonia* material, it is probable that his choice of these three quotations was influenced by the testimony tradition [4]. Moreover, although we cannot say how Sergius might have developed the connection between Ps.2.7 and Is.7.14 because the following folios are missing, it is difficult to see how the latter proves that the former does not apply to David. It looks rather as though Sergius is moving on to the beginning of his Testimony Book and citing Is.7.14 in order to prove that the Old Testament prophesies the Virgin Birth. We conclude, then, that the first page of Sergius's Disputation is a literary composition based rather on earlier models of dialogues against the Jews and on his Testimony Book than on any real discussion.

After the first folio, eight folios are missing, but on the basis of such collections of testimonies as that of Cyprian and that of Isidore of Seville [5], we may attempt to conjecture what these missing folios contained. Isidore's Bk.1, ch.10, has the heading 'Christ was born of a pure virgin' followed by the citation of Is.7.14, and this corresponds to Cyprian's Bk.II, ch.9, and the Disputation, i.3. His Bk.I.13 is entitled 'The Magi offered gifts', followed by the quotation from Ps.72 found in ch.i.6 of Sergius's Disputation. In between these chapters Isidore has I.11 en-

[1] Conybeare, *Dialogues*, p. 65f.

[2] McGiffert, *Dialogue*, p. 52.

[3] *Demonstrations*, I, 785.

[4] Cf. Cyprian, *Against the Jews*, II. 8f, the *Dialogue of Athanasius and Zacchaeus*, §1, Conybeare, *Dialogues*, p. 1f.

[5] *Against the Jews*.

titled 'Christ was born in Bethlehem', citing Mic.5.2, and corresponding to Cyprian's II.12; and ch.12, 'The Birth of Christ is shown by the sign of a star', citing Num.24.17, and corresponding to Cyprian's Bk.II.10. Apart from the rather remote possibility that Isidore drew upon the same Book of Testimonies as Sergius, it is a reasonable conjecture that such material as this was contained in the missing folios of the Disputation. It is also quite possible that the missing folios contained material akin to Isidore's Bk.I.8, entitled 'Christ sprang from the tribe of Judah', citing Gen.49.10 [6], a very well known testimony text which Sergius does not cite in the manuscript as we have it; and I.9, 'That Christ was born of the seed of David', citing Ps.132.11, II Samuel 7.12-16, Jer.23.5f, and Is.11.10 [7], none of which is cited in the manuscript.

The manuscript resumes at folio 2r (i.4) in the middle of the series of testimony texts in the form of a biography of Jesus in Old Testament prophecies, which we have discussed in the previous chapter. To the end of chapter iii the Disputation contains little more than a transcription of this collection of testimonies, though of course, Sergius may have added to it now and then. In this list of testimonies the Jew plays no part whatsoever. The Jewish objection (i.3) that Ps.2.7 refers to David is traditional and is found in almost all discussions of the text in anti-Jewish polemic [8]. The Jew is not mentioned here, neither does the use of the second person singular (i.3) necessitate the existence of a real opponent. Throughout the Disputation the whole Jewish race, past or present, is often adressed or subsumed under the second person singular [9].

At the end of chapter i the list of testimonies is interrupted after the citation of Mk.16.19, Mt.28.19, for Sergius clearly feels that the mention of the Holy Spirit needs the support of more testimonies. In line three of folio 4v, we find the bare words in red ink ܡܛܠ ܪܘܚܐ (concerning the Spirit), which looks like the heading of a testimony collection [10]. In this section (ii.1-2), which consists of a series of testimony texts for the existence of the Holy Spirit, the Jew again does not speak directly, but is treated as the representative Jew — 'any Jew'.

[6] Cf. CYPRIAN, *Against the Jews*, I. 21.

[7] Corresponding to CYPRIAN, *Against the Jews*, II. 11.

[8] Cf., for example, the *Dialogue of Athanasius and Zacchaeus*, §§49-51, CONYBEARE, *Dialogues*, p. 32f.

[9] The practice is traditional; cf., for example, the Ezra agraphon in ch. i. 17.

[10] See above, p. 19, 21.

In ii.3 the representative Jew is again introduced, and the sort of reply which he is likely to offer to what has been said in ii.1-2 is quoted :

> "Behold, three gods — the Father and the Son, and the Spirit; how does the statement of Moses remain (true) who said, 'God is One'?"

The author then supplies the reply which his Christian readers should offer to such a Jew : 'Do not accuse your prophets, O Jew, of acknowledging three gods etc.' and follows with an explanation of the doctrine of the Trinity, citing two well known testimony texts, Ps.33.6 and Is.48. 16 (the latter in a suitably adapted form). Quite naturally and easily at the beginning of ii.6 the author imagines himself confronting his readers' hypothetical Jewish opponent whom he addresses directly, 'O Jew'. Such apostrophes occur in many works which are clearly not dialogues in form, but it is easy to see how they led most naturally to the development of the dialogue form of Christian anti-Jewish polemic.

At the end of the excursus on the Trinity and Christology (ch.ii), we find the author directly addressing his Christian readers :

> "But to the faithful and discerning it is known that the Godhead is three persons..... But, nevertheless, you do not offer proper food to babes who need milk, for they cannot accept it, since it is harmful to them. For it is sufficient for you to say to the Jew, 'God is One with his Word and his Spirit; and yet, there is no other' " (ii.8).

It is clear from this that the author is providing material for Christians to combat Jewish arguments. It would have no place in a real discussion with a Jew.

At the beginning of chapter iii, the author returns to the catalogue of proof texts with the words, 'Let us return to our previous subject'. He concludes the catalogue at the end of the chapter with the revealing words :

> 'But they (i.e. these testimonies) are sufficient for believers, and that simple men may not go astray after the error of the Jews' (iii.5).

Clearly one of the author's principal reasons for composing his Disputation is the edification of Christians and, as we shall see [11], their preservation from apostasy to Judaism. This was a common, if not the preponderant, motive for the production of anti-Jewish polemical works by Christian writers [12].

[11] See below, pp. 74 ff.

[12] See below, pp. 74 ff and SILVESTER, *Discussion*, p. 85, BLUMENKRANZ, *Juifs et Chrétiens*, p. 75.

In chapter iv.1-3 the author turns to the subjects of sabbath and circumcision. The representative Jew is again addresed directly : 'Because you say, O Jew, that without sabbath and circumcision man is not pleasing to God...' (iv.1). There follows a series of arguments wholly composed of traditional material as the notes to the Translation demonstrate.

Chapter iv.4 begins a new section rather abruptly with the words ܘܡܛܠ ܒ̈ܢܝܐ (concerning children), again written in red ink. It is probably another heading to a collection of testimony material [13]. Again the arguments and examples used are composed from traditional material. The Jew, whether the particular Jew with whom Sergius is purported to have disputed or the representative Jew, is quoted as saying, 'Cursed be everyone who does not raise up seed in Israel' [14].

From iv.6 to the end of the chapter the author retails traditional Christian accusations against the Jews as murderers of the prophets who have always resisted God's will. The texts quoted are familiar testimony texts — Ezek.16, Is.1.4, Dt.32.32 — witnessing to the habitual perfidy of the Jews.

The beginning of chapter v marks a significant turning point in the literary structure of the work; the Disputation at last becomes a real dialogue :

> The Jew said : It is written, 'Cursed is everyone who hangs on a tree'.
>
> The Blessed Sergius said : But also thus again it is written, 'Cursed is everyone who does not do all which is written in this law'.

It may be noted, however, that the text of Dt.21.23 cited by the Jew, is not the Massoretic text but the Peshitta text of Gal.3.13. The Disputation is not then a transcript of the actual discussion, although we must always make the proviso that the scribe of the manuscript may have inserted the text with which he was most familiar. The phrase ܠܛܘܒܢܐ ܣܪܓܝܣ ܐܡܪ (the Blessed Sergius said) is unique in the work; normally we find only ܣܪܓܝܣ ܐܡܪ (Sergius said). The observation that in the manuscript the word ܠܛܘܒܢܐ (Blessed) is in red ink, while the rest of the phrase is not, prompts the suggestion that it is a scribal addition. If it is not, the phrase militates against the claim of the introduction and the colophon to the manuscript that the work

[13] Cf. APHRAATES, *Demonstration*, XVIII, entitled 'Against the Jews on Virginity and Asceticism'.

[14] See below, p. 12.

was written by Sergius the Stylite. It suggests rather that an anonymous author has employed the presumably well known figure of Sergius as an actor in his dialogue, and that subsequently the work itself was attributed to Sergius.

From this point to the end of chapter viii Sergius speaks. Chapters v-vi deal with the cross and the crucifixion, especially the Old Testament types of the former. In chapter vii Sergius deals with Jewish objections to the incarnation, and then in chapter viii he describes the present plight of the Jews, blaming their situation on their murder of Christ. The Jew is addressed directly on several occasions, sometimes by rhetorical questions like 'Is the lamb which saved Isaac, which was lifted up on the wood, accounted accursed by you?' (v.4), and sometimes by the interjection 'O Jew' (vi.3), or 'O hard-hearted Jew' (vii.8). Once Sergius cites what the Jew is purported to be saying, namely, 'The cross has no effect' (vi.6). But the substance of these chapters is once again drawn from traditional anti-Jewish polemical material [15]. It is possible that a few of the types of the cross adduced by Sergius are original, and perhaps even the elaborate etymology of the word ܦܨܚܐ (Passover) in v.13 is his own.

In chapter ix.1 the Jew speaks again, claiming that the Jews are the true sons of Abraham and of the prophets. No special knowledge of Judaism would be necessary for a Christian author to produce that statement! Sergius replies by saying that, since the Jews reject the prophecies of the prophets, they cannot be their sons. They have been put to shame by the Gentiles 'who have been taught by the prophets that which, in the name of the prophets you deny' (ix.2). The section which follows may be entitled 'The Gentiles have turned to Christ', and is certainly, along with its quotations from Ps.72, Gen.22.18, Jer.16.19, etc., based on testimony material [16].

Chapter x introduces, for the first time, a speech of reasonable length by the Jew. He agrees that the testimonies adduced by Sergius are compelling, and is particularly affected by the dispersion of the Jews. Nevertheless, he wants to know why Christians indulge in the worship of the cross, particularly by producing images of it, an activity which he regards as the equivalent of idolatry. At this point we appear to be confronted with material which has a real *Sitz im Leben* in the period in

[15] See the notes to the Translation.

[16] Cf. CYPRIAN, *Against the Jews*, I. 21-2, ISIDORE, *Against the Jews*, II. 1-2, 4, 7-8, and APHRAATES, *Demonstrations*, XVI.

which this work was produced, for the subject is not dealt with in earlier anti-Jewish works. But in the *Trophies of Damascus* [17], written in A.D. 681, the Christian participant in the dialogue defends the worship of the cross and images. Likewise Leontius, Bishop of Nicomedia, who lived A.D. 590-668, in his five books against the Jews [18], seems to have argued, as Sergius does (xii.6), that Christians do not really worship the wood of the cross [19]. The *Dialogue of Papiscus and Philo*, composed in two stages A.D. 600-1100, begins (§1) with an objection raised by the Jew to the use of images [20]. Thus from the end of the seventh century A.D. onwards this subject became a standard issue for discussion between Christians and Jews [21]. It is, then, a possibility that, in the sections dealing with the Christian worship of images, Sergius's Disputation is based upon a real discussion with a Jew, and is not merely fabricated on the basis of collections of testimony material. However, we cannot rule out the possibility that the testimony tradition, responding to new requirements, had already by the middle of the eighth century evolved a collection of testimonies to deal with these Jewish objections.

Chapter xi interrupts the discussion of the subject of images, while Sergius and the Jew turn aside to deal with the problem : which is the real Israel — the Church, or the Synagogue ? This break in the argument suggests that Sergius may be guided by the course which his argument with the Jew actually took; such arbitrary changes of subject are natural in real discussions. However, in this excursus the Jew seems to act as little more than a foil for Sergius's arguments, so that we must not be too hasty in assuming that we have a transcript from a real discussion. Certainly Sergius's argument, based on Gen.22.18 is by no means original, nor is the fact that the Jew allows Sergius to call Mt.16.13ff in evidence at all credible, while in ch.xi.17 the Jew is made to refer to I Samuel as 'the first book of Kingdoms'. While such a usage is not too difficult in a Syriac work coming from the region of Antioch, and hence from an area heavily influenced by Greek-speaking Christianity [22], to find it on the lips of a Jew is, to say the least, problematic. We must

17 Williams, *Adversus Judaeos*, pp. 162-6.

18 Williams, *Adversus Judaeos*,p.166. Williams thinks that the attribution to Leontius may be false, and that the material belongs to a later date.

19 So also Stephen of Bostra, Williams, *Adversus Judaeos*, p. 167.

20 McGiffert, *Dialogue*, p. 51.

21 Cf. Blumenkranz, *Juifs et Chrétiens*, p. 285ff.

22 Cf. Trans., ch. xi, n. 39.

therefore conclude that, while the break in the course of the discussion may reflect the circumstances of an actual disputation, the substance of this chapter is a literary creation.

At the beginning of chapter xii the Jew brings Sergius back to the subject of the worship of the cross, and accuses him of evading the question. Sergius tells the Jew to be patient and to listen in silence. while such remarks may belong to the literary artifice of the dialogue, it is not impossible that the Jew's persistence reflects that of the real Jew with whom Sergius is supposed to have disputed. At the least, it reflects real experience of debates with Jews. Throughout this chapter Sergius defends the Christian use of images, building principally upon the analogy of the worship of kings' images. The Jew is not convinced — an important point.

A folio is missing after 26v, but hints in ch.xii.14 and xiii.12 suggest that it contained a 'fearful oath' by the Jew 'not to deny the truth'. Sergius appears to be trying to pin the Jew down, and get him to acknowledge Jesus as the Messiah. The Jew says (xi'.14) that if the Messiah corresponds to the testimonies of the prophets, he will not reject or conceal the fact. Sergius takes this as a tacit acceptance of his position and says, 'Although you know this, why do you not acknowledge (him)?' The Jew replies :

'I do not acknowledge (him) for two reasons : one, that my heart will not allow me to leave the law of my fathers; and the other, that I fear my people lest they stone me or burn me with fire'.

What are we to make of this dialogue? Ostensibly it appears to be a transcript from a real discussion. If, however, we examine it more closely, the semblance of reality begins to break down. Firstly, there is a hiatus between the Jew's first speech and Sergius's reply. The Jew's statement that he will accept Christ is hypothetical. He does not concede that the Messiah is the one whom Sergius proclaims, yet Sergius proceeds as though the Jew has conceded this, and the subsequent speech by the Jew makes the same assumption. But the Jew's speech in xii.18 reverts to the hypothetical form — 'Whether I acknowledge (him) or not, is no concern of yours'. In the light of this, and the fact that at the end of the Disputation the Jew still does not accept Sergius's position, it seems that the Jew's speech, giving the reasons why he will not accept Jesus as the Messiah, is fabricated by Sergius to put the Jews in a bad light. For he is showing that, although they really know that Jesus is the Messiah, yet they refuse to acknowledge him as such purely on emotional grounds — clinging to the law of their fathers, and fear of reprisals from their fellow Jews.

Chapter xiii marks the start of a large division in the argument, extending to the end of chapter xv, in which Sergius defends the use of martyrs' relics. The Jew's speech in xiii.1 reveals a good knowledge of Christian practice with regard to the adoration of saints' bones and the depiction of their exploits on the walls of churches. Once again the Disputation is touching on a subject which is of specific relevance to the period in which it was composed, in contrast to much of the material hitherto dealt with. No section dealing with martyrs' relics is discernible in any of the earlier collections of testimonies. Dionysius bar Salibhi, however, in chapter viii.2-3 of his treatise *Against the Jews*, deals with the Jewish objections to Christian worship of the cross and saints' bones in very much the same terms as Sergius. Some of the details of Sergius's argument also find parallels in Aphraates' *Demonstrations*. It is inherently probable that as Christian practice with regard to images of the cross and saints' bones grew, teaching such as that found in Aphraates was developed and became the basis for a new collection in the testimony tradition. Some such collection seems to underlie both Sergius's Disputation and bar Salibhi's treatise. Nevertheless, we do get the impression from the discussion in this part of the Disputation that there is a substratum of reality in the dialogue, despite the fact that the Jew still seems to act as the foil for Sergius's arguments and never attains the dimensions of a real personality, and despite the fact that Sergius never seems to show any real knowledge of Judaism. The main argument in favour of this substratum of reality is that, throughout, the Jew remains unconvinced by Sergius's arguments, whereas in other clearly fabricated anti-Jewish dialogues the Jew or the group of Jews is invariably routed by the Christian, frequently by means of a miracle [23].

Two particular points in this section need to be mentioned. First, the Jew quotes frequently from the Peshitta text of the Old Testament, even when it diverges from the Massoretic text, and raises no objection to Sergius's use of Wisdom 3.1 (xiii.10), nor to his statement that four times Moses averted God's wrath by appealing to the names of the righteous fathers, whereas the Pentateuch reports only one such occa-

[23] So, for example, in the *Discussion of Silvester*, where the issue is decided when Silvester raises a bull which had previously been struck dead by a Jewish magician who uttered the sacred name in its ear — SILVESTER, *Discussion*, pp. 87ff.

sion. Second, in ch.xv.11, Sergius threatens the Jew, whom he regards as an enemy of God, with hell-fire. This may well be a reminiscence of a real discussion — Sergius, finding the Jew unconvinced by his arguments resorts, in the manner of many since, to threats about his opponent's eternal damnation. The Jew, unmoved, continues to question Sergius, this time about the use of pictures and icons in Christian churches. Sergius's reply occupies most of the next section of the Disputation which extends to the end of chapter xvii.

This section develops naturally out of the previous discussion of the worship of the cross and of saints' bones, and indeed, all three subjects are bound together by Sergius's recapitulation in xvii.11. Although the subject of this section could well have been raised and dealt with on the general lines depicted in the work, the actual text gives every appearance of being a literary production, with the Jew once again acting as Sergius's foil. It is particularly worth noting how the Jew in his long speech in ch.xvi.17f falls straight into a trap laid by Sergius. From the institution of the Passover in Ex.12f., and of the tassels on garments in Num.15.37-41, Sergius draws out the principle that the Old Testament sanctions the use of material objects to serve the purpose of teaching spiritual lessons. The Jew cannot, of course, disagree, and the way is then open for Sergius to apply this principle to the subject under discussion :

> 'This making of pictures and icons, which are inscribed with pigments in our churches, is confined to, and follows, the example of the scripture. And we depict in the church for the teaching and admonition of men every narrative which the scripture regarded worthy of being a reminder, that whatever the scripture relates for the hearing of the ear, the eye might see in the form of a picture' (xvi.19).

This argument, which seems to be unparalleled in the other Syriac literature, may well be original.

Chapter xviii marks the beginning of a clearly defined section in the structure of the Disputation, and for once the Jew speaks as one imagines a real Jew would :

> 'I myself know that you have too much to say, and everything which I ask you, you refute with idle talk. For the doctrine of the son of Mary is like this — a subtle contrivance of words' (xviii.1).

He then proceeds to raise the problem of the dietary laws enjoined in the Old Testament, with particular regard to the Christian consumption of the pig. That such a problem would be raised in a discussion between a Christian and a Jew is inherently probable. It is, of course, treated in other Christian anti-Jewish works. Christian apologia on this subject, apart from that found in the New Testament, goes back as far as the *Epistle of Barnabas*, x, and Justin's *Dialogue with Trypho*, xx. It merits a section in Isidore's *Contra Judaeos* (Bk.ii.18) where, as in the Disputation, the example of Elijah is adduced and the fact that God pronounced all things 'very good'. The fifteenth Demonstration of Aphraates is entitled 'Concerning the Distinction of Foods', and contains some material in common with Sergius's Disputation. It is, therefore, reasonable to assume that Sergius is drawing here upon traditional testimony material, for the arguments retailed by all these writers, besides others such as Ephraem [24] and Novatian [25], are identical, as are the proof texts which they cite. However, as far as can be ascertained, Sergius's argument that the Old Testament criteria for distinguishing clean and unclean foods are inconsistent (xviii.2-12), is original to the Disputation. Thus, although traditional anti-Jewish polemic serves as the basis for this part of the work, the author is adding original material of some importance.

In chapter xviii.15 the Jew makes an interesting speech in which he refers to Sergius's ascetic way of life upon his column. Probably we do have here reminiscences of a real discussion, and, if so, this is an important confirmation of the claims of the introduction and colophon of the manuscript regarding the literary structure and authorship of the Disputation. We must not, however, overlook the fact that this argument can be reversed : a scribe noting that the substance of the work is ascribed to a Christian called Sergius, and that this speech makes it clear that he was a stylite, could easily have made the step of attributing the Disputation to the otherwise unknown Sergius the Stylite. Nevertheless, another note of reality is struck by the Jews's persistence in pressing Sergius on the matter of the command to Noah to distinguish clean and unclean animals on entering the ark and on the matter of Moses' food laws (xix.10, 14), and by Sergius's inability to extricate himself from the difficulty.

The discussion of the Jewish food laws comes gradually to an end in chapter xx, and an argument about the proper subject of the later

[24] *Hymns on Unleavened Bread*, xix. 5.

[25] *De cibis Judaicis.*

chapters of Isaiah develops out of the Jew's citation of Is.66.17. Sergius, using traditional Christian exegis, separates out the promises contained in these chapters and refers them to Christians; the threats and curses he refers to the Jews [26]. The Jew, not unnaturally, protests.

The last major subject discussed in the Disputation is contained in chapter xxi, and it is in many ways the most interesting in the work, containing, as it does, a large number of extracts from Josephus's *War of the Jews* [27]. It can be broken up into three sections : (a) the Jew admits the miserable condition of his people (xxi.1-3); (b) Christ's prophecies concerning Jerusalem (xxi.4-5); (c) the witness of Josephus to the destruction of Jerusalem (xxi.6-15). For this general plan Sergius might well be dependent on Eusebius's *Ecclesiastical History*, where the same collocation of Christ's prophecies concerning Jerusalem with extracts from Josephus's *War of the Jews* may be found [28]. The use of Josephus, though not particularly common, is found elsewhere in the Christian anti-Jewish polemical tradition. The Latin text of the *Discussion of Silvester* appeals to Josephus [29]; Peter Damiani [30] refers like Sergius to Josephus's total for the numbers killed in the siege of Jerusalem; and Anastasius of Sinai [31] appeals to Josephus's testimony to Christ. It is more certain that Sergius is influenced here, as he is earlier in the Disputation [32], by those collections of testimony material which dealt with the destruction of Jerusalem and the dispersion of the Jews [33]. There are no, more persistent themes than these in Christian works written against Jews. We must conclude, therefore, that the general structure of this section owes more to literary precedent than to reminiscense of an actual conversation.

On the other hand, if an actual discussion lies behind this Disputation, it is not impossible that the Christian participant would have called Josephus in evidence. The Jew's speech in ch.xxii.1 strikes a note of reality :

> 'Then, when I approached you, I approached inadvisedly, for I was unaware that you (Christians) had all this knowledge'.

[26] See above, p. 29.
[27] See above, pp. 32-47.
[28] See above, p. 47.
[29] MOMBRITUS, *Sanctuarium*, p. 518.
[30] WILLIAMS, *Adversus Judaeos*, p. 373.
[31] WILLIAMS, *Adversus Judaeos*, p. 178.
[32] See ch. viii.
[33] Cf. CYPRIAN, *Against the Jews*, I. 6, ISIDORE, *Against the Jews*, II. 10-12.

The Jew is surprised by Sergius's knowledge of Josephus, and so are we; such knowledge (independent of Eusebius) is virtually unique in the Syriac anti-Jewish literature, and rare elsewhere. Perhaps therefore, we should modify our conclusions with regard to this section and say that, while it shows every sign of being a literary construction, we cannot rule out the possibility that it is also influenced by the course of an actual discussion with a Jew in which the author has either participated or which he has observed.

The final section of the Disputation provides the strongest evidence that some real experience of debating with Jews underlies the work. For this section, mainly devoted to the subject of Judaising Christians, shows every sign of being based on an actual conversation. The Jew continues, after the sentence quoted in the previous paragraph, as follows:

> 'But now I am amazed how, after knowing (all) this [34], there are among you some Christians who associate with us in the synagogue, and who bring offerings and alms and oil, and at the time of the Passover send unleavened bread (and), doubtless, other things also. They are not entirely Christians, and some of our men have said that, if they were truly Christians, they would not associate with us in our synagogue and in our law. And now, because of this, we are all the more scandalized' [35].

Sergius's Disputation is another witness to the perennial problem of Christian apostasy to Judaism, felt more acutely in the Syrian church than almost anywhere else, as a series of articles by S. Kazan demonstrates [36]. There can be little doubt that Sergius's Disputation was written primarily to counteract the situation portrayed in this final section of the work.

There is, then, a reasonable degree of certainty that this section of the Disputation is based on an actual discussion of the subject of Judaising Christians. Much of the dialogue in the section strikes a note of reality, especially when Sergius, like many other controversialists who are in an insecure position, descends rapidly to vilification of his opponent instead of attempting to meet his objections. For example:

[34] i.e. the evidence from Josephus.

[35] Ch.xxii. 1. For parallel situations to that described here by the Jew see below, p. 75f.

[36] *Isaac of Antioch's Homily.*

> "After all these miracles and wonders [37] you, the sons of 'the sons of vipers', say now, 'Christians scandalize us' " (xxii.16).

This is the sort of statement which, unhappily, one would expect to find in a real debate between Christians and Jews at this period. Not all the material in this concluding section can, however, be regarded as the verbatim report of an actual discussion. For the author weaves into it the theme of 'Christ, the Prophet like Moses', a subject touched upon earlier in the Disputation [38]. It is introduced in order to supply a fitting conclusion to the work:

> 'But because you boast in Moses, let us return to Moses, and as we began from him, so let us end with him. The Lord will raise up for you a prophet etc.' (xxii.18).

However, it is worth emphasizing that the Disputation ends not, as so often in other anti-Jewish dialogues, which the Jew giving way to the superior arguments of his Christian opponent, or being compelled to believe by means of a miracle, but with Sergius virtually declaring the Jew and his people irretrievably damned. We may feel reasonably confident that this conclusion is based on actual experience of debate with Jews.

We are now in a position to attempt to answer the questions which were raised at the beginning of this chapter. These are : Is the dialogue fictitious or real? What portrait does it give of the Jew, and does it show any first hand knowledge of Judaism? How well does it fit into the period in which it was written, and what was the purpose for which it was written?

2. *The Nature of the Dialogue*

Before we draw together the strands of our previous investigation, it may be of some use to refer to the conclusions which other scholars working in the field of Christian — Jewish polemic have reached as to the nature of the abundant literature composed in the form of dialogues or disputations. G. Bardy [39], after a discussion of the Christian apologetic (mainly anti-Judaic) dialogues, comes to the conclusion that, while some are accounts of real disputations, most are literary productions. Of Justin's *Dialogue with Trypho*, to which, as regards literary

[37] i.e. the miracles performed by Moses and Jesus.
[38] See ch. xvii. 7.
[39] *Dialog*, 928ff.

form, Sergius's Disputation most closely approximates, he says that, although it shows a pronounced literary character, it appears, nevertheless, to preserve the remembrance of a real discussion.

B. Blumenkranz, in a work devoted to the relations between Jews and Christians in the West in the period A.D.430-1096 [40], discusses at some length the literary nature of the dialogues written during that period. Although as evidence for the nature of a Syriac work this seems somewhat remote, the remarkable homogeneity of Christian anti-Jewish polemic makes his observations of some value. His general conclusion is that much real discussion lies behind the literary deposit [41], and he postulates a principle for ascertaining the real or fictitious nature of these dialogues — the ratio of Old Testament to New Testament quotations in each particular work. He cites the example of the authentic discussion of Gilbert Crispin, abbot of Westminster, with a Jew [42], where the ratio is 163 Old Testament quotations to 63 New Testament quotations. In the forged continuation added later to the dialogue, the ratio is 41: 30. For what it is worth, let us apply this test to the Disputation of Sergius the Stylite. We find that the number of Old Testament quotations, excluding texts cited more than once, is approximately 280; the number of New Testament quotations, excluding those which are themselves quotations from the Old Testament, is approximately 40. So the Disputation passes this test with flying colours. However, the test cannot be regarded as anything more than confirmatory evidence; it should not by itself be allowed to determine the reality or otherwise of a dialogue. Nevertheless, its basis is sound : in a real discussion between Christians and Jews the Book which they both equally regarded as authoritative would be the final arbiter; Jews would refuse to allow the New Testament to be called in evidence.

J. Juster in *Les Juifs dans l'empire romain* provides a comprehensive, though brief, survey of the literary deposit of the 'polémique antijuive des Chrétiens' [43]. He touches on the problem of the authenticity of the polemical dialogues and observes that, while they claim almost invariably to be the result of real discussions with Jews, there is a certain relationship between them all, and they are all cast in the same mould. However, he does qualify this observation in a footnote saying : 'On a

[40] *Juifs et Chrétiens.*

[41] *Juifs et Chrétiens*, pp. 68ff, 215.

[42] *Juifs et Chrétiens*, p. 223; cf. also WILLIAMS, *Adversus Judaeos*, pp. 375-383.

[43] Vol. I, pp. 43-76.

vraiment exagéré en prétendant que les polémiques antijuives ne sont pas du tout sorties de discussions réelles entre Juifs et Chrétiens' [44]. He then surveys the evidence which proves that Jews and Christians did frequently engage in debate. The conclusion from his survey would then seem to be that, while the written dialogues show signs of literary reworking, real contact between Jews and Christians underlies them. This position is also strongly supported by Marcel Simon, who stresses in particular the trustworthiness of patristic testimonies to contacts between Christians and Jews [45].

We must not, however, overlook the fact that some scholars have made very negative judgments as to the reality of the contacts between Christians and Jews presupposed by these dialogues. For example, A.C. McGiffert says that 'of the real attitude of the Jews toward the Christians, of the nature of their polemics against Christianity, if they still troubled themselves with such polemics, these works tell us nothing' [46]. Of the dialogues themselves he holds that 'it is plain, of course, that we cannot conclude the actual existence of the parties named in the dialogue. They may be, as they probably most often are, fictitious characters' [47]. And of the opening paragraph of the *Dialogue of Papiscus and Philo,* in which the Jew objects to Christian worship of images, and the subsequent section in which the Christian defends the practice, McGiffert argues that 'it is intended as a defense of the practice over against the attacks of iconoclastic Christians, with whom the strife was then raging', and has nothing to do with anti-Jewish polemic [48]. This observation, if correct, has interesting implications for the purpose for which Sergius's Disputation was written.

There is one other objective test which may be applied in order to ascertain the authenticity or otherwise of a Christian anti-Jewish dialogue — whether or not, at the end of the work, the Jew is converted. As a matter of historical fact we know that this anti-Jewish polemic almost invariably failed to convert the Jews to Christianity, so that when a dialogue claims that the Jewish participant is convinced by the arguments of his Christian opponent, we may justifiably be suspicious. Moreover, the large number of dialogues in which the Jew (or group of Jews)

44 *Les Juifs,* I, p. 53, n. 4.
45 *Versus Israel,* pp. 208-213.
46 *Dialogue,* p. 4.
47 *Dialogue,* p. 11.
48 *Dialogue,* p. 4.

is converted on the strength of a miracle performed by the Christian participant, may be suspected of concealing either the Christian's inability to convert his opponent by the force of his argument, or of reflecting the unfortunate attempts made to convert the Jews by force. In the Disputation of Sergius the Stylite the Jew is not converted, either by means of a miracle, or by the force of Sergius's arguments. Occasionally the Jew admits the strength of these arguments, but may we not detect a note of irony in the following example :

> 'The Jew (said) : I do not have anything to say. On that account the times and the events yield to you in every respect, and the words of the prophets suit you, as you wish' (x.1).

The nearest the Jew comes to admitting that Sergius may be right is in the following speech :

> 'The Jew (said) : I know that we have rebelled against the Lord our God from when our fathers sold Joseph, and in Egypt, and in the desert, and in the land of Canaan; as David said concerning us : We have sinned with our fathers, and we have gone astray and done evil (Ps.106.6). If again, as you say, the sin of (killing) the son of Mary was added to us, behold, a double evil ! Then woe to us ! What has happened to us that, instead of being the heirs and sons of Abraham, we are strangers and enemies ?' (xxi.1).

But we may note that the Jew's admission is still hypothetical, and the fact that seems to grieve him more than anything else is not the force of Sergius's arguments, but the sad plight of his people [49]. We must conclude, therefore, that not only does the Disputation pass Blumenkranz's test with comparative ease, but that, tested by the hypothesis suggested above, it gives every sign of reflecting a real situation.

Our discussion of the literary nature of the dialogue in the Disputation has, then achieved the following result. The work, especially in its opening sections, is a literary construction, based on collections of testimony texts and traditional anti-Jewish polemic. The first three chapters are nothing more than a transcript from a written book of testimonies and are constructed in the form of a treatise rather than a dialogue. No particular Jew is addressed or quoted in this section, only the representative Jew. It is thus interesting to observe that Rendel Harris says that 'we frequently find that a series of *Testimonies* is interpreted by a personal challenge to the Jew who is imagined to be listening to the

[49] See the rest of ch. x. 1.

demonstrations; and it was natural enough that this *argumentum ad hominem* should be varied by protestations on the part of the Jew against the conclusions that are being drawn. It was almost inevitable that when the testimony becomes a controversy, the collection of testimonies should become a dialogue; this will sometimes seem to turn *Testimonia* into a series of *Questions and Answers*' [50]. Is not this precisely the process that we see at work in the construction of Sergius's Disputation?

From chapter v onwards the work assumes the form of a dialogue which, as it proceeds, grows gradually more and more realistic, until in the last section of the Disputation we seem to be confronted with extracts from a conversation which actually took place. We have noted, in the discussion of the contents of the text, the occasional evidence for assuming that behind the literary framework there can be traced signs that the author is making use of a discussion (or discussions) which he had with a Jew or which he had himself observed. Reminiscence of such discussions will account for the preponderance of Old Testament over New Testament quotations, and for the fact that the Jew is not converted as the result of the dialogue. The extent to which the literary activity of the author has obscured his reminiscences of the real discussion is difficult to estimate, but we can see how, in different sections of the work, authentic dialogue lies closer to the surface than in others. The Disputation of Sergius the Stylite must therefore be regarded, not as the transcript of an actual discussion, but as a literary work, one of whose sources is an actual discussion with a Jew, which the author uses to varying degrees in the course of the work.

This conclusion does not conflict with the claims of the introduction and colophon to the manuscript that the work is a letter (or perhaps better, 'a treatise') written by Sergius the Stylite against a Jew with whom he had disputed. Sergius may have begun his treatise intending to set out all the evidence for the Christian position in the form of a collection of Old Testament testimonies and, as the work proceeded, it grew into a dialogue by the process outlined by Rendel Harris, a dialogue in which he made use of reminiscences of his discussion with a Jew. However, it is a curious feature of this work that Sergius is always introduced in the third person — 'Sergius said' — never in the first person. If we compare Justin's *Dialogue with Trypho*, we find that Justin com-

[50] *Testimonies*, II, p. 19; the italics are the author's.

poses of his work like a piece of autobiography. We could, therefore, suggest that the introduction and colophon are mistaken in attributing the work to Sergius, and that what we have is, say, a literary reworking by one of his disciples of a disputation which he had attended between Sergius and a Jew [51]. It may even be possible that the Disputation existed originally in an autobiographical form, and that a later scribe has converted it into a proper dialogue by introducing Sergius in the third person. If we choose to disregard the introduction and the colophon entirely, the possibilities become limitless. For we could say that an anonymous author chose Sergius, as a well known figure, to act as a participant in the dialogue which he was writing, and that subsequently the work was ascribed to Sergius himself. Or the original author may have written the introduction himself, ascribing the work to Sergius in order to reach a wider public; the practice is by no means unknown in early Christian literature. But with suggestions like these we are moving into the realm of pure conjecture; we have no information about Sergius the Stylite or his Disputation except that contained in this one manuscript. If he was a really well known figure, it is surprising that there is no mention of him elsewhere in Syriac literature, though it must be remembered that a large proportion of this literature has not survived.

Thus, if we disregard for lack of evidence those theories which ignore the introduction and the colophon, only three hypotheses as to the origin and authorship of this work have anything to commend them :—

(a) That Sergius the Stylite of Gousit wrote it, on the basis of a disputation which he had with a Jew.

(b) That it was written by a disciple (or other close connection) of Sergius on the basis of a disputation which he had attended between Sergius and a Jew.

(c) That it was written by Sergius in the form of an autobiography, which a scribe has subsequently altered into the form of a true dialogue.

Of these three hypotheses, the last has not much to commend it for it is difficult to see why a scribe should do this, and it is almost impossible to choose between the first two, for the only objective evidence we possess, with which to test them, is the introduction to the manu-

[51] Cf. BARDESANES, *Book of the Laws of Countries*, which records a dialogue between Bardesanes and a certain Avida, but was written down by Philip, one of Bardesanes disciples.

script [52]. And, as we have seen in a previous chapter [53], the only information this conveys, independently of the text of the manuscript, is the fact that Sergius the Stylite lived in Gousit. This small piece of evidence for the trustworthiness of the introduction does not, unfortunately, affect the issue either way. For if the work was written by one of Sergius's disciples, he could easily attribute it to him, since the bulk of the material probably derives from him anyway. It is best, therefore, however unsatisfactory it may be, to resist the temptation to single out one of these two theories as the most probable [54].

3. *The Portrait of the Jew and the Author's Knowledge of Judaism*

We have concluded above that the Jew is a real figure, but that the literary form in which the Disputation is cast has prevented his emergence as a concrete personality. It is worth noting, therefore, the manner in which Sergius refers to the Jew in the dialogue. Most frequently he refers to him as a 'wise man' [55]; occasionally he refers to him as a 'teacher of the law' [56]; and once he refers to him as a 'freeman' [57]. By itself the title 'wise man' is not specific, but the title 'teacher of the law' would seem to involve a claim that the Jew was a rabbi, though it is worth noting that the word used is not the technical term ܪܒܝ (rabbi), but the more general term ܡܠܦܢܐ (teacher). Against this apparent claim by the Disputation, it must be noted that it is very frequently a part of the literary form of these anti-Jewish dialogues for the Jew who participates in the discussion to be called a rabbi [58]. Moreover, the passage from xxii.1 quoted above [59] militates, if anything, against the suggestion that the Jew was a rabbi. For the words 'some of our men have said' look like those of an ordinary Jew referring to the opinion of the rabbis.

Apart from these few direct references, there is little else in the work to help us to determine the status of the Jew except the general im-

[52] The colophon is, of course, not independent of the introduction.

[53] See above, pp. 4-6.

[54] That Sergius is referred to throughout this book as the author of the Disputation is a mere convenience, and is not meant to indicate any choice between these two alternatives.

[55] See ch. ix. 9, xii. 3, xv. 2, etc.

[56] See ch. xvi. 4, xix. 9.

[57] Ch. xix. 15.

[58] So, e.g., in the *Discussion of Silvester*, which is clearly fictitious.

[59] On p. 63.

pression that although he seems reasonably well informed, he displays little special knowledge of Judaism. But no conclusions can easily be drawn from the general impression that the Jew makes, for we cannot tell how much the portrait given of him owes to the literary artifice of the author. We have noted above that sometimes whole speeches made by the Jew are clearly fabricated by the author, and that in most other cases he acts merely as Sergius's foil, seeking information or asking leading questions. It is only in rare instances that the Jew attains the dimensions of a real personality, such a case being the two occasions when we are allowed to observe the Jew's deep grief over the plight of his people [60]. On the whole, the portrait given of the Jew, despite the literary reworking, strikes one as fairly realistic. His persistent questioning and his refusal to accept Sergius's frequently contorted reasoning, contrasted with his occasional willingness to concede that Sergius has put forward a good argument, provides a picture of the Jews which contrasts strongly with the bitter and slanderous portrayal found in such works as the *Discussion of Silvester.*

A problem, closely related to that of the portrait of the Jew, is the knowledge of Judaism displayed in the Disputation. If the Jew with whom Sergius disputed was really a rabbi, we could expect his opinions to be reflected in the Talmud and Midrash. However, when we come to gather together and list the points made by the Jew in the Disputation, we find that there is remarkably little of any substance. As has been already observed, he serves mainly as Sergius's foil and, in most cases, his speeches are confined to asking questions. Elsewhere, his opinions are directly drawn from some text of scripture with little element of interpretation.

The following examples merit closer attention :—

(a) In i.3, Sergius quotes a Jewish interpretation (not explicitly that of the Jew in the Disputation) of Ps.2 which applies it to David. As we have noted earlier [61], this was probably a traditional opinion in the Christian anti-Jewish polemical tradition as to the way in which the Jews interpreted the text. However, in the Midrash to the Psalms [62], and in the Talmud [63], the Psalm is taken to refer to the battle of God and Magog, and therefore v.7 is inter-

60 See ch.x.1 and xxi.1.

61 See p. 51.

62 *Psalms Midrash,* I, p. 35ff.

63 *b.Berakoth,* 7b, 10a.

preted of the Messiah 'in the time to come'. Dionusius bar Salibhi's Jewish opponents interpreted Ps.2.7 as a reference to the people of Israel regarded collectively as God's son [64].

(b) The Jewish accusation in ii.3 that Christians worship three gods would be well known and shows no special knowledge [65].

(c) The quotation 'cursed be everyone who does not raise up seed in Israel' (iv.4) shows accurate knowledge of the attitude of rabbinical Judaism to asceticism [66].

(d) The Jew quotes Dt.21.23 according to the text of Gal.3.13 [67], and it is probable that the author was dependent upon Paul for this section of the dialogue. However, there is no doubt that Jews did use this text against Christians [68].

(e) In ch.ix.8, the Jew maintains that Ps.72 refers to Solomon, and it is a traditional Christian opinion, going back as far as Justin, that the Jews interpreted it in this way [69]. However, the Midrash to the Psalms tends rather to apply the Psalm to 'king Messiah' [70], despite the fact that the heading in the Massoretic text refers it to Solomon.

(f) In ch.xii.2, the Jew seems to admit that the prophecies which Sergius has adduced do refer to the Messiah. This is probably an accurate reflection of Jewish opinion. Where they would differ from Christians is precisely stated by Sergius in xvii.12 :

> 'Let us bring in one (subject) to the debate and discussion, and let us seek the truth that it may stand in the midst and settle the dispute between you and me, which is this — whether the Messiah has come or not'.

It is interesting, however, to note that Herford [71] finds no evidence in Jewish literature of disputes between Christians and Jews on the question of the Messiah.

(g) We have already concluded that the Jew's speech giving the

[64] *Against the Jews*, v. 9.

[65] For vague allusions to this accusation in Jewish literature see Herford, *Christianity in Talmud*, pp. 291-306, Simon, *Verus Israel*, pp. 299ff.

[66] Cf. *Mishnah*, *Yebamoth*, 6.6, *b.Yebamoth*, 61a-66a, and Simon, *Verus Israel*, *pp*, 250-3.

[67] In ch. v. 1.

[68] Cf. *Tosephta*, *Sanh.* ix. 7, cited in Herford, *Christianity in Talmud*, p. 86f.

[69] Cf. the Translation, ch. ix, n. 14.

[70] *Psalms Midrash*, I, p. 557ff.

[71] *Christianity in Talmud*, p. 349.

reasons why he refuses to believe [72] is fabricated by the author [73]. Nevertheless, there is plenty of evidence for very strong Jewish hostility to converts to Christianity [74].

(h) The Jew's statement that the dead are unclean [75], although based on the Old Testament, represents a very strong Jewish feeling [76].

(i) The Jew's claim that the miracles of Jesus and the saints are phantasies [77], should be compared with the Talmudic accusation that they were the result of magic [78].

(j) The Jew's statement that the law restrains man's bestiality [79] is true to Jewish teaching that the Torah was ordained as an antidote to the evil Yetzer [80], and that neglect of the law leads to social chaos [81]. Nevertheless, as we have argued above [82], this speech by the Jew falls neatly into a trap laid by Sergius, and we may therefore suspect that, although it is clearly based on knowledge of Jewish teaching, it is a literary construction.

(k) The Jew's application of Jer.31.22 to a woman [83], certainly represents the rabbinic opinion in *b. Yebamoth*, 62b.

(l) The Jew's mode of referring to Jesus as 'the son of Mary' may reflect Jewish accusations that he was illegitimate [84].

(m) The Jew's statements regarding the uncleanness of the pig [85] represent Jewish sentiment on the matter fairly accurately [86].

72 See ch. xii. 16.

73 See above, p. 58f.

74 Cf. HERFORD, *Christianity in Talmud*, pp. 173ff.

75 Cf. ch. xiv. 2.

76 Cf., for example, *b. Shabbath*, 64a.

77 See xiv. 8.

78 See *b.Sanhedrin*,43a, *Jerusalem Talmud, Sanhedrin*, 25d, discussed by HERFORD, *Christianity in Talmud*, p. 115f. For doubts whether these really concern Jesus of Nazareth see KLAUSNER, *Jesus of Nazareth*, pp. 27ff, but for confirmation from patristic sources that Jesus was regarded by the Jews as a magician see SIMON, *Verus Israel*, p. 397.

79 In xvi. 18.

80 Cf. *b.Kiddusin*, 30b.

81 Cf. *b.Shabbath*, 33a.

82 See p. 60.

83 See xvii. 4.

84 See the Translation, ch. xviii, n.2.

85 See ch. xviii, passim.

86 Cf. b.Baba Kamma, 82b, and the *Jewish Encyclopaedia*, XI, p. 609.

This survey of the knowledge of Judaism reflected in the Disputation serves to reinforce the conclusions reached earlier about the nature of the work. For in some places it represents Jewish teaching fairly accurately, while in others it tends to present more what Christian tradition said Jews thought. There is not, however, enough evidence to decide one way or the other the problem of the Jew's status; the most that can be said is that there is nothing to disprove the apparent claim that he was a rabbi.

4. *The Purpose for which the Disputation was written*

As we have seen above in the discussion of the contents, Sergius's Disputation makes perfectly clear in three places the purpose for which it was written. These are ii.8, iii.5, and most of the last section of the work, chapter xxii. The author's purpose is to strengthen Christians who are in danger of apostatizing to Judaism. The method chosen is the traditional one of demonstrating that the heir to the Old Testament is the Church, not the Jews, whose rejection by God is emphasized by the destruction of Jerusalem and their consequent dispersion. We must, therefore, ask what other evidence there is to prove that Christian apostasy to Judaism was a real danger at the time when this work was composed.

First, however, it is necessary to observe what the Disputation has to say about these Judaising Christians. We have already quoted the Jew's speech in which he states that some Christians at the time of the Passover bring offerings, alms, oil, and unleavened bread to the Jewish synagogue [87]. Sergius admits that this happens and suggests that those involved are 'weak Christians who, doubtless, are the children of heathen and their mind has not yet been cleansed from the fear of their fathers' idols. Or they are the children of Hebrews and the former custom still prevails over them' (xxii.5). In xxii.12, Sergius again mentions Christians who 'give oil or bring unleavened bread' to the synagogue, and in xxii.15, he quotes the rationale adopted by these Christians :

'If Christianity is good, behold, I am baptised as a Christian. But if Judaism is also useful, behold, I will associate partly with Judaism that I might hold on to the sabbath'.

Apart from a few other allusions which add nothing new, this is the total of what the Disputation has to say on the subject.

[87] See above, p. 63.

It is possible to cite evidence proving that the Disputation of Sergius the Stylite is witnessing here to a situation endemic in Syria from the first to the thirteenth century A.D. Fom the warnings of the *Didascalia* in the third century to the canons of the Jacobite church in the thirteenth the Christian authorities strove to counteract the perennial attraction of Jewish observances for Christians. Not only in Syria but throughout the Orient, and occasionally in the West, the Church was perpetually confronted with the problem of Judaising Christians as Marcel Simon's comprehensive study of the phenomenon has demonstrated [88]. The Church's anti-Jewish polemic was motivated, not by any abstract theological considerations, but by a very real threat to its position.

If we accept the theory that Christians are at least included in the term 'Minim' by which the Talmud and the Midrash refer to deviants from Jewish orthodoxy [89], then the frequent references found in this literature to the problem of their participation in synagogue services [90], are early evidence for the kind of situation mirrored in Sergius's Disputation. Chapter xxvi of the *Didascalia* represents a Christian attempt to wean Jewish Christians in Syria from their attachment to Jewish observances, while very clear light is thrown upon the situation in Antioch at the end of the fourth century by John Chrysostom's *Eight Homilies against the Jews*. A detailed study of these homilies by Simon [91] from the angle of the light which they throw on the Judaising movement concludes that the real problem underlying them is that of Christians participating in Jewish festivals, with some going as far as getting circumcised. This time, however, it is specifically Gentile Christians who are involved.

All the Syriac anti-Jewish literature has been studied by Stanley Kazan [92] to see what light it throws on Christian/Jewish relations, and his conclusions fully support the suggestion that the Disputation of Sergius the Stylite was written to deal with a real and pressing problem. He summarises the evidence from Aphraates' *Demonstrations* to prove that they were written to provide Christians with arguments with which

88 *Verus Israel*, pp. 356-393.

89 See Simon, *Verus Israel*, pp. 214-238.

90 Cf. Herford, *Christianity in Talmud*, pp. 97ff.

91 *Recherches*, pp. 140-153. Cf. also Kazan, *Isaac of Antioch's Homily*, OC, 49, pp. 57-60, and Downey, *A History of Antioch*, p. 447ff.

92 *Isaac of Antioch's Homily*.

to combat Jews, and to strengthen the faith of Christians who were weakening in the face of Jewish attacks [93]. Jacob Neusner's recent study of Aphraates and Judaism confirms that this was the primary motivation behind Aphraates' work [94]. It is not difficult to prove that Ephraem's anti-Jewish statements 'seem to reflect a situation in which the Jews were proselytising among the members of the Syrian church in Nisibis' [95]. Of even greater interest is the fact that "the situation reflected in Ephraem's 'Hymns on Unleavened Bread' seems to be one in which Christians were celebrating the Jewish Passover by eating unleavened bread" [96]. Isaac of Antioch, whose *Homily Two Against the Jews* is edited by Kazan in this series of articles, witnesses to the fact that the same state of affairs existed in his days [97] as had existed in those of John Chrysostom; his homilies inveigh against Christians who practise circumcision and celebrate Jewish festivals [98].

From the fifth to the thirteenth century there is a gap in the witness of the Syriac tradition of anti-Jewish polemic to the existence of Judaising Christians. Kazan concludes rightly that Jacob of Sarug in the sixth century was not faced with this problem, nor can we glean any evidence from Dionysius bar Salibhi's *Against the Jews*. However, the existence of canons promulgated in the Jacobite church in the thirteenth century to deal with the problem we are considering, shows that the attraction of Jewish observances for Christians had not waned in the interval. These canons forbid the participation of bishops and other clerics in the Jewish Passover celebrations, enjoin the faithful to work on the sabbath and not observe it in the Jewish manner, and they forbid Christians to receive unleavened bread from the Jews [99].

The Disputation of Sergius the Stylite fills the gap in the witness of Syriac literature to the attraction of Jewish rites for Christians. Although there does not seem to be direct evidence confirming the Disputation's statements, the existence of many parallel situations both before and after the date of its composition creates a presumption that

93 *Isaac of Antioch's Homily*, OC, 46, p. 90f.

94 *Aphrahat and Judaism*, pp. 124f, 144ff, 168f.

95 Kazan, *Isaac of Antioch's Homily*, OC, 47, p. 89.

96 Kazan, *Isaac of Antioch's Homily*, OC, 47, p. 90.

97 The first half of the fifth century.

98 Kazan, *Isaac of Antioch's Homily*, OC, 47, pp. 94-7.

99 Summarised in Kawerau, *Die jakobitische Kirche*, p. 106, from Bar Hebraeus's *Nomocanon*. Cf. also Kazan, *Isaac of Antioch's Homily*, OC, 49, p. 69.

its testimony is trustworthy. Particularly interesting is the evidence that the problem was felt acutely in Antioch, since we have good reason to believe that the Disputation was written not far from that city [100]. Here we may include as confirmatory evidence that the Disputation deals with real problems which were exercising the church in the period in which it was written, the fact that the main body of the work (chapters x-xvii) is occupied with subjects particularly relevant in the eighth century — the worship of the cross, of relics, and the use of pictures and icons [101]. The first would be particularly relevant since we know that the Jews were joined by the Muslims, then in control of Syria, in their condemnation of Christian worship of images of the cross [102], while in the light of McGiffert's comments on the *Dialogue of Papiscus and Philo* [103] it is reasonable to suppose that Sergius's apologia may be directed at iconoclastic Christians as well as against Jews. We may therefore conclude, that the Disputation of Sergius the Stylite reflects a real historical situation, both in the subjects chosen for discussion and in its allusions to Judaising Christians.

100 See above, p. 5.

101 Cf. Emerau, *Iconoclasme*.

102 Cf. Hage, *Die syrisch-jakobitische Kirche*, pp. 70f, 86. For the role of the Jews in the iconoclastic controversy see Parkes, *Conflict*, pp. 291-4.

103 See above, p. 66.

* I.1. The letter[1] of the Blessed Sergius the Stylite of Gousit, which was composed by him against a Jew who contended that God has no son, and (that) God has not begotten. *p. 1

2. Moses said : *Hear, O Israel : The Lord God is one Lord*[2]; *and you shall love the Lord your God with all your strength, and with all your mind, and with all your soul*[3]. But he, this one God, said by the mouth of David the prophet in the second psalm : *The Lord said to me, 'You are my son, and today I have begotten you'*[4]. Behold he, God, said that he has a son, and that he has begotten. Believe him, therefore, and do not withstand God or struggle with him. He said these things, not we! But because he has spoken, truly we did not believe man; we, therefore, have believed God in fear and trembling. 3. But if you say, 'This is said concerning David'[5], behold Isaiah the prophet said : *Behold, a virgin shall conceive and shall bear a son, and his name shall be called*[6]....... [7]
4. .....Israel. And (concerning the fact) that for the sake of the salvation of men he came down from heaven, and put on a body, and was revealed upon earth, Job said : *I know that my saviour lives, and at the last will be revealed upon earth*[8]. 5. And (prophesying) that he would be circumcised and presented[9] in the temple, Moses said :*Every first*

[1] In the colophon the work is (more aptly) called a 'disputation'. The translation 'treatise' would be more appropriate here than 'letter' and for this translation of ܐܓܪܬܐ see CURETON, *Ancient Syriac Documents*, p. 192. The work is certainly not cast in the form of a letter but of a treatise which develops into a dialogue.

[2] Or : The Lord God, the Lord is One.

[3] Dt.6.4f. Cf. DBS, *Against the Jews*, v.3, APHRAATES, *Demonstrations*, I,48.

[4] Ps.2.7. Cf. DBS, *Against the Jews*, ii.11, v.8, JACOB OF SARUG, *Against the Jews*, II,1.305, APHRAATES, *Demonstrations*, I,804, SILVESTER, *Discussion*, p.73.

[5] See the Introduction, p. 71f.

[6] Is. 7.14. Cf. KAZAN, *Isaac Antioch's Homily*, OC, 45, p. 49, DBS, *Against the Jews*, iv.14, ix.6, JACOB OF SARUG, *Against the Jews*, I,11. 275,339, III, 1.231f., SILVESTER, *Discussion*, p. 74, and HARRIS, *Testimonies*, II, p. 59f. For the collocation of Dt.6.4f, Ps. 2.7, and Is. 7.14 in the testimony tradition see the Introduction, p. 52.

[7] Eight leaves are missing between folios 1v and 2r; for conjectures as to the contents of the missing leaves see the Introduction, p. 52f.

[8] Job 19.25. Cf. DBS, *Against the Jews*, iii. 11, v.8, JACOB OF SARUG, *Against the Jews* III, 1. 241f.

[9] For the participle with modal force cf. NÖLDEKE, *S.G.*, §276. For a discussion of the formula used to introduce these testimony texts see the Introduction, p. 21.

born (who) opens the womb shall be called holy to the Lord [10]; and : *They shall offer for him a pair of turtle-doves or young pigeons* [11]. This was fulfilled in our Lord alone; for sexual intercourse first opens the womb of every woman who gives birth, but our Lord opened the womb of his mother, yet did not break the tokens of virginity. **6.** And (prophesying) that the Magi would offer presents to him, David (said) : *The kings of*
*p. 2 *Sheba and Seba * shall offer presents to him. All kings shall worship him and all nations serve him* [12]. **7.** And (prophesying) that Herod would kill the children, Jeremiah said : *A voice was heard in Ramah, weeping and much lamentation. Rachel is weeping for her children and she refuses to be comforted* [13]. And (prophesying) that he would enter Egypt, Isaiah said : *Behold, the Lord rides upon swift clouds and enters Egypt* [14]; the swift clouds are the arm of the Virgin Mary. And (prophesying) that he would come out of Egypt, the prophet (said) : *Out of Egypt have I called my son* [15]. **8.** And (prophesying) that he would live in Nazareth, Isaiah said : *He shall be called a Nazarene* [16]. John the Teacher explains and says that in the Hebrew language 'nurbā' is called 'naṣor' [17]. And (prophesying) that he would send John to preach before him, Isaiah said : *A voice which cries in the desert, 'Make level the way of the Lord, and make straight in the plain pathways* [18] *for our God* [19]. **9.** And (prophesying) that he would live among men, Jeremiah said : *This is our God, and we take account of no other beside him. He found all the way of righteousness; he gave it to Jacob, his servant, and to Israel, his beloved. After these things he appeared on earth, and lived among men* [20]. And (prophesying) that he would be baptised in the river by John, Daniel said : *And I, Daniel looked, and behold, two others stood, one on this bank of the river and one on that. And the man clothed in magnificent raiment*

[10] Ex. 13. 2,12f, but based mainly on Lk. 2.23.

[11] Lev. 12. 6-8, but based mainly on Lk. 2.24.

[12] Ps. 72. 10f. Cf. DBS, *Against the Jews*, iii. 1, and Introduction, p. 24.

[13] Jer. 31. 15, but following the text of Mt. 2. 18.

[14] Is. 19.1. Cf. *The Pseudo-Matthaean Infancy Gospel*, 23.

[15] Hos. 11.1, but following the text of Mt. 2.15. Cf. JACOB OF SARUG, *Against the Jews*, II, 1. 321f, and APHRAATES, *Demonstrations*, I, 773. Note the collocation of Is. 19.1 and Hos. 11.1 in ATHANASIUS, *De Incarnatione*, 33.5.

[16] Mt. 2.23; cf. Is. 11.1

[17] See the Introduction, p. 50f.

[18] [ܫ]ܒ̈ܝܠܐ (pathways) added in the margin by or.scr.

[19] Is. 40.3. Cf. DBS, *Against the Jews*, v. 17.

[20] Baruch 3.35ff. Cf. SILVESTER, *Discussion*, p. 74, DBS, *Against the Jews*, v. 16.

and (*who*) *stood above the waters of the river said*........ [21]. **10**. And (prophesying) that the Father would call out above the Son over the Jordan, David said : *The voice of the Lord is upon the waters : the glorious God thunders, the Lord upon many waters* [22]. And (prophesying) that the Spirit would descend upon him, Isaiah said : *And the Spirit of the Lord shall rest and abide upon him* [23]. **11**. And (prophesying) that he would go forth and conquer Satan outside in the desert, his stronghold, Zechariah said : *I saw Joshua* [24], *the high priest, standing, and Satan standing at his right hand and seeking to harm him. And he* [25] *said to him, 'Satan, Satan, the Lord rebuke you* ! *The Lord, who has chosen Jerusalem, rebuke you* [26]. * And (prophesying) that he would choose for himself the *p. 3
twelve and the seventy disciples, behold Ezekiel said : *Behold, I am sending many fishermen, and they shall catch them* [27]. **12**. And (prophesying) that he would teach them and that during the first year no one would withstand him, Isaiah said : *The Spirit of the Lord is upon me, because the Lord has anointed me and sent me to bring good tidings to the humble, to bind up the broken-hearted, to proclaim liberty to the captives and release to the prisoners, and to proclaim the acceptable year of* (*his*) *good will* [28]. **13**. And (prophesying) that he would perform healings, David said : *The Lord gives bread to the hungry* [29] — when he blessed the bread; *the Lord releases the prisoners* — those who are possessed; *the Lord opens* (*the eyes of*) *the blind* — the blind men; *the Lord straightens the crooked* — that woman [whom] the Adversary bowed down for eighteen years, and he (Jesus) laid his hand upon her and she was made straight [30]. And Isaiah said : *Truly he has borne our sorrows, and endured our pains* [31]. **14**. And (prophesying) that he would raise the dead,

21 Dn. 12.5f.

22 Ps. 29.4.

23 Is. 11.2. Cf. Aphraates, *Demonstrations*, I,21.

24 In Syriac, the same word as 'Jesus'. For the link Jesus/Joshua cf. Harris, *Testimonies*, II, p. 54ff.

25 S. scr. has corrected to P by adding ܡܠܐܟܐ (angel) in margin.

26 Zech. 3.1f. See the Introduction, p. 9f.

27 Jer. 16.16, wrongly ascribed to Ezekiel. Cf. Dbs, *Against the Jews*, vii. 37.

28 Is. 61.1f; cf. Lk. 4.19, and the Introduction, p. 8. Cf. also Ephraem, *Sermon c. Jews*, 213.

29 ܠܟ̈ܦܢܐ (to the hungry) added above the line.

30 Ps. 146.7f; for the New Testament allusions cf. Mk. 6.41, 5.1-13, Mt. 20.30-34, and Lk. 13.10-17, and the Introduction, p. 7.

31 Is. 53.4. Cf. Dbs, *Against the Jews*, iii. 12.

Isaiah said : *Your dead shall live, O Lord, and their bodies shall rise* [32]. And (prophesying) that he would ride upon a colt, Zechariah said : *Rejoice greatly, O daughter of Zion, and shout aloud, O daughter of Jerusalem ! For behold, your king comes to you, righteous, and a saviour, and humble, and riding upon an ass and upon a colt, the foal of an ass* [33].

15. And (prophesying) that he would give a new covenant, Jeremiah said : *And I will give them a new covenant, not like that former one which I gave to their fathers* [34]. And (prophesying) that he would seal the law [35], Isaiah said : *Bind up the testimony, and seal the law* [36]. And the angel said to Daniel, 'When Christ comes, *vision and prophets will cease*, and he will give a new covenant — *and the holy of holies*' [37]. **16**. And concerning (the fact) that he would be betrayed by his disciple, the psalm says : *He who eats my bread, whom I trust, has greatly deceived me* [38]. And concerning the false witnesses he writes : *False witnesses rose up against me, and they asked me something which I did not know* [39]. And (proph-
*p. 4 esying) that he would be crowned * with thorns, Jeremiah said : (*With*) *the thorns of its transgressions this people surrounded me* [40]. **17**. And (prophesying) that he would be scourged, David said : *The scourgers scourged upon my back, but he prolonged their affliction* [41]. And (prophesying) that he would be crucified, Ezra said : *You* [42] *bound me not as the Father, who delivered you* [42] *from the land of Egypt. When* (*you*) *were crying before the seat of the judge, you* [43] *humiliated me*; *you* [43] *delivered*

32 Is. 26.19. Cf. Aphraates, *Demonstrations*, I, 382, and the Introduction, p. 28.

33 Zech. 9.9. Cf. Ephraem, *Sermon c. Jews*, 217 F, 222A, and dbs, *Against the Jews*, iv. 17, v. 11.

34 Jer. 31.31f. Cf. Aphraates, *Demonstrations*, I, 500,534, dbs, *Against the Jews*, ii.3, iv. 6, iv. 20, and Jacob of Sarug, *Against the Jews*, III, l.235.

35 i.e. terminate the dispensation of the law.

36 Is. 8.16. Jacob of Sarug, *Against the Jews*, I, l.288, interprets this differently.

37 Cf. Dn. 9.24, and the Introduction, p. 8.

38 Ps. 41.9. Cf. Silvester, *Discussion*, p. 75, and the Introduction, p. 20.

39 Ps. 35.11 (27.12). Cf. Silvester, *Discussion*, p. 75, dbs, *Against the Jews*, vi. 8, and the Introduction, p. 20.

40 An agraphon; see the Introduction, p. 10.

41 Ps. 129.3. Cf. Jacob of Sarug, *Against the Jews*, I, 1,265. If the reading ܘܐܓܪ (and he prolonged) for P's ܘܐܓܪܘ (and they prolonged) is not just a scribal error, Sergius could be subtly altering the sense of the verse to say : the Jews caused Christ to be scourged, so God has prolonged his affliction of them.

42 Plural.

43 Singular.

me up to be hung upon the tree [44]. **18.** And (prophesying) that he would be mocked, Jeremiah said : *I have become a laughing-stock to this people* [45]. And (concerning the fact) that they gave him vinegar and bitter herbs, David said : *They gave (me) bitter herbs for my food, and when I was thirsty they gave me vinegar to drink* [46]. And (concerning the fact) that they shared out his garments, David said : *They shared out my garments among themselves, and for my clothing they cast lots* [47]. And (prophesying) that he would be pierced with a spear, Zechariah said : *They shall look on me whom they have pierced* [48]. **19.** And (prophesying) that the sun would be darkened but would shine in the evening, Zechariah said : *And I will darken the earth in broad daylight* [49]. And Moses said that on the fourteenth (day) of the month the Lamb of God would be slain, 'he who takes away the sin of the world' [50], and that not a bone of him would be broken [51]. And Isaiah bore witness : *Like a lamb he was led to the slaughter*; and : *The Lord has laid on him the sins of us all* [52]. **20.** And (prophesying) that he would be buried, Jeremiah said : *And by his burial the dead shall live* [53]. And (prophesying) that he would rise from the dead, David (said) : *For you have not left my soul in Sheol, or allowed your holy one to see corruption* [54]. And (prophesying) that he would command his disciples : *Go and preach my gospel in all the world, and baptise them in the name of the Father, and of the Son, and of the Holy Spirit......* [55]

[44] An agraphon; see the Introduction, pp. 11-13.

[45] Lam. 3.14/Jer. 20.7; see the Introduction, p. 13.

[46] Ps. 69.21. Cf. KAZAN, *Isaac of Antioch's Homily*, OC, 45, p. 53, DbS, *Against the Jews*, iv. 19, vi. 12, JACOB OF SARUG, *Against the Jews*, I, 1.260f, APHRAATES, *Demonstrations*, I, 811, SILVESTER, *Discussion*, p. 75.

[47] Ps.22.18. Cf. DbS, *Against the Jews*, vi.11, SILVESTER, *Discussion*, p.75, APHRAATES, *Demonstrations*, I, 808, JACOB OF SARUG, *Against the Jews*, I, 1.262f.

[48] Zech. 12.10. Cf. DbS, *Against the Jews*, vi. 12.

[49] Amos 8.9; see the Introduction, pp. 26-28.

[50] Jn. 1.29.

[51] Cf. Ex. 12.5,18,46, Num. 9.12, Jn. 19.36.

[52] Is. 53.6f. Cf. DbS, *Against the Jews*, iii.12, vi.8, and APHRAATES, *Demonstrations*, I, 58.

[53] An agraphon; see the Introduction, p. 13f.

[54] Ps. 16.10. Cf. APHRAATES, *Demonstrations*, I, 809.

[55] Mk. 16.15, Mt. 28.19. The expected Old Testament quotation is missing because Sergius digresses to consider the Holy Spirit; the chain of testimony texts is resumed at iii.1.

II.1. Concerning the Spirit [1]. If the Jew [says] [2] that there is no Holy
*p. 5 Spirit, behold David said : * *Take not your Holy Spirit from me* [3]. And Isaiah said : *And they provoked and grieved his Holy Spirit, and the enemy overthrew them* [4]. **2.** And Daniel wrote : *And the angel laid his hand upon the head of Habakkuk, and lifted him by the hair of his head, and set him down in Babylon above the den, by the strength of the Holy Spirit* [5]. And Moses said : *And the Spirit of the Lord was hovering ove. the face of the waters* [6]; and again : *My Spirit shall not abide in man for ever, for he is flesh* [7]; and again : *Do not be jealous, my son* ! *Would that he had made ......For the Lord has bestowed upon them his Holy Spirit instead of the evil spirit which is consuming them* [8]. And Haggai said : *My Spirit abides among you* [9]. **3.** But if the Jew says, "Behold, three gods — the Father, and the Son, and the Spirit ! how does the statement of Moses remain (true) who said, 'God is one' ?" ; (then reply) : Do not accuse your prophets, O Jew, of acknowledging three gods — the Lord, and his Word, and his Spirit. They are one; one (in) three, and three (in) one.

4. For God without the Word and the Spirit is incomplete. But neither was he ever without his Word and his Spirit, nor can he be; nor can his Word and his Spirit separate from him. Do not blaspheme against your prophets, for we have learnt this from them. And if they are accounted true by you, accept them, and try to see that the prophets acknowledge one God in one indivisible Trinity. **5.** Behold David, for he said : *By the Word of the Lord the heavens were made, and all its hosts by the Spirit* [10] *of his mouth* [11]. And Isaiah said : *The Lord God sent me*

[1] A section title written in red ink in the MS.

[2] There are faint traces of a scribal correction which may have been adding here the word ܐܡܪ (says).

[3] Ps. 51.11.

[4] Is. 63.10. Cf. DBS, *Against the Jews*, iii.6.

[5] Bel and the Dragon 36.

[6] Gen. 1.2.

[7] Gen. 6.3.

[8] Num. 11.29. The phrase ܟܠܗ ܥܡܗ ܕܡܪܝܐ ܢܒܝܐ (all the people of the Lord prophets) seems to have dropped out. The final clause has no basis in Num. 11.29, but cf.I Sam. 16.14.

[9] Hag. 2.5.

[10] Or : 'Breath'. Sergius makes use of the ambiguity.

[11] Ps.33.6. Cf. DBS, *Against the Jews*, v.5, JACOB OF SARUG, *Against the Jews*, I,1.91f, SILVESTER, *Discussion*, p.73.

to you and his Word and his Spirit [12]. God is one with his Word and his Spirit from everlasting to everlasting, and without beginning and without end. **6.** Tell me, O Jew, this one God whom you acknowledge, has he a Word and a Spirit or not? If he has not, he is incomplete, and if * *p. 6 he has, behold, (it is) as the prophets acknowledge — he was [never] [13] without the Word and the Spirit, nor could he be without the Word and without the Spirit. **7.** And if '*the Word abides for ever*' [14], as David said, and does not go from him, and does not perish, and subsists and exists in a true hypostasis [15], so also does the Spirit of God. I have acknowledged and I do acknowledge one God with his Word and his Spirit. And you also, you acknowledge and do not dispute [16] how he exists with his Word and his Spirit, that you may not be consumed by the '*fire which is not quenched*' [17]. But believe, as he declared to you by the prophets, and be silent! **8.** But to the faithful and discerning it is known that the Godhead is three persons, one nature [18]. And one of these three persons — that is to say, the Word — united our nature to himself by means of the God-bearing [19] holy Mary, without confusion and without division. But, nevertheless, do not offer proper food to babes who need milk, for they cannot accept it, since it is harmful to them. For it is sufficient for you to say to the Jew, 'God is One with his Word and his Spirit; and yet, there is no other'.

III.1. Let us return to our previous subject. And (prophesying) that he would ascend to heaven, David said: *You ascended to the height, and you led away captives, and you gave gifts to men* [1]. And (prophesying)

[12] Is. 48.16. Cf. DBS, *Against the Jews*, v.16, JACOB OF SARUG, *Against the Jews*, I, 1.167, and the Introduction, p. 8.

[13] Adding ܠܐ (not); cf. ii.4.

[14] Ps. 119.89? or a mistake for Is. 40.8 or Num. 23.19.

[15] ܩܢܘܡܐ, here the Syriac equivalent of ὑπόστασις.

[16] Or: 'do not inquire too closely how......'

[17] Cf. Is. 66.24.

[18] ܟܝܢܐ (nature); the normal Syriac word used to represent οὐσία in the Trinitarian formula is ܐܝܬܝܐ or ܐܝܬܘܬܐ (cf. JACOB OF SARUG, *Against the Jews*, III,1.39f), or the loan word ܐܘܣܝܐ (cf. the title/introduction to DBS, *Against the Jews*). Sergius is using ܟܝܢܐ here as it is used in BARDESANES, *Book of the Laws of Countries*, PS,II,559 (and often) — 'that which belongs in common to the members of any particular order of beings', BETHUNE-BAKER, *Nestorius and his Teaching*, p. 217. For a similar formula to Sergius's cf. PHILOXENUS, *Discourses*, tx., p. 32.

[19] The equivalent of θεοτόκος and Deipara.

[1] Ps. 68.18.

that the gates of heaven were opened to those who are worthy [2], David said : *Lift up your heads, O gates ! and be lifted up, O everlasting gates ! and the king of glory shall come in* [3]. **2**. And (prophesying) that he would sit at the right hand of the Father, David said : *The Lord said to my Lord, 'Sit at my right hand'* [4]. And (prophesying) that he would come
*p. 7 upon the clouds * of heaven, Daniel said : *And I saw one like a son of man coming upon* [5] *the clouds of heaven* [6]. **3**. And (prophesying) that all who lie in the dust would be raised, Ezekiel said : *And they stood upon their feet, an exceedingly great host* [7]. Again Daniel said : *And many of those who lie in the dust shall awake, some to everlasting life, and some to destruction and to the reproach of their fellows for ever* [8]. **4**. And (prophesying) that the Lord would judge by fire, David said : *God will come, and he will not be silent*; *and fire will consume before him, and blaze greatly round about him* [9]. And Isaiah said : *The Lord will judge by fire* [10]; and again : *And you shall go forth and see the dead bodies of the men who have rebelled against me, whose worm shall not die, and whose fire shall not be quenched*; *and they shall be a spectacle to all flesh* [11]. **5**. These things Christians uphold : they are written in the Gospel. What is there here that the prophets did not say or teach ? We were able to bring forward many testimonies to this fact. But him whom these things do not convince, ten thousand others would not either. But they are sufficient for believers, and that simple men may not go astray after the error of the Jews [12].

[2] An alternative translation based on the emendation of ܠܐܝܠܝܢ ܕܫܘܝܢ to ܠܗܘ ܕܫܘܐ would be : 'to him who is worthy'. The text is usually applied to Christ in anti-Jewish polemic ; cf. Eph.4.8, Daniélou, *Theology*, p.241, and Harris, *Testimonies*, II, p. 40f.

[3] Ps. 24.7 ; cf. Dbs, *Against the Jews*, vii.7. Contrast the very different use of this text in the *Acts of Pilate*, XXI.

[4] Ps. 110.1. Cf. Dbs, *Against the Jews*, ii.11, vii.7, Kazan, *Isaac of Antioch's Homily*, OC, 45, p. 51ff.

[5] ܥܠ (upon) added in margin by or.scr.

[6] Dn. 7.13 ; cf. vi. 4. Cf. also Ephraem, *Sermon c. Jews*, 214, Dbs, *Against the Jews*, iv. 17, v. 11, Jacob of Sarug, *Against the Jews*, 1.237f, J, fol. 204r.

[7] Ezek. 37.10. Cf. Aphraates, *Demonstrations*, I,386.

[8] Dn. 12.2.

[9] Ps. 50.3. Cf. Dbs, *Against the Jews*, v.11, viii.5.

[10] Is. 66.16. Cf. Aphraates, *Demonstrations*, I,32.

[11] Is. 66.24. Cf. Dbs, *Against the Jews*, viii. 5, Aphraates, *Demonstrations*, I, 32, and the Introduction, pp. 14, 28 f.

[12] Cf. Silvester, *Discussion*, p. 85, and the Introduction, pp. 54, 74 ff.

IV.1. Because you say, O Jew, that without sabbath and circumcision man is not pleasing to God and does not inherit the kingdom, behold Adam, Abel, Seth, Enosh, Kenan, Mahalalel, Jared, Enoch, Methuselah, Lamech, Noah, Shem, and Melchizedec : they did not circumcise, and they did not keep the sabbath [1]. Yet they pleased God more than you who circumcise and keep [the sabbath] [2]. And each of them has now departed to life. * *p. 8 **2.** And behold Abraham, Isaac, Jacob, Joseph, and the twelve heads of the tribes : none of them kept the sabbath, yet they pleased God more than you, who keep the sabbath. **3.** You circumcise a child on the sabbath ; behold, you have broken the sabbath! And if you do not circumcise on the sabbath, you have made void that (commandment) about the eight days old child. Behold, see that they both break each other ! [3] When has the sun ceased from its course on the sabbath, or the springs from flowing, or the trees from growing ? Also God does not cease work on the sabbath [4].

4. Concerning children [5], and your saying, 'Cursed be everyone who does not raise up seed in Israel' [6] — then, according to what you say, the angels, who do not raise up seed, are accursed [7]. And children, who die and do not raise up seed, are cursed by you. And Elijah, Elisha, and Jeremiah, and many other prophets and priests, who consecrated their flesh to God and did not take wives and beget children, are accounted accursed by you [8]. **5.** Daniel, Hananiah, Azariah, and Mishael, who were eunuchs, that is to say *εὐνοῦχοι* [9], who did not raise up seed, are they accounted accursed by you ? Snakes and scorpions who beget young and raise up seed, are they indeed accounted blessed by you ?

[1] For this argument, which is as old as Justin (see *Trypho*, 19,27), cf. APHRAATES, *Demonstrations*, I, 476,548f, 557ff, KAZAN, *Isaac of Antioch's Homily*, OC,45, p. 33f, DBS, *Against the Jews*, ii. 5,12f, JACOB OF SARUG, *Against the Jews*, II, 11. 184ff, 225ff, H, fol. 31v, and HARRIS and MINGANA, *Odes*, II, pp. 223-6.

[2] ܫܒܬܐ (sabbath) seems to have dropped out of the text.

[3] The argument goes back to Jn. 7.22-4. Cf. JUSTIN, *Trypho*, 27, JACOB OF SARUG, *Against the Jews*, II, 1.181f, DBS, *Against the Jews*, ii.13.

[4] cf. DBS, *Against the Jews*, ii.13, APHRAATES, *Demonstrations*, I,548, JACOB OF SARUG, *Against the Jews*, II, 11.150ff, *Didascalia*, xxvi. Perhaps this argument is implicit in Jn. 5.17. For Jewish attempts to combat it see HERFORD, *Christianity in Talmud*, p. 228.

[5] A section title written in red ink in the Ms.

[6] See the Introduction, p. 72.

[7] Cf. APHRAATES, *Demonstrations*, I,841.

[8] Cf. APHRAATES, *Demonstrations*, I,834.

[9] See the Introduction, chapter II,n.58.

6. O foolish and senseless people! A people whose whole mind is (fixed) on earth(ly things), and to whom heavenly things mean nothing, as David said concerning you: *He remembered that they were (made) of flesh, and of that wind which goes and does not return* [10]. It is indeed their carnal mind which does not return to righteousness and to spirituality, but seeks and thinks on everything which is of the flesh.

*p. 9 **7.** The prophets said that when the Messiah came, the law * would be sealed and the testimony bound up [11]. If you are a true Jew, accept your prophets, and do not reject anything from them. But if you reject (them), you have shown yourself not to be a friend of the prophets but a hater and murderer of the prophets. And if, when they were alive, you [12] were their enemy and persecutor, now that they have died, will you accept their words? **8.** But it is evident that as in their lifetime you killed and stoned them, so also today you oppose and dispute their prophecies. And although the prophecies of the prophets, and the events of the times, and the chronology and the reckoning of the years and of the weeks, are revealed, made known, and attested, you persist in perversity and you are not ashamed. You reverence neither God nor the events, but you stand in awe of men. **9.** Therefore, rightly did Ezekiel and the prophets, his fellows, denounce you, representing you as a prostitute as a way of rebuking you. He calls your city the sister of Sodom, and your father an Amorite, and your mother a Hittite [13]. Why do you glory in the name of Abraham, when you are the '*offspring of iniquity and a fornicating and false seed*' [14], as Isaiah testifies. Also Moses, in whom you boast, said thus concerning you: *For their vine is from the vine of Sodom, and from the grove of Gomorrah* [15]. **10.** What advantage is the circumcision of Abraham to you? How does it help you in these bitter reproaches? Jeroboam, Ahab, and the rest of the evildoers like them — these are your true fathers [16], who also were circumcised like you. Now if they inherit the kingdom of heaven by their circumcision, so also you (will inherit) with them and like them [17].

[10] Ps. 78.39.

[11] An inference from Is. 8.16f; cf. i.15.

[12] 2nd sing. — this shows how completely Sergius identifies the Jew with his forbears.

[13] Cf. Ezek. 16.3, 45f, and Aphraates, *Demonstrations*, I,766.

[14] Is. 57.4.

[15] Dt. 32.32. Cf. Kazan, *Isaac of Antioch's Homily*, OC, 45, p. 53, Aphraates, *Demonstrations*, I,225, 860,937.

[16] ܐܒܗ̈ܝܟ (your fathers) added in margin by S. scr.

[17] Cf. Aphraates, *Demonstrations*, I,472f.

V.1. The Jew said : It is written, '*Cursed is everyone who hangs on a tree*' [1].

2. The Blessed Sergius said [2] : But also thus again * it is written, *p. 10 '*Cursed is everyone who does not do all which is written in this law*' [3]. But no man has kept it, and none can keep it. All the world was under the curse of the law and under the guilt which the sentence on Adam transmitted [4]. But Christ came, and he became a curse for us, and he took the sin of the world and hung it upon the wood of his cross. For he is '*the Lamb of God* (*who*) *takes away the sin of the world*' [5]. **3.** Isaiah testified, saying : *He is killed for our sins*, and *the Lord has laid on him the sins of us all* [6]. And Moses, who lifted up the bronze serpent upon wood in the desert [7], testifies that by his cross he would crucify sin. And by that wood on which it was hung God wished that they should be saved from the serpents. **4.** Again, is the lamb which saved Isaac, which was lifted up on the wood [8], accounted accursed by you ? And the ark, which the priests carried with poles is it accounted accursed by you ? And (concerning) the cross, (about) which you say, 'A carpenter made it, and if you wish, you can burn it with fire and make (another) like it' [9] — then the carpenter, who made the ark of the covenant of the Lord, can go and burn it with fire and make (another) like it [10]. For before it all Israel worshipped the Lord. **5.** The rod of Moses, by which he performed signs and miracles, he, Moses, a man, picked it from a tree [11]. Why did he divide the sea with a rod ? [12] Tell me ! Why did he

[1] Dt. 21.23, but following the text of Gal. 3.13.

[2] Cf. the Introduction, p. 55f.

[3] Dt. 27.26, but following the text of Gal. 3.10.

[4] Cf. Rom. 5.12-14.

[5] Jn. 1.29.

[6] Is. 53.5f. Cf. DBS, *Against the Jews*, iv. 19, APHRAATES, *Demonstrations*, I, 808,813.

[7] Cf. Num. 21.9, and JACOB OF SARUG, *Against the Jews*, III, 1.197f.

[8] Cf. Gen. 22.9ff, and JACOB OF SARUG, *Against the Jews*, III, 1.183f, J, fol. 203v.

[9] Sergius is anticipating the Jew's objection that the cross (presumably Christian replicas of it) is no special object containing any hidden power; it can be burnt and another made like it.

[10] Sergius meets the objection by saying that this applies equally to the ark of the covenant, to which the Israelites attached a special significance. He may well also be alluding to the Jewish practice of keeping the scrolls of the Law in replicas of the ark.

[11] i.e. the fact that Moses' rod was picked from a tree does not invalidate the contention that it possessed a special hidden power.

[12] Cf. Ex. 14.16.

break through the rock with it and the water flowed ? [13] Tell me ! Why did he lay the rod before the Lord and (why) did it put forth buds and bear ripe almonds ? [14] Why did he put it in the ark of the Lord and command all Israel to sacrifice to the Lord before that (piece of) wood, and (why) did all Israel worship and sacrifice before it, both in the desert and in the promised land, unless the secret of the wood was that eternal
*p. 11 life was in it? [15] * Why did you [16] not burn it with fire ? **6.** The prophets, righteous men, and apostles, whom you [16] killed, did a carpenter make them ? And if you destroyed these men, who are the creation and image of God, will you not surely burn the cross ? You sacrificed your sons and daughters to demons [17], but this [18] you do not do. You burnt the law in which is the name of God, so (witnesses) David [19]; but the cross you do not burn. Behold, you are like Nebuchadnezzar who burnt the temple of the Lord. Did not Zedekiah [20], the king of Judah, burn the book of Jeremiah [21] ? **7.** None shall boast in pride; in pride, no excels you. But nevertheless, we know this, that if you or any other dares to insult [22] this cross, which the prophets proclaimed and extolled, this world is given over to the insolent to fulfill their will. But we worship it and glory in it until he who was crucified upon it is revealed upon the

[13] Cf. Ex. 17.6f, Num. 20.11

[14] Cf. Num. 17.7f.

[15] For Moses' rod as a symbol of the cross cf. JACOB OF SARUG, *Against the Jews*, I, 11.193ff, DBS, *Against the Jews*, viii.2.

[16] 2nd sing.

[17] A familiar accusation in anti-Jewish literature, based on Ezech. 20.26, Jer. 32. 35, Jud. 11, etc. Cf. DBS, *Against the Jews*, i.12.

[18] i.e. burn the cross.

[19] Cf. perhaps Ps. 74.7f; the reference seems to be misplaced.

[20] A mistake for Jehoiakim; cf. Jer. 36.

[21] Sergius continues to meet the Jew's objection that the cross is a mere piece of inert matter. He is saying that, although the Jews destroyed the prophets etc., that does not mean that they lacked supernatural power. Hence the rhetorical question : 'Did a carpenter make them ?' i.e. are they no more than inert matter ? Three other examples of this principle are then adduced. David witnesses (?) that the Jews burnt the law, but this does not mean that it was not holy. Nebuchadnezzar burnt the temple, and likewise this does not mean that it was not holy. Lastly, the same principle applies to Jehoiakim's burning of the book of Jeremiah. However, Sergius's argument is confused, for while he is trying to show that it does not matter whether the cross (i.e. Christian replicas of it) is burnt or not, nevertheless, he regards it as significant that the Jews do not actually burn it, no doubt, in his view, because of the supernatural power contained in it.

[22] ܠܡܨܚܪܘ (to insult) added below line by or.scr.

clouds of heaven, as Daniel proclaimed [23]. And '*he shall judge the world with righteousness*', as David said, '*and the peoples with integrity*' [24].

8. But because you are a people whose '*mind is reprobate*', as Moses said concerning you, and '*there is no understanding in*' you [25], and (because) another prophet said that '*unless you believe, you shall not understand*' [26], hear the symbols of the cross. Moses, for forty years by night and day, set up a cross in the desert, when he made Israel encamp in four companies around the tabernacle [27]. **9.** God set up a cross in the midst of paradise — the source which divided into four heads [28]. God set up the world like a cross — the East, the West, the North, and the South [29]. God made a cross in heaven from the stars. Jacob made a cross with his hands when he crossed them on the head of Ephraim and of Manasseh, * and by the cross he blessed them [30]. **10.** Moses again *p. 12 made a cross on the top of the mountain by stretching out his hands, and Aaron and Hur supported his arms in the shape of the cross beams [31], and by the symbol of the cross he conquered Amalek [32]. Again Moses commanded the Israelites to make a cross of blood on the two doorposts and on the lintels of the doors, when the Angel destroyed the firstborn of Egypt [33]. And by this symbol of the cross the firstborn of Israel were delivered from the sword of the Angel. **11.** Although your heart is stopped up and you do not understand, understand even now that the blood of ten thousand lambs did not restrain the Angel from destroying the firstborn. If it had not been a symbol of the blood of Christ, the Angel [34] would not have seen (it) on the doors. **12.** In this way the symbols, types, and the allegories, which are inscribed in the books of the prophets, declare (the things) concerning Christ, the

[23] Cf. Dn. 7.13.

[24] Ps 98.9.

[25] Dt. 32.28. Cf. Aphraates, *Demonstrations*, I, 852.

[26] Is. 7.9.

[27] Cf. Num. 2.

[28] Cf. Gen. 2.10.

[29] Cf. Daniélou, *Theology*, pp. 285ff.

[30] Cf. Gen. 48.14. Cf. Ephraem, *Commentary on Genesis and Exodus*, tx., p. 110.

[31] Emending ܠܓܘܕ̈ܐ (troops) to ܠܓܒ̈ܐ (sides), hence, 'cross beams'.

[32] Cf. Ex. 17.8ff. Cf. Aphraates, *Demonstrations*, I, 122,960, Ephraem, *Hymns on Unleavened Bread*, xx. 8-11.

[33] Cf. Ex. 12.7. For the typological and allegorical interpretation of the Passover in §§10-15 cf. Melito, *On the Pascha.*

[34] Syr. : 'he'.

Son of God. They were written concerning him, as he said in the Gospel: *Moses wrote concerning me* [35]. And again he said: *For if you believed Moses, you would also believe me* [36]. **13.** Observe also what the name of the Passover [37] means; it is to be interpreted, 'joy'. For the Lord said to Moses: *I will see the blood, and I will pass over* [38] *you* [39]. It is certain, therefore, that it means 'the joy [40] of God': the symbol of the blood of his Son makes him rejoice. **14.** Your deliverance from Egypt by means of the blood of a lamb proclaimed and symbolized the deliverance of all nations through the cross, from error as from Egypt, and from the subjection of Satan as from the power of Pharaoh [41]. And the lamb which has no blemish in it [42] is Christ, the Lamb of God, '*he who takes away the sin of the world*' [43], as John said. This — '*there is no*
*p. 13 *blemish in him*', (and) this — '*he did no iniquity*, * *neither was deceit found in his mouth*' [44], is as Isaiah said concerning him. **15.** If you will understand (it), the cross of blood upon the doors represented the stretching forth of his hands and of his arms upon the cross [45]. And the doors are the mouths of believers who receive him by faith and with him seal their doors, that is, their mouths and their very selves [46]. He who destroyed the firstborn, who did not enter the house upon which the cross of the blood of the lamb was represented, signified Satan, who turns away from the person who is faithfully and truly fervent in the love of the cross. **16.** But there is little time for us to collate by itself each single thing...... [47] which is inscribed in the prophets and on the face of nature which declares the cross of Christ, the Saviour of all. For

[35] Jn. 5.46.

[36] Jn. 5.46.

[37] Pṣḥ vocalized peṣḥā. The same root, vocalized peṣāḥā means: 'joy'.

[38] The verb pṣḥ in the Aph'el theme means: 'to gladden' and 'to pass over, to keep the Passover'. If, however, the Pe'al theme were to be read, it could mean: 'I will rejoice'.

[39] Ex. 12.13.

[40] Peṣiḥuṯā.

[41] Cf. Ephraem, *Hymns on Unleavened Bread*, i.7, Aphraates, *Demonstrations*, I,521, 957.

[42] Cf. Ex. 12.5.

[43] Jn. 1.29.

[44] Is. 53.9. Cf. Aphraates, *Demonstrations*, I,313,516.

[45] Cf. Daniélou, *Theology*, p. 272f.

[46] This exegesis supports well the connection which Daniélou makes between this testimony, cross typology, and liturgical symbolism.

[47] There is a tear through the MS at this point leaving only the first and last letters of a word visible. We may conjecture: ܝ[ܕܥܝܢ]ܢ (we know).

'*you have eyes but you do not see*' [48], as the prophet said concerning you. You have outward eyes, not the understanding of the mind, or (rather), although you do understand, you struggle against the truth.

VI.1. But let us speak a little more about those things which the scriptures and nature expound to us. God said : *Let us make man in our image and according to our likeness* [1]. Though this [2] sentence provides many meanings for us concerning Christ [3], nevertheless, (let us) follow only one (which) it demonstrates. For man, when he was created, was created in the figure of a cross [4]. **2.** If you, who have hated the cross, pray and stretch forth your hands in prayer, you demonstrate the cross, albeit unwillingly. When you put on your coat, you demonstrate the cross — (likewise) in the window of your house, in the yoke and ploughshare of your plough. Unless a bird stretches out its wings and its feet, it cannot fly on thin air. **3.** O Jew, open your eyes and observe the bird, which by the power * of the cross cleaves and passes through (the *p. 14 air). It provides a type that except by the power of the cross no man can fly on the clouds to meet our Lord in the air [5], when he comes at the end and everything has been subjected to him, as is written concerning him [6]. **4.** For he is that Son of man of whom Daniel said that he was brought near to the Ancient of days, to whom he gave dominion that all the nations should serve him [7]. For he shall rule the kingdom which shall not be destroyed, as Daniel decreed. At that time, all his enemies shall be put under his feet [6], and '*every knee shall bow, which is in heaven, and on earth, and under the earth, and every tongue confess that Jesus Christ is Lord to the glory of God, his Father* [8]. **5.** For there are many things written by the prophets and (present) in nature, (which) show that by the power of the cross of Christ everything exists, and that there is no salvation and no resurrection, neither in this world nor in that which is to come, neither can the haters of the cross live or exist,

[48] Is. 6.9, but following the text of Mk. 8.18.

[1] Gen. 1.26.
[2] ܗܢܐ (this) added in margin by S. scr.
[3] A reference to the use of Gen. 1.26 as a proof text for the Trinity.
[4] Cf. Daniélou, *Theology*, pp. 274ff.
[5] Cf. I Thess. 4.17.
[6] Cf. I Cor. 15.27, but the ultimate reference is to Pss. 8.6, 110.1.
[7] Cf. Dn. 7.13f.
[8] Phil. 2.10f.

except by the power of the cross. **6.** Although these things are so and bear witness to themselves, are you telling me that the cross has had no effect? Behold, we have learnt and demonstrated all these things from the writings of your prophets. And if before the coming of Christ the fathers and the prophets thus extolled the symbols of the cross, now that he has come and fulfilled the words and description [9] of the prophets, and has suffered for us and been crucified, as the prophets proclaimed beforehand, and in him all those of mankind in whom he delights had life and salvation, are you urging upon me that the cross has had no effect? **7.** You do not know the power of the cross because your heart is blind to understanding on account of your evil will, as the *p. 15 prophet said concerning you: * *They have gone after the evil will of their heart* [10]. But I will not listen to you, and I will not be contentious against God like you. But I will make the sign of the cross all the time, over everything which I approach in the love and in the faith [which is in] Christ. **8.** If for the sake of this cross you kill [me, then] I shall be counted worthy of the [holy] inheritance of the prophets and apostles whom your fathers killed. As David says: *For your sake we are killed all the day long, and we have been accounted as sheep for the slaughter* [11], that whether we die or live, we may be counted worthy with them of the kingdom of heaven, through the prayers of all the saints, for ever, Amen.

VII.1. If you are offended because the Son dwelt in the womb of a pure virgin and put on a body, though there is the testimony of the prophet Isaiah [1], (and) though he did not break the tokens of virginity, because the Father dwelt in the thorns of a thorn bush and did not consume it [2], what then do you say, and which is more excellent — a thorn bush full of thorns, or a pure, undefiled virgin, a daughter of Abraham and a daughter of David? [3] **2.** If it is written concerning the Son that he put on a body [4], it is written concerning the Father that

[9] i.e. the description they gave of Christ in their prophecies.

[10] Jer. 9.14.

[11] Ps. 44.22, but following the text of Rom.8.36.

[1] Cf. Is. 7.14.

[2] Cf. Ex. 3.2.

[3] Sergius may be directly or indirectly dependent upon Ephraem for this parallel — cf. EPHRAEM, *Commentary* (*Syriac*), I.25.

[4] Cf. Jn. 1.14 S[c], and APHRAATES, *Demonstrations*, I, 282,392.

'*he was covered with light as* (*with*) *a mantle*' [5]. And if it is written concerning the Son that he increased [6], it is written concerning the Father that '*the Lord God increased greatly*' [7]. And if it is written concerning the Son that he ate and drank, it is written also concerning the Father that he ate and drank with Abraham [8]. **3.** And if it is written concerning the Son that he slept [9], it is written concerning the Father: *Awake, and do not sleep, O Lord* [10]! and again: *The Lord awoke as one who sleeps* [11]. And if it is written concerning the Son that he was weary from the strain of the way [12], it is written: *You have wearied the Lord with your words* [13]. **4.** If it is written concerning the Son that he went down * into Egypt [14], also concerning the Father it is written [that] he *p. 16
said to Jacob: *I will go down with you, and I will bring you up* [15]. And if it is written concerning the Son that he rested [16], also concerning the Father it is written that he rested on the seventh day [17]. **5.** If it is written concerning the Son that he used to go from place to place, also concerning the Father it is written that he used to journey from one resting place of the tabernacle to another [18]. And if the Son asked Legion, '*What is your name?*' [19], also the Father asked Satan, '*Whence do you come?*' [20] And if the Son asked, '*Where have you laid Lazarus?*' [21], also the Father asked, '*Where are you, Adam?*' [22], and (he asked) Cain, '*Where is Abel, your brother?*' [23] **6.** If it is said that the Son was sub-

[5] Ps. 104.2.
[6] Lk. 2.52.
[7] Ps. 104. 1.
[8] Cf. Gen. 18.1ff, and DBS, *Against the Jews*, iv.8.
[9] e.g. Mk. 4.38.
[10] Ps. 44.23.
[11] Ps. 78.65. Cf. DBS, *Against the Jews*, iv.10, vii. 4.
[12] Jn. 4.6; cf. S[c].
[13] Mal. 2.17. Cf. DBS, *Against the Jews*, iv.9, APHRAATES, *Demonstrations*, I, 864.
[14] Cf. Mt. 2.14.
[15] Gen. 46.4.
[16] Cf. Jn.4.6 S[c].
[17] Cf. Gen. 2.2.
[18] Lit.: 'from tabernacle to tabernacle'. Cf. II Sam. 7.6, I Chron. 17.4.
[19] Lk. 8.30.
[20] Job 1.7. This could be read: 'Whence have you come?' but since P reads, ܐܬܐ ܐܢܬ, ܐܬܐܢܬ is probably the ptc., combined with the 2nd m.s. pronoun; cf. NÖLDEKE *S.G.*, §64.
[21] Jn. 11.34
[22] Gen. 3.9.
[23] Gen. 4.9.

jected to the Father[24], it is said concerning the Father that he was subjected to Israel. For he said to them[25] : *You have subjected me with your sins, and you have wearied me with your iniquities*[26]. And if the Father was subjected to the creation and is blameless, how much more the Son to the Father! 7. If the Son sought help from an angel[27], in the same way the Father laid a curse upon Meroz because they did not[28] come to the help of the Lord[29]. And if the Son grieved and was sorrowful at the time of his death[30], in the same way the Father regretted that he had made man and he grieved in his heart[31]. And if it is written concerning the Son that he descended and ascended[32], in the same way it is written[33] concerning the Father that he descended to mount Sinai and ascended[34]. 8. O hard-hearted Jew, God does not speak with us as he (really) is, for we would not be able to understand, but he has spoken with us according to our capacity. See what the people said to Moses, when they heard the mighty sound of the trumpet and (saw) the mountain blazing with fire : *You speak with us, but let not God speak with us, lest we die*[35]. For God is superior to all minds, and to every thought, and to all human understanding; he is inscrutable, incomprehensible, and infinite.

*p. 17 * **VIII.1.** Behold we have demonstrated all these things from your scriptures. If we said anything which is not in your scriptures, you would not accept (it). But investigate and see that when you went down into Egypt, the prophets went down with you — Jacob, Joseph, Moses, Aaron, (and) Miriam. Two hundred years[1] passed, and see how many

[24] Cf. I Cor. 15.28.
[25] Lit. : 'to it', i.e. to Israel.
[26] Is. 43.24. Cf. DBS, *Against the Jews*, iv.9, APHRAATES, *Demonstrations*, I, 565.
[27] Cf. Lk. 22.43.
[28] ܠܐ (not) added at top of page by S.scr.
[29] Cf. Jud. 5.23.
[30] Cf. Mt. 26.37f, Mk. 14.33f.
[31] Cf. Gen. 6.6, and DBS, *Against the Jews*, iii.7.
[32] Cf. Eph. 4.9.
[33] ܕܟܬܝܒ (it is written) added in margin by S. scr.
[34] Cf. Ex. 34.5.
[35] Ex. 20.18f.

[1] The traditional Christian and Jewish computation based on Ex. 12.40 LXX (215 years). Sergius gives the nearest round number; cf. Gal. 3.17, and APHRAATES, *Demonstrations*, I, 54, 940, II, 85.

prophets (there were)! **2**. There were prophets among you, both in the desert and also in the land of Canaan, and (the succession of) prophets never broke off from you. And when you went down to Babylon, Daniel, Hananiah, Azariah, Mishael, Ezekiel, Ezra, Mordecai, (and) Esther (were there). Seventy years passed, and see how many prophets (there were)! And when you went up from Babylon see again Ezra the scribe, Zerubbabel, Haggai, Zechariah, (and) Malachi. **3**. But behold, after Christ came, prophecy, priesthood, and kingdom ceased from you, according to the word of the angel which he spoke to Daniel [2]. And your back is bowed in subjection to all the nations all the time, as David said concerning you [3]. **4**. Because you gave bitter herbs to eat [4] to him who gave you manna to eat [5], behold, you [6] are eating bitter herbs everywhere in subjection under tribute. And you are drinking the sour vinegar of reproach and shame in every place, so that even those men who are strangers to the Christian faith are hostile to you because you gave vinegar [7] to him [8] who gave you sweet [7] water in the desolate, stoneless wilderness [9] by means of the secret rod of the cross. **5**. Behold, your eyes are darkened today, seven hundred years [10] without prophet, without king, without priest [11], without temple, without city, without altar, and without the putting on of the ephod, as Hosea prophesied [12]. And you live in the vain hope that you will be gathered together. For the Lord has laid upon you a deceiving spirit, and he has plunged you into darkness. **6**. For when you served idols God did not leave you without prophets, priests, and leaders. But now that you worship God, * as you assert, and do not reverence idols, and observe *p. 18
circumsion and sabbath, why had this wrath been laid upon you for

[2] Cf. Dn 9. 24-7. For the argument (which goes back as far as JUSTIN, *Trypho*,52) cf. APHRAATES, *Demonstrations*, I, 886, Jacob of Sarug in H,fol. 43r, and DBS, *Against the Jews*, iii. 20, iv. 1-3.

[3] Cf. Ps. 69.24.

[4] Cf. Mt. 27.34, Jn. 19.28ff.

[5] Cf. Ex. 16.13ff, Num. 11.7ff.

[6] ܐܢ̈ܬܘܢ (you) is the probable reading of an indistinct marginal note.

[7] A play on words in the Syriac — ḥalā (vinegar), ḥalyā (sweet).

[8] Cf. Jn. 19.29f.

[9] Cf. Ex. 15.25.

[10] Cf. ch. viii. 6, xiv. 5 and see the Introduction, pp. 1-6.

[11] Cf. EPHRAEM, *Sermon c. Jews*, 211f.

[12] Cf. Hos. 3.4, and DBS, *Against the Jews*, ii.16, iii.19, APHRAATES, *Demonstrations*, I, 509.

seven hundred years, and (why) has he not sent to you even one consolation, or prophet, or worthless dream ? [13] **7**. If you were consumed with zeal for God and you crucified and killed the deceiver of your people, it would have been right for the justice of God to have exalted you to honour and to have made you famous among all the nations. For God has never treated unjustly the zeal of one who was zealous on his behalf, to which Phinehas and Elijah bear witness — one received the covenant of priesthood [14], and Elijah ascended to heaven in a chariot of fire [15]. **8**. So also with you — if God had been pleased with the deed which you did, heaven and earth would have taken arms against him who deceived you, but you he would have exalted above. But from the day that you crucified the Son of God you have gone down beneath [16], but he, above, to the highest heaven. **9**. That which has been written concerning David and Saul has been fulfilled : *The house of David grows stronger and stronger, and the house of Saul grows weaker and weaker* [17]. For if you were the sons of the prophets you would assent to and accept the writings of the prophets. But now, you have made it quite clear that you are not the sons of the prophets.

IX.1. The Jew said : Now if you can, make the Father known to us apart from Abraham and the prophets. For we are truly the sons of Abraham; and if sons of Abraham, we are the sons of the prophets. And this is known to everyone.

2. Sergius (said) : You [1] boast in the name of Abraham, although you are far from the truth, but you do not obey the writings of the prophets. *p. 19 Therefore it is clear that you are not the sons of the prophets, * but the sons of the murderers of the prophets. Therefore you reject the prophets because you do not accept their prophecies. And now you are put to

[13] Cf. Dbs, *Against the Jews*, i.12.

[14] Cf. Num. 25.10ff.

[15] Cf. II Kings 2.11. Sergius is using Phinehas's killing of the Israelite who married a Midianite woman (Num. 25.6-8), and Elijah's slaying of the false prophets of Baal (I Kings 18.40), as examples of how God can bless acts of murder. Cf. Dbs, *Against the Jews*, i.13,iii.23, and for the comparison of Elijah and Phinehas in Jewish thought see Moore, *Judaism*, III, p. 165, n. 253.

[16] A familiar theme of Christian anti-Jewish polemic, developed at greater length in ch.xxi. Cf. Aphraates, *Demonstrations*, I,60,428, Dbs, *Against the Jews*, 1.2, 12f, Kazan, *Isaac of Antioch's Homily*, OC,49, p. 77.

[17] II Sam. 3.1.

[1] 2nd pl.

shame [2] by the nations who have been taught by the prophets that which, in the name of the prophets, you deny. Therefore you lay claim to the prophets in name only. **3**. Who indeed kills his enemy, and after his death loves him or receives his words? Now your fathers — that is, the house of Ahab, Manasseh, and the rest who were like them — killed the prophets. How can the son of Manasseh, who sawed Isaiah asunder [3], accept the prophecy of Isaiah concerning Christ, or (those) of the prophets, his colleagues? **4**. But because you have seen that the nations have hated the worship of idols and turned to Christ, you (for your part) have turned to establish the law, which in its time you hated, even as you will always be perverse. Again, understand this also, if you [4] will, that with the coming of Christ behold, the worship of idols ceased from the Nation and from the nations [5], so that they should not again sacrifice their sons and daughters to demons, as they used to do formerly [6]. **5**. It was especially right that you should wonder and be amazed at this and not doubt that Christ is the Son of God, because in him was fulfilled the prophecy of Isaiah, who said : *The idols shall completely pass away, and they shall enter into the caves of rock and into the holes of the earth, from before the terror* [7] *of the Lord, and from before the glory of his power, when he rises to subdue the earth* [8]. Tell me now, what prophet or priest or any of the fathers was able to cause the idols to pass away from the earth, except he who is the mighty Lord? For he said that from before the terror * of the Lord [7] they would pass away, *p. 20
when he rises to subdue the earth.

6. The Jew said : What does 'when he rises to subdue' mean?

7. Sergius (said) : 'When he rises to subdue' means this : he rose from the dead, when he had conquered death. He rose and subdued the earth by his disciples, and brought the nations and tongues into subjection, that might worship his cross, as David proclaimed beforehand : *All the nations shall be blessed in him, and they shall all praise him* [9]. Again (he

[2] Or : 'you stand ashamed before....'

[3] Cf. *The Ascension of Isaiah*, v. 1,11.

[4] Sergius reverts to the 2nd sing.

[5] The Nation = the Jews, the nations = the Gentiles.

[6] Cf. ch. v.6, n.17.

[7] Or : 'worship, fear'; Sergius is making use of the ambiguity, since he understands by ܕܚܠܬܗ ܕܡܪܝܐ (the terror of the Lord) the worship of Christ, the Lord.

[8] Is. 2.18f.

[9] Ps. 72. 17.

said) : *All kings shall worship him* [10], *and all nations serve him* [11]. Behold then, David witnesses that in Christ all the nations have been blessed. And also that which God said to Abraham has been fulfilled in him : *In your seed all the nations of the earth shall be blessed* [12]. Again, another prophet said : *The nations shall say, 'Surely the idols which our fathers left us as an inheritance are nothing'* [13].

8. The Jew said : That (passage), '*All kings shall worship him*', was said concerning Solomon [14]. For the scripture says that all the kings of the earth sought to see his face and to hear his wisdom [15]. And the queen of Sheba came from the ends of the earth to greet him with presents and gifts; and all kings came like her.

9. Sergius said : Tell me, O wise man, does the scripture testify that Solomon, to whom the kings came, turned them [16] from the fear of idols to the worship of the one God ? Or can you give proof of this ?

11. The Jew (said : Scripture does not say that he turned them from the fear of idols, but by all means he made the one God known to them.

11. Sergius (said) : Know, O wise man, that while Solomon reigned alone for forty years, he did not serve the Lord all these years. For it is
*p. 21 written : *In the time * of Solomon's old age his wives turned away his heart and he served their gods* [17]. If then the son of David turned aside from the law of his father and went after strange gods [18], how could the heathen and the sons of the heathen continue in his teaching ?

12. Therefore it is certain that it was not fulfilled in Solomon, but a pattern like a kind of type was effected in it [19]. For Solomon is not '*from before the sun*' [20], he did not '*descend like rain upon* [21] *the mown*

[10] ܠܗ (him) added above the line by S.scr.

[11] Ps. 72.11; cf. ch. i.6.

[12] Gen. 22.18. Cf. DBS, *Against the Jews*, vii. 12, Jacob of Sarug in J, fol. 205r, APHRAATES *Demonstrations*, I, 52 (and often) SILVESTER, *Discussion*, p. 82.

[13] Jer. 16.19. Cf. APHRAATES, *Demonstrations*, I, 764.

[14] Cf. the Introduction, p. 72, and JUSTIN, *Trypho*, 34, *Dialogue of Athanasius and Zacchaeus*, § 99, DBS, *Against the Jews*, v. 12.

[15] Cf. I Kings 10.24.

[16] ܐܢܘܢ (them) added in margin by S. scr.

[17] I Kings 11.4.

[18] ܐܠܗܐ (gods) added in margin by S. scr.

[19] ܒܗ (in it) probably refers to Ps. 72, which is regarded as containing typological references to Christ.

[20] Ps.72.17. Cf. DBS, *Against the Jews*,v.9, and JACOB OF SARUG, *Against the Jews*, II, 1, 312.

[21] ܥܠ (upon) added above the line by or. scr.

grass' [22], he did not *'rescue the children of the poor'* [23], and *'right'* did not *'flourish in his days'* [24]; and the other things which are said in the prophecy. How could right flourish in the days of him who multiplied his sacrifices [25] upon all the mountains to all the gods of the nations? **13.** But open your eyes and see that they have all been exactly fulfilled in Christ, the Son of God. Behold, the weeks of which Daniel spoke bear witness. Behold the years of the kings which agree one after the other. Behold the chronologies and the events with signs and miracles of every kind — God who thundered with a voice from heaven, *'This is my Son and my Beloved, in whom I am well pleased* [26]; angels descending and ascending to him [27]; demons who obey his command [28]; the dead who rise at his voice [29]; and the rest of the other marvellous things which, if every one of them had been written down, the whole world would not have been sufficient for the books which would have been written, as John, his disciple, said [30]. But after the prophets who preached about him, and after the set time of the weeks which have been fulfilled [31], and after the accuracy of the events which stand (as confirmation) [32], what answer have you now to return?

* **X.1.** The Jew (said): I do not have anything to say. On that account the times and the events yield to you in every respect, and the words *p. 22 of the prophets suit you, as you wish. But this especially rebukes me to silence — that we are humiliated more than all the nations upon the face of the earth, and we are dispersed in all the uttermost parts (under) heaven. We do not have any resting-place nor are we (together) in one region. **2.** However, I have this to say: whether or not the Messiah

22 Ps. 72.6. Ephraem, *Sermon c. Jews*, 214, identifies the 'mown grass' with the Virgin Mary; cf. also dbs, *Against the Jews*, iii. 11. v. 9,12.

23 Ps. 72.12f.

24 Ps. 72.7.

25 Or: 'his high places'.

26 Mt. 3.17, 17.5; see the Introduction, p. 8.

27 Cf. Jn. 1.51.

28 Cf. Mk. 1.25f, 5.8ff, etc.

29 Cf. Mk. 5.41ff, Lk. 7.14f, Jn. 11.43f.

30 Cf. Jn. 21.25.

31 An allusion to Dn. 9.24-7; cf. dbs, *Against the Jews*, ix.10-12.

32 i.e. after the Messianic prophecies have been so accurately fulfilled in the events of Christ's life.

has come, why do you worship the cross? For it is written: *You shall not make for yourself any image or any* [1] *likeness (of anything) which is in heaven above or which is in the earth beneath* [2]. But you, behold, you have filled the earth with crosses (made) of every material found by you — of wood and stone, of bronze and iron, and the rest. And with regard to this, in what way are they less than idols? [3] It is written: *The idols of the nations are silver and gold, and the rest* [4]. Now if you love Christ and believe in him, worship Christ, and that should be enough for you. Thus you do not need the cross [5], for this image which is visible in the world is useless.

3. Sergius (said): Now you have compelled me to utter the saying of the wise Ben Sira: *The man who teaches a fool is like one who glues potsherds together* [6]. But a man's enemy scarcely [7] loves him, though sometimes he does not harm him [8]. Let Christ be an example to us, whom, although he did not harm you in any way, behold, you hate without a cause. As it is written: *They hated me without a cause* [9]. **4**. So the examples which we have cited from the prophets have not, as it seems, taught you anything. Tell me then, why he changed the figures of the sons of Jacob into sheaves of the field? [10] God spke figuratively in the
p. 23 dreams of Joseph. Again (he compared) Rachel and Jacob to the sun and the moon, and again, his brethren to eleven stars. And where is it (said) that Rachel came to worship him, as Jacob interprets [11], since she died before (that) time [12]. And why did he show Pharaoh the years of

[1] ܘܟܠ (or any) added above the line by or. scr.

[2] Ex. 20.4, Dt. 5.8.

[3] MS: 'in what way are you less than idols'. Emending ܐܢܬܘܢ (you) to ܐܢܘܢ (they) gives a tolerable sense, which fits the context.

[4] Ps. 135.15. Cf. DBS, *Against the Jews*, viii. 2.

[5] Lit.: 'For the cross is, for you, superfluous'.

[6] Ecclus. 22.7.

[7] Reading ܠܡܚܣܝܣ (scarcely) for the unintelligible reading of the MS.

[8] This and the following sentence can be taken in one of two ways. Sergius could be saying that the Jew, being Christ's enemy, can hardly be expected to love him, although Christ has done him no harm. Or he could be saying that a man has great difficulty in loving his enemy though at times he manages to avoid actually harming him; Christ, by inference, not only manages to avoid harming the Jew who is his enemy, but actually loves him.

[9] Ps. 35.19,69.4, but following the text of Jn. 15.25.

[10] Cf. Gen. 37.5ff.

[11] Cf. Gen. 37.10.

[12] She died before Joseph had his dreams; see Gen. 35.18f.

plenty and of famine in cows and ears of grain?[13] **5.** Also he compared Nebuchadnezzar to a tree[14] and the world to an image[15], and he showed Daniel beasts coming up from the sea[16]. Many similar things were spoken by the prophets in allegories and parables. '*Behold, I will open my mouth in parables*', said David[17]. Show me where David went down into a deep pit[18]; or where dogs surrounded him[19], as he says; or that they pierced his hands and his feet[19]; or that they shared out his garments[20]; or that he ate bitter herbs and drank vinegar[21]. There are many things which he spoke about his own person, yet not one of them happened to him, if things are as reported. Show that David had a horn![22] Or what righteous man has a horn upon his head like a he-goat, as he said: *The horns of the righteous shall be exalted*[23]? Or where did the Lord break the cedars of Lebanon[24], or as Isaiah said: *Lebanon shall fall in its glory*[25]? **6.** However, we cannot discuss one by one each (statement) which was spoken by the prophets typologically. But if you are a worshipper of God these should be sufficient to convince you. So know that all Christ's dispensation was spoken of in symbols and types — his annunciation, his conception, his birth, his upbringing, his miracles, his crucifixion, his death, his descent into the grave, his resurrection from the dead, his ascension to heaven, and his session at the right hand; and that he is to come[26] on the clouds of heaven in the glory of his angels; and that he will judge the world with righteousness; and that, like a just judge, he will reward everyone according to his deeds.

* **XI.1.** But if you are a disciple of the prophets, accept and obey the *p. 24
prophets. For it is certain that if you do not obey the prophets you can-

[13] Cf. Gen. 41.1ff.
[14] Cf. Dn. 4.10ff.
[15] Cf. Dn. 2.31ff.
[16] Cf. Dn. 7. 3ff.
[17] Ps. 78.2.
[18] Cf. Pss. 40.2,88.6.
[19] Cf. Ps. 22.16.
[20] Cf. Ps. 22.18.
[21] Cf. Ps. 69.21.
[22] e.g. Ps. 132.17.
[23] Ps. 75.10.
[24] Cf. Ps. 29.5.
[25] Is. 10.34.
[26] Sergius slips into the testimony style here.

not call yourself a Jew. For the name 'Judaism' is to be interpreted 'confession' [1]. And if you strive against the prophets you have become a denier and not a Jew [2]. For until Christ you were correctly called 'Jews' and 'Israel', but since Christ, and henceforth, the name of Jews and of Israel is, for you, superfluous, and it is not right that you should be called either Jews or Israel.

2. The Jew (said) : And what is our name then ?

3. Sergius (said) : This is your correct name — deniers, crucifiers, and rejecters; deniers, because you denied that Christ is the Son of God; and crucifiers, because you crucified him without a criminal charge [3]; again rejecters, because, behold, you reject those things which are written by the prophets and are apparent in the events. You are like a blind man who has never seen the light and (who) contradicts those who can see, saying that the sun has not risen, although it is no longer dark. And though the sun burns his body with its heat, he denies that there is either sun or light.

4. The Jew (said) : And what is a real Jew and Israel ?

5. Sergius (said) : The true confessor; he is the real Jew [4], as it is written that Jacob said in his blessings : *O confessor, your brethren shall praise you* [5]. Because Christ was thus to arise from Judah, Jacob made beforehand a confession by the name 'Judah'. Henceforth, not everyone who is born from Judah is a Jew, but everyone in whom is born the true confession of Christ, even if he is from an alien people. For God said to Abraham : *In your seed all the nations shall be blessed* [6]. Do you think then, that in Ishmael and in the sons of Keturah, or in the wicked sons
*p. 25 of Jacob, * the heathen nations are truly blessed ? Do not err ! The heathen cannot be blessed by wicked men, but by Christ, the Blessed and the Righteous One. In him the accursed nations have been blessed. For it is written : *You have rebuked the nations, and cursed are those who wander from your commandments* [7]. So then, according to the word of

[1] This etymology, deriving both words from the root ܝܕܐ, which in the Aph'el theme means 'to confess, acknowledge', can be traced back as far as the third century — see the *Didascalia*, XIII, and cf. DBS, *Against the Jews*, i.3.

[2] i.e. a confessor.

[3] i.e. without being able to convict him of any real offence.

[4] Most of Jacob of Sarug's sixth homily against the Jews (J, fols. 202v-205r) parallels Sergius's argument here.

[5] Gen. 49.8; Sergius has substituted ܡܘܕܝܢܐ (confessor) for the ܝܗܘܕܐ (Judah) of P.

[6] Gen. 22.18; cf. ix.7.

[7] Ps. 119.21.

David, everyone who wanders from the commandments is bound under a curse, in accordance with that which (is written) : *Cursed is everyone who does not do all which is written in this book* [8]. Now present to me one out of all the seed of Abraham who has not wandered from the commandments except Christ, concerning whom the prophet Isaiah witnessed and said : *He did no iniquity, neither was deceit found in his mouth* [9].

6. Therefore it is certain that (the prophecy) '*in your seed all the nations shall be blessed*' [6] has been fulfilled in Jesus Christ — that is, in the Christian faith. Everyone who is outside the Christian faith, whether from the Nation or from the nations [10], is subject to the curse, and is nowhere near to the blessing of the faithful Abraham : *Abraham believed God, and it was reckoned to him for righteousness* [11]. As to Abraham, so to everyone who believes in Christ, faith [12] is also reckoned for righteousness. Therefore it has been made known and confirmed that those who believe in Christ are the sons of Abraham and the Israel of God [13].

7. The Jew (said) : Then if it is as you say, why are you not called 'Jews' and 'Israel'? If you are the true Jews and the true Israel, it is right [14] that you should be called Jews and we by a name that suits us. But why then do you shrink from the name of 'Jews'?

8. Sergius (said) : If both we and you were thus called by the same name, (one) people would not be distinguished from another or (one) person from another, and there would be great confusion in the world. * It would not be right for corn and straw to be mixed up together under *p. 26
the one name. Therefore it pleased God that the ancient name should remain upon you as a reproach, but we have been called Christians — (that is), confessors. **9**. This name makes a distinction between confessors and deniers, that the real Jews might be named 'Christians', and instead of the 'Synagogue' the body of confessors [15] might assume the name 'Church'. For Isaiah said to the Synagogue : *And you shall be*

[8] Dt. 27.26; cf. ch. v.2.

[9] Is. 53.9; cf. ch. v.14.

[10] Cf. ch. ix, n.5.

[11] Gen. 15.6. Cf. Aphraates, *Demonstrations*, I,34 (and often), and DBS, *Against the Jews, ii.5*.

[12] Lit. : 'it'.

[13] Cf. Gal. 6.16, and DBS, *Against the Jews*, iv.7.

[14] S.scr. adds ܗܘܐ in margin, altering the sense to : 'it was right.....'

[15] Lit. : 'it'.

called by a new name which the mouth of the Lord will give [16]. Rightly then, the synagogue of confessors has been named 'the Church', which was decreed by the mouth of the Lord. For the truth required (it) thus.

10. The Jew (said) : Show me how and where it was decreed.

11. Sergius (said) : If you will believe the Gospel, thus it written, that when Jesus had multiplied the bread and five thousand men besides women and children had been satisfied by five loaves, he asked his disciples, '*Who do the crowds say that I am?' The disciples answered, 'Some say that you are Elijah, or Jeremiah, or one of the prophets'. And he said to them, 'But who do you say that I am?' Simon, who was called Cephas, answered and said, 'You are the Messiah, the Son of the living God'. Jesus answered and said to him, 'Blessed are you, Simon Bar-Jona! For flesh and blood has not revealed* (*this*) *to you, but my Father who is in heaven. Therefore I tell you that you shall be called Cephas, and on this rock I will build my church, and the bars of Sheol* [17] *shall not prevail against it* [18]. Behold, as Isaiah said, the synagogue of God was called by a new name, which the mouth of the Lord gave [19]. And he made a dis-
*p. 27 tinction between the synagogue of the sinners * and of the righteous. Again, he called his servants by another [name], as he said through Isaiah : *And the Lord will kill you, but his servants he will call by another name* [20]. And this is 'Christians' which means 'the Messiah's men' [21].

12. Understand then, like a wise man, that even in the time of Elijah the people was divided [22] into two factions. For he said to them, '*How long will you divide into two factions? If the Lord is God, follow him; but if Baal, follow him*'. [23] In the same way Jehu also showed (this), when he deceived the wicked worshippers of Baal and said, '*Search and see if there is any of the servants of the Lord among you in all the house of Baal* [24].

16 Is. 62.2. Cf. Ephraem, *Sermon c. Jews*, 220B, and for a similar argument by Augustine cf. Simon, *Verus Israel*, p. 386.

17 For the reading ܡܘܟܠܐ ܕܫܝܘܠ (bars of Sheol) cf. Ephraem, *Commentary* (*Syriac*), XIV. 1, and Burkitt, *Evangelion*, II, pp. 119, 156,170.

18 Mt. 16.13ff.

19 The exegesis depends on the early Christian equation of κύριος χριστός with 'the Lord' of the Old Testament.

20 Is. 65.15; cf. ch. xx. 12, Aphraates, *Demonstrations*, I, 909, and the *Dialogue of Athanasius and Zacchaeus*, §57.

21 Cf. iv.5 and the Introduction, ch. II, n.58.

22 ܦܠܝܓ (divided) added in margin by or.scr.

23 I. Kings 18.21.

24 II Kings 10.23.

And they said, 'There is none'. Then his sword prevailed over them. **13.** So this holy portion of the Lord was called by a new name, 'the Church' and 'Christians'. And the Gentiles have adhered to it and they have been grafted in [25] through the Christian faith, and they have been blessed. That which God said to Abraham stands firm and has come to pass : *In your seed all the nations of the earth shall be blessed* [26]. They have become all one flock and (there is) one shepherd, Christ [27]. **14.** For all the prophets meditated on this portion of the Lord. For things to come make clear a prophecy, and as it [28] draws near, it [29] is proved by later events [30]. Therefore David said : *In the portion of the Lord I meditated, that I might keep your commandments* [31]. And the excellent promises and good pledges, which are written in the prophets, were spoken concerning this holy portion. (For example) : *Zion shall be redeemed by Judgement, and her captivity by righteousness. But the wicked and the sinners will be crushed together* [32]. And again : *The deliverer will come from Zion, and he will turn away iniquity from Jacob* [33]. And Hosea said: *I will betroth you to me * in righteousness, and I will betroth you to me* *p. 28 *in faithfulness* [34]. **15.** There are many things like these concerning the nations who are grafted into this holy portion through the Christian faith. When David saw the multitude of crowds and tongues who, with all kinds of musical notes and pleasant melodies, sing praises with his psalms, he said in the joy of his heart : *I will give thanks to you in the great church* [35], *and among many nations I will praise you* [36]. And again (he said) : *All the ends of the earth shall remember and turn to the Lord, and all the families of the nations shall worship before him. For the kingdom is the Lord's, and he rules over the nations* [37]. Again (he said) : *The rulers*

[25] Cf. Rom. 11.17.

[26] Gen. 22.18; cf. ch. ix.7, xi.5.

[27] Cf. Jn. 10.16.

[28] i.e. the event prophesied.

[29] i.e. the prophecy or the event prophesied.

[30] Lit. : 'Far off things'. This must mean either that the prophecy is proved by the occurrence of the event prophesied at a later date, or that the significance of the event is proved by reference to prophecy uttered at a far earlier date.

[31] Ps.119.57.

[32] Is. 1.27f.

[33] Is. 59.20, but following the text of Rom. 11.26.

[34] Hos. 2.19f.

[35] Or : 'congregation', but 'church' is what Sergius saw in the text.

[36] Ps. 35.18.

[37] Ps. 22.27f. Cf. Aphraates, *Demonstrations*, I, 776.

of the nations shall turn to the God of Abraham [38]. **16**. Say then, O deceiver, who errs wilfully and through ignorance, when, and where, and at what time, did David give thanks to God in the great church [35], and sing praises among the nations, if it was not in the church of Christ, as I have said ?

17. The Jew said : Among the Philistines, and among the Moabites and the Ammonites, as the first book of Kingdoms [39] shows.

18. Sergius (said) : The book of Kingdoms shows that he fled and hid himself and begged bread like a poor man, and was afraid lest any man should know that he was David. And the book says that he made his spittle run down on his beard near Achish, king of Gath, from fear lest he should die, while it was an important matter in his eyes whether he could save himself from death [40]. But the book does not say that he turned a (single) man to the knowledge of the law nor, in his lifetime, did any of the nations sing praises with his hymns. **19**. But now, through the Christian faith, behold, all nations meditate on his hymns, and sing praises with his psalms. His prophecy, which I quoted, has been fulfilled : *I will give thanks to you in the great church, and among many nations I will praise you* [36]. And now answer me ! Will you accept the prophecy of the prophets or struggle against God who is in the prophets ?

*p. 29 * **XII.1**. The Jew said : O obstructive man ! I have asked you why you worship the cross, but you have eluded me in many ways. And I have pursued after you to bring you back to the question, but still you go round me in circles on the way. Do not elude the question ! You have realised that I am disturbing you with this (question). **2**. Tell me then, why do you worship the cross ? Tell me exactly, and explain your worship to me, but do not tell me again the story of Christ. For I know these things which are in the prophets, who spoke about him [1]. This I must demand — that you explain to me why you worship the cross, so (much so) that you have filled the earth with crosses in every place.

3. Sergius (said) : Be patient with your question like a wise man, and

[38] Ps. 47.9; cf. the Introduction, p. 8.

[39] This is the Septuagint title for I Samuel, but it was used in Syriac-speaking areas heavily influenced by Greek Christianity.

[40] Cf. I Sam. 21.13f.

[1] Cf. the Introduction, p. 72.

listen calmly to our discourse. For this is philosophy — patience. For it is not right that the word of faith should come into existence in a tumult, but in sobriety and self-control. Listen then ! Has not the rod of Moses persuaded you that by the secret of the cross which is in it he performed all the miracles both in Egypt and in the desert ? [2] And the rest of the examples from the prophets which we have brought forward and which we have omitted, do they not persuade you ? **4.** Let us tell you one example from the world, namely, the rank of kingship, which is as follows. As even you know, when a king has begun to reign and sat upon his royal throne, the hosts of his servants draw near to worship him, not needing anyone to give a description of him — what the king is like, or of his ornaments, or his royal attire — because they see him face to face and worship him * with awe. **5.** But (for) those who are afar off *p. 30 and (for) the cities of his realm, because they cannot assemble and come to one meeting-place and render the worship which is due to their lord, he is carefully depicted with choice pigments on images and pictures. Great care is taken, as far as possible, that they take exactly the shape of (his) person, crown, and throne, And they are given to the cities and regions under his rule, and the heralds and the authorities exhort the crowds to accept the image of the king with the praises and honours which befit kingship [3]. **6.** These crowds, as it were, really see the person and figure of the king [4], offering worship with love to the image of their lord. Likewise the king also himself accepts that those who honour and worship his image, worship and honour his real self. Likewise again, also the king's enemies and adversaries, even if they cannot harm the king in person, if the king's image falls into their hands, vent their hatred upon it, and assuage their wrath by destroying it. **7.** Behold, I have given you a clear example, if you wish to be instructed. Understand by means of this simile why we worship the cross. The cross is the image of Christ, and in its form the sign of the crucifixion as shown to us. And, as it were, we see Christ crucified (and) we worship the likeness [5] with love. **8.** Therefore in our love for him, we depict him in every place, remembering his victory over death and the

[2] Cf. ch. v.5.

[3] Cf. Wisdom of Solomon 14.17.

[4] i.e. the reality represented by the image.

[5] i.e. what it represents. For a similar rationale of the worship of the cross cf. DbS, *Against the Jews*, viii.2.

deliverance from Satan and sin which he wrought by it [6]. And because we know that it is a terror to the demons and the rebellious powers, we sign ourselves with it both at our going in and at our coming out, at our eating and at our drinking, at our waking and at our sleeping. **9**. For *p. 31 we know that *it is the power * of God unto salvation of all who believe* [7]. As it is written : *Behold, I am laying in Zion a stone of stumbling and a stone of offence, and he who believes in it shall not be afraid* [8]. We believe and we boast in his crucifixion, the prophets being with us and strengthening us so that we may not become weak. **10**. Even if we suffer reproach for his [9] sake we do not mind, but we rejoice because it is written : *The reproach of those who reproached you fell upon me* [10]; again (it is written) : *Your enemies have reproached me, O Lord, and they have reproached the footsteps of your Messiah* [11]. What have you to say against these things, you who reject the truth ?

11. The Jew (said) : This cannot be — that the worship of both Christ and the cross is the same thing. If you worship Christ, you do not need to worship the cross. And if you worship the cross, what good is Christ to you ?

12. Sergius (said) : Fear God, O man, and judge what is right and do not reject the truth, and remember the example which I put forward to to you, of the king and his image. Who is there, who is in subjection to the king, who can despise or insult the king's image without passing a sentence of death upon himself. It is certain that after the insult he will either be burnt or cut in pieces. Those who are near to the king, worship the king, but for those who are distant the king's image is necessary, that by worshipping the image they may show that they are the king's servants and subjects. If there is anyone who despises and insults the king's image, he is rebellious and insolent. And when, on one *p. 32 occasion, the king comes to one of the cities under his rule, * its inhabitants do not any more need to worship his image as long as the king is present in person. **13**. So also we, until Christ comes, we worship his cross, which is the symbol of his crucifixion. For he said to us : *Do thus*

[6] i.e. the cross.

[7] Rom. 1.16.

[8] Is. 28.16; cf. Rom. 9.33, I Peter 2.6, and Ephraem, *Sermon c. Jews*, 219D, dbs, *Against the Jews*, marginal note to v.7, and Jacob of Sarug, J, fol. 204r.

[9] Or : 'its' i.e. the cross's sake.

[10] Ps. 69.9; cf. Rom. 15.3.

[11] Ps. 89.51.

in remembrance of me until I come [12]. But when he has come, we shall not need to worship the symbol, for we shall be with him, and we shall rejoice in his kingdom and enjoy ourselves at his table. In that day his friends shall rejoice but his enemies shall lament for themselves, when they have seen the sign of his cross between earth and heaven bearing and being borne from one end to the other [13], and (heard) the sound of the trumpet blowing [14], which is more powerful than that of Mount Sinai. And then, with one gesture of command, the dried bones of the departed shall be gathered together, as Ezekiel prophesied beforehand [15]. For the dead shall be raised and the living shall draw near and be present together at the one meeting-place of just judgement, that everyone may be rewarded according to his deeds [16]. Then the Risen One shall come upon...... [17]

14. ..... I can flee from it [18]. I speak the truth as I know (it) and do not conceal (it). Now if the Messiah is, as he is reported in the books of the prophets, he whom you proclaim and no other, and there is no other Messiah of God; and (if) the prophets, the events, and the set times, bear witness as you have demonstrated above, then I will not reject or conceal (it) on account of the oath which you made me swear [19]. If any other comes, he is false and a liar.

15. Sergius (said) : Although you know this, why do you not acknowledge (him)?

16. The Jew said : I do not acknowledge (him) for two reasons : one, that my heart will not allow me to leave * the law of my fathers; and the *p. 33
other, that I fear my people lest they stone me or burn me with fire [20].

17. Sergius (said) : This is a marvel — that the judgement of man is more important to you than the judgement of God. Now I advise you not to fear the judgement of man who comes to an end and passes away, but fear the judgement of God [21] who has no end and is eternal.

[12] I Cor. 11.24,26.

[13] Lit. : 'from the ends to the ends'. Probably we have here echoes of Jewish Christian speculation on the cosmic role of the cross; cf. Daniélou, *Theology*, pp. 265-292.

[14] Cf. Mt. 24.31, I Cor.15.52, I Thess. 4.16.

[15] Ezek. 37.1ff; cf. ch. iii.3.

[16] Cf. Mt. 16.27, Rom. 2.6.

[17] A folio is missing here in the MS after 26v. Presumably it continued with an allusion to Dn.7.13f; cf. the Introduction, p. 58.

[18] The Jew is speaking now.

[19] Cf. ch. xiii.12, and the Introduction, p. 58, 72f.

[20] See the Introduction, p. 58f.

[21] ܕܐܠܗܐ (of God) added in margin by S.scr.

18. The Jew (said) : Whether I acknowledge (him) or not is no concern of yours. But prepare yourself and answer the things which I am going to ask, lest you render void your faith and fall into censure on account of the things which you hold.

19. Sergius (said) : The truth to which I hold fast stands firm on its own, for the truth cannot be overcome.

XIII.1. The Jew (said) : It is written in the law : You shall not touch the bone of a dead man [1], especially those who are priests [2]. But you, behold you carry the bones of the dead in your pockets, and you defile yourselves with dead bodies, and you are unashamed. And not only this, but also you pray to and worship dry and withered bones. You rub the dust from them on your bodies, and you regard (this practice) as something important [3]. But if he who touches a bone with the tip of
*p. 34 a finger is unclean until * the evening how much more shall he to whom a dead man's putrefying matter clings be unclean! But you build churches for them, and you paint pictures for them [4] with pigments. And you dedicate them to martyrs and call them a house of prayer. Though you have testimonies concerning Christ from the books of the prophets, there is nothing at all about these things. For Moses gave commandment concerning the bone of a dead man, and Isaiah said : *They defile their vessels with dead bodies* [5], *and they eat* [*pigs'*] *flesh, and vermin, and mice*; *they shall be consumed together says the Lord* [6]. Behold then, you [7] defile yourselves with dead bodies and bones, and you eat the pig and the rest of the things which God through the law [has forbidden] [8]. In all these things you are condemned and, as it seems to me, you do not have even one excuse. But now, give an answer.

2. Sergius (said) : These are your questions — the bone of a dead man, and images which are icons [9], and pigs' flesh. With which do you wish to begin?

[1] Cf. Num. 19.11-22.
[2] Cf. Num. 6.6, Lev. 21.11.
[3] A scribe has added ܪܒܐ (important) at the top of the page.
[4] i.e. for the churches.
[5] Is. 65.4.
[6] Is. 66.17.
[7] ܐܢܬܘܢ (you) added in margin by S. scr.
[8] The reading 'has forbidden' is based on a partly illegible marginal note by S. scr.
[9] The Gk. loan word ܐܝܩܘܢܐ (εἰκών).

3. The Jew (said) : Concerning the bone of a dead man first.

4. Sergius (said) : Whom do you call dead ? Tell me.

5. The Jew (said) : I call dead everyone from whom his spirit has departed. For David said : *His spirit departs and he returns to his earth, and on that day all his thoughts perish* [10]. And Solomon (said) : *The body returns to its dust, and the spirit to the Lord who gave it* [11]. Therefore all flesh in which there is no spirit is dead.

6. Sergius (said) : Are both the righteous and the sinners included without distinction under this name 'death' ?

7. The Jew (said) : The scripture makes no distinction. For it says : *His spirit departs* * *and he returns to his earth* [10]. This is sufficient evidence. *p. 35

8. Sergius (said) [12]: Then why did God say : *I am the God of Abraham and of Isaac and of Jacob* [13] ? If they are dead and are like all the sinners and the heathen, then he ought not to single out a man's name, but (say), 'I am the God of all the dead', as Moses said : *O God, the God of the spirits of all flesh* [14]. For the living and true God is the God of the living not of the dead [15]. For he set himself apart and made known that he is not the God of the erring or of the heathen. Therefore he commands and says : You shall not go after the gods of the nations, for I am the Lord your God, the God of Abraham, and of the rest [16]. You tell me now how he can be both the God of Abraham and of the wicked and impious. Be straight with me [17] and speak the truth.

9. The Jew (said) : I cannot say that the God of Abraham is the God of the wicked and impious, because it is written : *The wicked says in his heart, 'There is no God'* [18]. And again (it is written) : *The impious shall turn to Sheol, and all the nations who forget God* [19].

10. Sergius (said) : Behold then, acknowledge that the sinners and the impious, even though they are alive in the body, are dead to God. Thus also the righteous, although they are dead in the body, are alive to God.

[10] Ps.146.4.

[11] Eccl. 12.7.

[12] In what follows Sergius is clearly drawing on Mt. 22.23-33; cf. Aphraates, *Demonstrations*, I, 993.

[13] Ex. 3.6.

[14] Num. 16.22.

[15] Cf. Mt. 22.32.

[16] Cf. Ex. 20.3 for the first clause, Ex. 3.6,6.7 for the second.

[17] Lit. : 'Direct your word straight to me'.

[18] Pss. 14.1,53.1.

[19] Ps. 9.17.

For it is written : *The souls of the righteous are in the hands of God* [20]. Again it is written : *On whom shall I look and in whom shall I dwell, but in* [21] *the meek and the contrite in spirit, who trembles at my word* [22]. Again it is written : *You are the temple of God, if you amend your ways and your deeds before him* [23]. And again he said : *I will dwell in them and walk in them, and I will be their God and they shall be my* [24] *people* [25]. What is God — life or death ?

*p. 36 **11**. The Jew (said) : He is life. * For he is the life of everything which is alive, and apart from him there is no life, but absolute death [26] and everlasting destruction.

12. Sergius (said) : Then where do the living dwell ? Death has no authority (over them) [27], in the same way as darkness cannot [28] enter a house to which the sun gives light. For he said : *I will dwell in them and walk in them* [25]. If God is life and he dwells in the righteous, behold, we do not honour the bones of a dead man but the life and power of God which dwells in them [29]. Moses laid down the commandment : You shall not touch the bone of a dead man. From it your contention that we worship the bones of dead men derived strength. Tell me now, are you under a fearful oath to God not to deny the truth ? [30] But judge truly the question which I am going to ask you : is it right and just that he who lays down a law should abide by the law, or he who did not lay it down ?

13. The Jew (said) : Truly it is right for him who lays down a law to abide by the law which he has laid down, that he may not be a hypocrite. If he does not, he cannot blame anyone else who breaks his law.

14. Sergius (said) : Moses laid down the commandment : You shall not touch the bone of a dead man, and he who touches (it) shall be

[20] Wis. 3.1.

[21] As the argument develops it becomes clear that Sergius is using these texts to prove that God dwells *in* the righteous. So 'in', rather than 'with', is the best translation here.

[22] Is. 66.2. Cf. Aphraates, *Demonstrations*, I, 829.

[23] Jer. 7.4f.

[24] ܠܝ (my) added in margin by S.scr.

[25] Lev. 26.12, II Cor. 6.16. Aphraates, *Demonstrations*, I, 10,793 cites this and Jer. 7.4f together.

[26] ܡܘܬܐ (death) added twice in margin and once above the line by scribes.

[27] Or : 'Then where does the life dwell ? Death has no authority (over it).....'

[28] ܡܨܐ (can) added in margin by S. scr.

[29] Cf. Dbs, *Against the Jews*, viii.2.

[30] Cf. ch. xii.14, and the Introduction, p. 58.

unclean until the evening [31]. And again he said : *Cursed is everyone who does not keep all which is written in this law* [32]. Tell me, were the bones of Joseph those of a dead or a living man ?

15. The Jew (said) : As we Hebrews maintain, those of a dead man.

16. Sergius (said) : Then show me where he who laid down the commandment cast the bones of the righteous Joseph.

17. The Jew (said) : I cannot show (anything) except that he carried the body around on all the journeys of the Israelites for forty years, until they entered * the promised land [33]. And they were buried in the *p. 37
inheritance of Joseph by Joshua, the son of Nun, the son of Ephraim, the son of Joseph [34].

18. Sergius (said) : Tell me, is Moses under the curse which he pronounced : *Cursed is everyone who does not do all which is written in this book* [32]. He laid down the precept concerning the bone, but he carried [35] the bones. And he cursed him who transgresses anything which he commands. Come, condemn Moses ! Come ! Your boast is in Moses, your master and teacher. If Moses is condemned, so am I. And if Moses is innocent, so am I, like him. Come, answer me ! Why are you silent ? [36]

19. The Jew (said) : Although Moses did indeed carry the bones, he did not worship (them) as you have done. And you cannot show that he did worship (them).

20. Sergius (said) : Neither can you show that he did not worship (them). But as he carried, so also he worshipped and honoured (them) although he did not worship (them) as God, but as a righteous man whose intercession God accepts. And as he presented the names of Abraham, Isaac, and Jacob, in his prayer [37], so also he mentioned the bones of Joseph before God [38]. And if there had been another just man between Abraham and himself, he would also have made mention of him before God, that with him [39] they [40] might repair the breaches of your sins. For David said : *If Moses, his chosen, had not stood in the*

[31] Cf. Num. 19.11-22.
[32] Dt. 27.26 ; cf. Gal. 3.10, and ch. v.1.
[33] Cf. Gen. 50.25f, Ex. 13.19, Josh. 24.32.
[34] Cf. APHRAATES, *Demonstrations*, I, 376.
[35] Accepting the S.scr. 's addition of ܗܘܐ ;cf. text.
[36] Cf. DBS, *Against the Jews*, viii.2.
[37] Cf. Ex. 32.13.
[38] An inference by Sergius, for it is nowhere stated in the Pentateuch.
[39] i.e. the other 'just man'.
[40] i.e. the righteous fathers.

breach before him and averted his wrath that he might not destroy them [41], it is certain that they would have been destroyed, as the sons of Aaron were destroyed [42], and as the two hundred and fifty priests whom the fire which went out from before the Lord burnt up [43], and as the company of Korah and Dathan perished [44], and as the rest of the wicked men whom the fire round about the camp consumed [45]. See that four times God threatened to destroy them, but Moses took up like *p. 38 presents and offerings the names of the righteous* fathers and presented (them) to God [46]. Then his wrath was assuaged. Are these things (so) or not?

21. The Jew (said): They are, and I cannot deny (it), for they have their own attestation.

XIV.1. Sergius (said): Come then, let us search for the truth. For these men are alive for ever — (this is) the orthodox faith. For I said to you, 'Whom do you call dead?' And you said to me, 'Everyone from whom his spirit has departed'. Then according to your definition, everyone who is dead to this life is unclean, and everyone who is alive in this physical life is clean.

2. The Jew (said): The scripture said: He who touches the bone of a dead man shall wash his body with water and be unclean until the evening [1]. And in this it does not distinguish between the righteous and the sinner. Therefore I say that everyone who is dead is unclean.

3. Sergius (said): Are the heathen, the Magi, the enchanters, the idolaters, the adulterers, the thieves, the murderers, and the transgressors of God's law and commandments, holy until they die?

4. The Jew (said): I do not say (on my own authority) that they [2] are holy, but because the scripture requires (it).

5. Sergius (said): But behold, the scripture says: *Kings (who) do*

41 Ps. 106.23.

42 Cf. Lev. 10.2.

43 Cf. Num. 16.35.

44 Cf. Num. 16.31ff.

45 Cf. Num. 11.1.

46 Cf. Ex. 32.13f, Dt. 9.27. The Pentateuch reports only one occasion on which Moses specifically mentioned the names of the fathers, but see Num. 11.2,14.12ff, 16.22.

1 Cf. Lev. 11.24f, Num. 19.11f.

2 ܡܝ̈ܬܐ (the dead) has been added here incorrectly by S.scr.

iniquity are unclean [3]. And David said concerning the Lord : *his soul hates the wicked and the lovers of iniquity* [4]. Therefore it is clear that the wicked is unclean and defiled both in his life and in his death. This is truly death, and he who cleaves to him defiles himself. But the righteous and he who loves God is clean and holy both in his life and in his death; the divine power dwells in his bones. And the bones of Elisha — which gave life to the dead man who touched them and returned with those who were digging his grave — bear witness [5]. Behold, let your whole people be gathered, you * who live and speak, and pray over *p. 39 one dead body, and call on God to whom you pray, and mention Abraham, Isaac, and Jacob, your fathers, and let the power of your prayer be seen in the coming to life of the dead body. And if you cannot do this, although you cannot, why do you deny the truth and find fault with our glorious faith ? And (why) are you not ashamed that, behold, for seven hundred years [6] no man has been found among all your people who prays either for a dead or for a sick man, and is heard ? But by this it is clear to ordinary people that you are exasperating, and also that God is exasperated by you. But you do not understand, and still you harden your hearts to his exasperation.

6. The Jew (said) : But where are the signs that are performed among your people ?

7. Sergius (said) : Who can number the signs and miracles and mighty works which have been performed among our people in all nations, in all places, in the name of Christ, through his disciples and the saints after them, even until this day ? In all generations you see with your eyes you do not wish to believe, because you are the children of those who saw his wonderful deeds but (who) afterwards said to Aaron, '*Make us gods that they may go before us*' [7]. If you were not their children you would have seen the dead who were raised, the lepers who were cleansed, the blind (whose eyes) were opened, the lame who leapt like harts, as Isaiah prophesied beforehand [8], and the evil spirits who were driven out, and others without number. For on account of them the nations turned to the God of Abraham. What place or city, or even just a village, is

[3] Untraceable; cf. perhaps Dt. 17.14-20,25.16.

[4] Ps. 11.5.

[5] Cf. II Kings 13.20f.

[6] Cf. ch. viii.5f.

[7] Ex. 32.1 ; cf. ch. xxii.16.

[8] Cf. Is. 35.5f, and Dbs, *Against the Jews*, v.10.

there in which God has not placed the treasure of one of his saints, from
*p. 40 whose bones flow cures and healing * like Elisha's. There are thousands and ten thousands living and speaking among you, while you are deprived of (even) one simple sign.

8. The Jew (said) : They are phantasies, and not true.

9. Sergius (said) : You are like your fathers who, when they saw the evil spirits coming out, said, '*This man casts out demons by Beelzebub*' [9]. And they said about the blind man (whose eyes) were opened, '*It is not he, but he is certainly like him*' [10]. And (because) they did not know what to say about Lazarus who rose from the dead, they wished to kill him that he might not say that it was Jesus who had raised him up [11]. But what can you say without burying yourself in falsehood ? Then let the word of the prophet Isaiah tell you — he who foresaw your slander said : *Woe to those who call evil good and good evil, and put light for darkness and darkness for light, and put bitter for sweet and sweet for bitter* [12] ! And again he said : *Woe to the sinful people, a people weighed down with iniquity* [13] ! **10.** Behold, see now the magnitude of your iniquity — that pure and holy men are regarded by you as evildoers and impious. Pure and holy men in whom the Spirit of the Lord dwells are regarded by you as unclean and defiled, and 'he who touches them defiled' [14]. But Moses, who carried the bones of the holy man, proves to you that the bones of the saints are not unclean but (only) those of wicked men, who are unclean both in their lives and in their deaths. And the holy bones of Elisha, from which life sprang up for the dead man, put you to shame [15]. Even your own (bones) are regarded by you as unclean and 'he who touches (them) defiled'. The companions [16] of Hananiah and of Daniel, to whom beasts and flames showed honour and did not harm
*p. 41 their bodies [17] — holy bodies, * in which holiness dwelt — why did they become unclean after their death, as you say, and 'he who touches them defiled' ?

[9] Lk. 11.15.

[10] Jn. 9.9.

[11] Cf. Jn. 12.10f.

[12] Is. 5.20.

[13] Is. 1.4f.

[14] Cf. Num. 19.11ff.

[15] Cf. II Kings 13.20f.

[16] ܒܝܬ ܚܢܢܝܐ stands for Hananiah, Azariah, and Mishael (cf. Dn. 1.6f); see PS, *Thes.*, col. 485.

[17] Cf. Dn. 3.27,6.22.

11. The Jew (said) : But can you show that you have the bones of the companions of Hananiah and of Daniel ?

12. Sergius (said) : Although I do not have the bones of the companions of Hananiah, I do have like them victory over the beasts and fire. Now they held out against and endured all tortures that God might not depart from them, he who said : *I will dwell in them and walk in them, and I will be their God* [18]. And in antiquity Daniel, and Hananiah and his companions, and the Maccabees, and the old man Eleazar [19], and Shamuni and her seven sons [20], and many others, gave themselves up to death in their integrity, for the sake of the law of their God, that they might not change (their) worship of him. Sometimes God showed his power in the miracles which he did, but sometimes he disregarded his servants and left them to die. Recently, in like manner, sometimes miracles occured and many were converted, (while) there are some who ended their lives in the contest. We regard both the former and the latter [21] as servants of God, and we honour them as servants of God.

13. The Jew (said) : Honour and worship are two different things, and I observe that you worship and honour (them) as gods.

14. Sergius (said) : Tell me, if you enter and worship before a king, do you worship a judge and all the ranks of authority or all the order of rulers with the same (position of the) head with which you have worshipped the king [22] ? You change (the position of the) head according to the authority of each one of them.

15. The Jew (said) : It is impossible for me to change the (position of my) head according to each one of them as they are lifted up and brought low [23]. So I worship the king and the lower ranks of the kingdom with the same (position of the) head. But the mind distinguishes the honour * of each one of them according to the measure of his rank. *p. 42

16. Sergius (said) : If you cannot change (the position of) your head, with the result that you worship the judge, the military commanders,

[18] Lev. 26.12, and II Cor.6.16; cf. ch. xiii.10,12.

[19] Cf. II Macc. 6.18ff.

[20] Cf. II Macc. 7, IV Macc. 5-17. For the name 'Shamuni' in the Syriac tradition see Aphraates, *Demonstrations*, I, 221, Ephraem, *Madrasha on the sons of Shamuni*.

[21] i.e. those who worked miracles to escape martyrdom, and those who were martyred.

[22] Sergius is making use of the fact that there is only one word in Syriac to describe worshipping God and doing obeisance to secular authorities; cf. DBS, *Against the Jews*, viii.3, Aphraates, *Demonstrations*, I, 800f.

[23] Perhaps an ironic comment on the frequency with which officials were promoted and demoted.

the rulers, and every man who has the honour of authority, with the same (position) with which you have worshipped the king, why then do you complain of me that with the bending of one (position of the) head I honour the King and his servants [24]? I also have a mind which distinguishes the rank of each one of them. When I offer to God, as the Lord of all, the worship which is due to him as the King of all the worlds, so (I do) to the martyrs as the servants and great friends of the king [25], who have demonstrated their love for him by enduring [damaging] tortures. Although I do not forget that the King is the King, I need both the servants, the stewards, and the attendants of the King, that they might intercede with the King, my Lord [26], against whom I have sinned, and because I know that he does the will of those who fear him.

17. The Jew (said): Give me a clear example and a trustworthy testimony for these things which you have related.

18. Sergius (said): You ought not to have forgotten what I said — that for the sake of Abraham, Isaac, Jacob, and the holy bones of Joseph, the people was delivered many times from wrath in the desert [27]. For God said to Moses: *I act kindly towards thousands of generations on account of* [28] *those who love me and keep my commandments* [29]. **19**. When Sennacherib came up against Jerusalem and the city and its inhabitants were in distress, Hezekiah, the king, sent his servants and the oldest priest [30] to Isaiah asking him to pray for them that the remnant which had been left might not perish. When the prophet had prayed and made supplication, a word came forth to him from before
*p. 43 the Lord * and he said: *I will protect this city and save it for my sake, and for the sake of David, my servant* [31]. **20**. What more clear and certain example is then required by you? But if you wish to be convinced by the truth, then do not dispute, but accept and believe the things which

[24] i.e. God and his saints.

[25] Cf. DBS, *Against the Jews*, viii.3.

[26] Again DBS, *Against the Jews*, viii.3, closely parallels Sergius's argument.

[27] Cf. ch. xiii.20.

[28] This, although not the sense of the original text of Exodus, fits Sergius's argument better; otherwise why should he introduce the quotation in this context? EPHRAEM, *Commentary on Genesis and Exodus*,tx.,p.149, takes the biblical text in this way and interprets the ܠ as ܡܛܠ (on account of)

[29] Ex. 20.6, Dt. 5.10.

[30] An alternative trans. based on a slight emendation would be: 'the senior priests' — bringing the text into line with II Kings 19.2 P, Is. 37.2 P; cf. text.

[31] Is. 37.35, 38.6, II Kings 19.34,20.6.

are written — namely, that the bodies of the just give help to the places in which they are buried, and to the men who in faith honour them. For as the friends of a king, while they are persuading him, procure from him a gift for the man who perhaps is unworthy, so the bones of the saints give help to the districts in which they are buried. **21**. Let the bones of the prophet convince you, he who came from Judah to Bethel when Jeroboam and the people were offering up sacrifices on the altar to the golden calves which he had made and set up in Bethel [32]. How did the bones of the aged prophet who dwelt in the city escape? — because he protected his dead body (by having it buried) in the grave of the prophet of God [33], who proclaimed against the altar of Bethel the judgement brought about by [34] the sin of the priests and the people — (namely), the burning of the bones of the wicked by Josiah, the righteous king [35]. It is written that when Josiah saw the sign which was over the grave of the prophet he asked, '*What is the sign which I see?*' And they said to him, '*The grave of the prophet who prophesied this deed [which] you have done*'. *And he commanded*, '*Let no-one disturb his bones*' [36]. **22**. Thus the righteous are a protection, both in their lives and in their deaths, to the places and districts where they are present. Along with these which we have set forth, Sodom, in which there were thousands and ten thousands of men, bears witness. If only ten righteous men had been interspersed among them, it would not have been overthrown [37].

XV.1. The Jew (said): The things which you have said are compelling. Nevertheless, I wish to inquire again into this: You shall not touch the bone of a dead man [1].

2. Sergius (said): Know, like a wise man, that all the attention of the righteous man and of him who fears God is directed towards [2] God, as * David said: *On the portion of the Lord I directed my thoughts, that I* *p. 44
might keep your commandments [3]; *and in your law I meditated that I*

[32] Cf. I Kings 13.1ff.
[33] Cf. I Kings 13.30-32.
[34] Lit.: 'of'.
[35] Cf. I Kings 13.2.
[36] II Kings 23.17f.
[37] Cf. Gen. 18.32.

[1] Cf. Num. 19.11-22.
[2] Lit.: 'in'.
[3] Ps. 119.57.

might not forget your words [4]; *I will never* [5] *forget your commandments, for in them is my life* [6]. And he called him blessed who is like this, and said : *Blessed is the man who has not walked in the way of the wicked, nor stood in the counsel of sinners, nor sat on the seat of scoffers*; *but his delight is in the law of the Lord, and on his law he meditates day and night. And therefore he who is like this shall be like a tree planted by a stream of water, which yields* [7] *its fruits in its season, and whose leaves do not drop off* [8].

3. As a tree planted by a water course does not fear heat, and is not deprived by lack of water, so is the man of God. God is to him like the spring of water to the tree. He is planted by his side, and he draws from him everlasting life; and the impulse of his thoughts originates in him [9]; and the Spirit of God dwells in him as in a holy temple, as he said : *I will dwell in them and walk in them* [10]. **4.** But why do you think concerning the man who is like this that, because his temporal life has ended, his holiness and the power of his God concealed in him, as in Elisha, has also died with him? You will say that his bones are unclean. But as he is holy during his life, so also after his death. But the wicked and impious, the heathen and the sorcerer, and all the lying workers of iniquity, are unclean and defiled both in their lives and in their deaths. *p. 45 For as the servants of God mediate on him and he dwells in them, * so likewise does Satan (dwell) in his disciples. **5.** *The wicked devises impiety in his heart because there is no fear of God before his eyes*; *for it is hateful in his eyes that he should abandon his sins and hate them. The word of his mouth is trouble and deceit, and he does not wish to do good. But he devises trouble upon his bed, and he walks in a way that is not right in order that he may do evil* [11]. This man is defiled and unclean both in his life and in his death. Demons dwell on the bones of this man, and Satan also dances inside his grave and on his corpse. For in him and those like him the word which the prophet David spoke is fulfilled : *The rebellious shall dwell in the tombs* [12]. Flee from the graves

[4] Ps. 119.16.
[5] ܠܐ (not) added above and below the line by S.scr.
[6] Ps. 119.93.
[7] ܝܗܒ (yields) added above the line by or. scr.
[8] Ps. 1.1-3.
[9] i.e. in God.
[10] Lev. 26.12, II Cor. 6.16.
[11] Ps. 36.1-5.
[12] Ps. 68.6.

of such men! For the bones of such men are the abode of demons, and the meeting-place of fierce [13] devils. For Moses said : *You shall not keep a sorcerer alive* [14]. And he shall have no burial, but after his death his bones shall be burnt with fire, in order that his grave and his bones may not be [15] an abode for devils [16]. Are things as I have said, and has the truth become apparent, or will you still go on disputing?

6. The Jew (said) : They are as you have said, and the truth bears witness concerning them. But we Jews continue to hold [17] that which is written : He who touches the bones of a dead man shall wash his flesh in water and be unclean until the evening [18]. And in this we make no distinction whether he is righteous or a sinner, but (we hold) only that one should never touch the bone of a dead man. For the scripture does not distinguish (between them).

7. Sergius (said) : But because of this — because you do not make distinctions in your reading — error has taken possession of you [19]. Then make distinctions with regard to the question which I am going to ask * you. Which do you prefer — to cling to the bone of the righteous *p. 46
man [20] who has died, or to associate with a wicked man who is still alive?

8. The Jew (said) : As before God, it is indeed much better for me to approach a righteous man rather than to associate with a wicked man. For I do not forget that David said : *With impious men I shall not have fellowship* [21]. And he who cleaves to the wicked learns from his ways.

9. Sergius (said) : Then wherefore your accusation against us that we honour the bones of the righteous and the saints? For we trust, and also we know by experience, that the power of God dwells [22] in their bones. And cures and healing flow from them to those who touch them in faith, as life flowed from the bones of Elisha to the dead man who touched him. This testimony of Elisha is sufficient for us in place of ten

13 Or : 'accursed devils'.
14 Ex. 22.18.
15 ܢܗܘܐ (may be) added in margin by S.scr.
16 This looks like a midrashic expansion of Ex. 22.18.
17 Lit. : 'thus hold'.
18 Cf. Lev. 11.24ff, Num. 19.11ff.
19 Or : 'has ruled over you'.
20 ܕܙܕܝܩܐ (of the righteous man) added in margin by S.scr.
21 Lit. : 'eat salt'. Ps. 141.4.
22 The MS is pointed to give the past tense 'dwelt', but the force of the argument requires the punctuation and trans. 'dwells'; cf. text.

thousand arguments. And it is certain that many (arguments) will not convince the man who is not convinced by this. But he persists in his presumption until he comes to that teacher which will give him instruction.

10. The Jew (said) : And what is this ?

11. Sergius (said) : Everlasting fire, the worm which does not die [23], (and) barren darkness. When the flame of retribution roars before him, then he will accept instruction. And that which the Lord said will be fulfilled : *Ah, I will take vengeance on my enemies, and I will avenge myself on my foes* [24]. And again (he said) : *Woe to those who call evil good and good evil !* [25]

12. The Jew (said) : But can you show me that we are the Lord's enemies ?

13. Sergius (said) : The prophet of God, David, has testified, saying : *The enemies of the Lord* [26] *have denied him, and therefore their ruin shall be eternal* [27]. And you will not suppose that the prophet of God lies, (will you) ? What the prophet says, God says. Again he said : *I have hated your enemies, O Lord, and raged against those who rise up against*
*p. 47 *you.* * *And I have hated them with a perfect hatred* [28].

14. The Jew (said) : But how have we risen up against the Lord ?

15. Sergius (said) : As it is said in the second psalm : *They took counsel together against the Lord and against his Messiah* [29]. For you took counsel and you agreed among yourselves to resist the will of the Lord and to reject his Messiah, and you chose that a murderer and a robber should be given to you instead of the Lord's Messiah [30]. And the evil and sin which you committed is not enough for you, but still you pervert the straight ways of the Lord in which righteous Christians walk, while you, the wicked, stumble in them.

16. The Jew (said) : How do we strumble in them ? Explain to me !

[23] Cf. Is. 66.24, Mk. 9.48.

[24] Is. 1.24.

[25] Is. 5.20.

[26] i.e. Christ.

[27] Ps. 81.15.

[28] Ps. 139.21.

[29] Ps. 2.2. Note how Sergius omits the subject of the sentence, 'the kings of the earth', in order to make it serve his purpose better. Cf. Acts 4.25f, Dbs, *Against the Jews*, vi.3, and ch. xxi.13.

[30] Cf. Acts 3.14.

17. Sergius (said) : We journey in the way of righteousness and of faith, and God is our guide through the writings of his prophets. But you brand with blame and disgrace the faultless Way, and you speak evil against us, the upright. Your hands are entangled in evil, and you do not wish to know the truth, or although you know (it), you deny and suppress (it).

18. The Jew (said) : Say how !

19. Sergius (said) : You have forgotten what I told you — that you cleave to unclean and defiled sorcerers, and you are accomplices in their polluted deeds with adulterers, fornicators, murderers, and all evildoers [31]. Doubtless it does not enter your mind that you have even (one) ordinary sin or little defect ! But although, together with and among them, you are filled with every sin and provocative act, you find fault with us on account of the bones of the saints and the righteous, concerning whom God has witnessed that they are pure and holy through the signs and miracles * which he has done and is doing by their *p. 48
bones. **20**. But you resist God in your evil will, and where God pronounces (something) holy, you say, 'It is unclean'; and where you pronounce (something) unclean, it is clean. Therefore he said to you through David : *How long will you judge unjustly, and show partiality to the wicked ? Rescue the poor and the needy from the hand of the wicked.* For they, the wicked, in their wickedness, *did not know nor did they understand that they were walking* — that is to say, were judging — *in darkness.* And therefore, through the magnitude of their iniquity and evil, *all the foundations of the world were shaken* — that is to say, all the inhabitants of the world were agitated [32].

XVI.1. The Jew (said) : Enough ! For you have wearied me with your words. Let us approach another question. Let us see what you (can) say to us.

2. Sergius (said) : You question me and I will answer you according to the facts [1]. But nevertheless, I have told you that it is impossible for the truth to be overcome [2].

3. The Jew (said) : Behold, you have instructed me about the Mes-

[31] This must have been contained in one of the missing sections of the MS.

[32] Ps. 82.2,3-5; cf. the Introduction, p. 7.

[1] Lit. : 'as it is'.

[2] Cf. ch. xii.19.

siah, and you have instructed me about the bones of the dead, those whom you call martyrs. Instruct me now about the pictures and images which are the icons with which you have filled your churches — pictures and likenesses of every kind. For it is written in the law : *You shall not make for yourself any image or any likeness (of anything) which is in heaven above, or which is in the earth beneath, or which is in the water under the earth. You shall not worship them, and you shall not serve them* [3]. *I am the Lord your God who brought you up from the land of Egypt* [4].

*p. 49 **4.** Sergius (said): Now as * a wise man and teacher of the law [5], tell me the reason for this commandment; whence was it ? For every commandment [6] had one.

5. The Jew (said) : The reason for it was paganism, the multitude of gods, and the various religions of all kinds to which every region inhabited by men adhered.

6. Sergius (said) : And what were your people in that time ? Were they pagans or not ?

7. The Jew (said) : I cannot say that they were not pagans. For Moses said to God, when he was commanded by him to go down into Egypt : *Behold, when I say to them, 'The God of your fathers has sent me to you', and they say to me, 'What is his name ?' what shall I say to them ?* [7] This shows then that the name of the Lord had been no longer mentioned by their mouths as well as being forgotten from their minds. But perhaps there was someone who was aware of the God of our fathers. For it was impossible that absolutely everyone should have forgotten. But for the most part paganism abounded amongst them. For he said : *You shall have no other gods besides me* [8]; and afterwards he said : *You shall not make for yourself any image or any likeness* [3]. This was the reason for this commandment.

8. Sergius (said) : Indeed, I also know that this was the reason, and because of this I have questioned you — that you might testify to the reason. Now tell me, in the fear of God, in what way is this which we do similar [9] to the situation of that time ?

[3] Ex 20. 4f, Dt. 5.8f.
[4] Ex. 20.2, Dt. 5.6.
[5] See the Introduction, p. 70.
[6] ܦܘܩܕܢܐ (commandment) in margin.
[7] Ex. 3.13.
[8] Ex. 20.3, Dt. 5.7.
[9] Lit. : 'near'.

9. The Jew (said) : If it is not similar [9], you tell (me) what difference there is between that (situation) and this. For I hold thus — when compared, they are the same. He said : *You shall not make...* [3] But if you know something else, speak ! For to this we have been called — that we should seek the truth.

10. Sergius (said) : Do you know that when God commanded Moses about the Passover, he said : *When, in time to come, your son will ask and say to you, 'What does this service mean ?' say to him, 'With a mighty hand and an uplifted arm the Lord brought us out of * Egypt, when he killed all* *p. 50 *the first-born of the Egyptians'* [10] ?

11. The Jew (said) : Yes, it is true.

12. Sergius (said) : Again, when he who gathered wood on the sabbath day forgot, and the commandment came upon him and he was stoned, God commanded that they should make fringes on their cloaks — a reminder lest they should forget the commandments of the Lord and die [11].

13. The Jew (said) : And this also is true.

14. Sergius (said) : If they are true, as they are true, come, let us lay them down as solid stones beneath a building, and let us build upon them the argument which concerns us. Now I will fix your attention on their reminder [12], and do not forget (it), for doubtless I shall have to establish on them at length foundations (consisting) of suitable narratives. For it is impossible for a building to be constructed with one foundation. But tell me, which matters does the scripture relate — those which are regarded worthy as a reminder, or those which are not regarded worthy ?

15. The Jew (said) : Those which are regarded worthy are mentioned.

16. Sergius (said) : Why did he do this [13], and why was it necessary for them to be written down ?

17. The Jew (said) : It was indeed exceedingly necessary. For they were written down lest men should perish in stupid ignorance through forgetting them from their minds and not having them mentioned in (their) ears. For if, now that they have been written down and proclaimed, foolish ignorance still takes hold of the world, if they had not been written down, what would the world have come to ? For he said to

[10] Cf. Ex. 6.6,12.26,13.14f, Dt. 4.34.

[11] Cf. Num. 15.32-41. Cf. Jacob of Sarug, *Against the Jews*, II, 11.121ff.

[12] i.e. Israel's fringes.

[13] i.e. command the memorials of the dedication of the firstborn and the fringes.

Pharaoh in the scripture : *For this purpose I have raised you up — that I might show forth my power in you, and that my name might be proclaimed in all the earth* [14]. For as it was necessary for the battle of the Lord with Pharaoh to be written down, so it was necessary that all these matters which have been written down should have been written down. **18**. David (said) : *One generation shall relate your deeds to another* [15].
*p. 51 And again (he said) : *The things which we have heard * we have known, the things which also our fathers told us, so as not to hide* (*them*) *from their children but to tell* (*them*) *to the next generation* [16]. He commands [17] our fathers to inform their children in order that the next generation might know, and that the children who are being born and raised up might tell their children that their hope should be in God, and that, not forgetting the works of God, they should keep his commandments. For the children who are being born today or in every generation, whence do they know except from the teaching and from the instruction of the scriptures and the fathers ? If this were not so, men would be like beasts, and their fierceness would surpass every mad beast. For even though the scriptures, the laws, and the severe punishments of judges, now exist, wilful men still dare to trample under foot the precept [18] of justice. And if, as we have said, the scriptures and the laws had not terrified (them), it is certain that the world would have already come to an end and would not exist.

19. Sergius (said) : I confess to God that, behold, I have heard the truth from your mouth. Now therefore that you opened for me a convenient door, listen to me in the fear of God. This making of pictures and icons, which are inscribed with pigments in our churches [19], is confined to, and follows, the example of the scripture. And we depict in the church for the teaching and admonition of men every narrative which the scripture regarded worthy of being a reminder, that whatever the scripture relates for the hearing of the ear, the eye might see in the form of a picture. **20**. For Moses wrote : *In the beginning God created the*

[14] Ex. 9.16, but based mainly on Rom. 9.17.

[15] Ps. 145.4.

[16] Ps. 78.3f.

[17] Lit. : 'as he commands'; it is better to separate the two halves of a very involved sentence.

[18] Perhaps read the plural : ܦܘܩܕܢ̈ܐ (precepts).

[19] Or : 'in the naves of our churches'.

heaven and the earth [20]. So where we (wish to) depict 'in the beginning' [21], we draw the likeness of the various things which were created in the six days. As the mind of man is able to provide a likeness and a representation, so (we make one) of Abel, of Noah, of Abraham, of Jacob, Joseph, Moses, * and of the rest, one after another until Christ; and of *p. 52
Christ and all his saving work, and after Christ of every saint who set foot in the struggle of the contest against sin, the sentences of whose judgement [22] have been written down like those of Daniel and the companions of Hananiah [23]. **21.** When men enter to worship, and see these narratives inscribed on the walls of the church in front of their eyes, will they not ask the learned, 'What does this mean?' And the learned will teach and inform them in every way in accordance with it [24]. Then the ignorant will learn, and by teaching knowledge will enter, and from knowledge will be born the fear of God. For it is written : *The earth shall be filled with the knowledge of the Lord as the waters which cover the sea* [25]. **22.** Behold then, the earth has been filled with the knowledge of the Lord [26] through Christ, as it is written : *My salvation shall extend to the ends of the earth* [27]. Behold, the mountains, the hills, and the valleys, are full of the knowledge of the Lord. Tell me, when and where was the prophecy of Isaiah fulfilled which says : *Sing to the Lord a new song, his song from the ends of the earth, (you) who go down to the sea with its fulness, and the islands and (you) who dwell in them. The desert and its towns* [28] *shall rejoice, and the meadows Kedar inhabits. Those who dwell in the crags shall sing to him; and they shall shout from the tops of the mountains. And they shall give praise to the Lord, and declare his praise in the islands* [29].

XVII.1. How long will you refuse to understand that these things have been fulfilled and come to pass in Christ? For we do not have pic-

20 Gen. 1.1.

21 i.e. the story of creation.

22 i.e. the saint's martyrology in an abbreviated form or as a legend acoompanying the picture.

23 i.e. in the book of Daniel.

24 i.e. the picture and its accompanying legend.

25 Is. 11.9; cf. Hab. 2.14.

26 ܕܡܪܝܐ (of the Lord) added in margin by S. scr.

27 Is. 49.6. Cf. Aphraates, *Demonstrations*, I, 773.

28 ܘܩܘܪܝܗ (and its towns) added in margin by a scribe correcting to Is. 42.11 P.

29 Is. 42.10-12. Cf. Dbs, *Against the Jews*, vii.8.

tures for the purpose which you think we do [1], and we do not err with regard to them as you erred in every way, as the prophet Ezekiel re-
*p. 53 buked you. For through every door * which the Lord caused him to enter he saw the variety of your abominations — of the sun, of the moon, of Babylonian pictures, of the women weeping for Tammuz, and of many others with a variety of all sorts of paganism [2]. **2.** But behold, God transformed these heathen pictures into holy ones, and instead of the name of gods and goddesses being commemorated through the images of idols, behold, through the icons the name of holy men and women is commemorated, those who fought valiantly and bravely, and who trod under foot all the torments of the times of distress, and laid hold on the crown of victory through the faith of our Lord Jesus Christ. **3.** But you, in your folly and enmity towards Christ, call this observance, by which God is honoured by his servants, images and idols, so as to be always perverse and provocative. And you make the prophets liars and you pervert their words according to your evil will. Where their prophecies concerning Christ are clear and evident, you make yourselves like a dumb, senseless stone. For I have told you that all the evil and hateful things which Satan brought into the world, Christ has transformed into good and honourable things. Entirely for this purpose [3] Christ came — *that he might destroy the works of Satan* [4]. But behold, the good things appear to you as evil! *Woe to those who call evil good, and good evil!* [5] *Behold, I create new heavens and a new earth* [6]; and again: *For the former things shall be forgotten and shall not come into mind* [6]. *Behold, I create a new thing upon the earth: the female shall embrace the male* [7]. Tell me, what does this mean?

4. The Jew (said): This is certainly said about a woman [8].

5. Sergius (said): If it is said about a woman, it is not a new thing
*p. 54 and he who says that he creates a new thing is a liar. * For women are always embracing men, and what is there new about this [9] — *behold, I*

[1] Lit.: 'as you think about us'.

[2] Cf. Ezek. 8. Cf. APHRAATES, *Demonstrations*, I, 769.

[3] For Sergius's use here of ܚܠܗ ܕ, a use not recorded in the dictionaries, cf. ch. xviii. 15 and EPHRAEM, *Sermones de Fide*, III. 251.

[4] I Jn. 3.8.

[5] Is. 5.20.

[6] Is. 65.17.

[7] Jer. 31.22.

[8] See the Introduction, p. 73.

[9] Lit.: 'and where is that'.

create a new thing [7]. And again (he said) : *Cast out the old before the new* [10]; *and leavened bread shall not be seen in any dwelling-place of yours* [11]; *and every person who eats leavened bread shall be cut off from his people* [12], *for he has broken my covenant* [13].

6. The Jew (said): About the unleavened bread at the feast of the Passover — he commanded that they [14] should be made in order that they might remember the Exodus from Egypt, and that they might not forget the deliverance which he wrought for them from subjection to Pharaoh's oppression.

7. Sergius (said) : Remember what I said — that as the dream of Pharaoh was a symbol for the famine which was about to come, and (as) he expressed the years figuratively in cows and ears of grain [15], so through unleavened bread he indicated to you that you should reject the ancient customs as leavened bread before the new and pure unleavened bread of the new gospel of the new prophet, Christ, whom the Lord raised up for you from your brethren [16], according to the word of Moses who said : *Every person who does not give heed to that prophet shall be cut off from his people* [17]. See now how much the person who eats leavened bread and the person who does not give heed to the prophet are equal to each other ! [18] (See) that the meaning hidden in them is the same, and the sentence of judgement passed on them is the same — that is to say, everlasting destruction ! **8.** If then, you fear the decreed destruction, reject the old which is hidden in you, and do not let leavened bread be seen anywhere in the dwelling-place of your soul. Receive (and) refresh yourself with the sweet and wholesome wine which has come from the cluster which sprang up and rose from the

[10] Lev. 26.10.

[11] Ex. 13.7, Dt. 16.4.

[12] Ex. 12.15,19; cf. Gen. 17.14, Lev. 23.29f. 'Leaven' is here identified with the 'old, which the Jew must now reject; cf. ch. xvii.7, and cf. the use of 'leaven' in Mt. 16.6,11f, I Cor. 5.7f, and Ephraem, *Commentary on Genesis and Exodus*,tx., p.141, *Hymns on Unleavened Bread*, XVII. 5.

[13] Gen. 17.14; cf. Lev. 26.15.

[14] i.e. the unleavened loaves.

[15] Cf. ch. x.4.

[16] Cf. Dt.18.15ff, and ch. xxii, n.18.

[17] Dt. 18.19, but based on Acts 3.23.

[18] Sergius is using an exegetical principle favoured by the rabbis : he deduces that the offences are identical from the fact that the punishment prescribed for them both is the same. Cf. Rosenblatt, *Interpretation of the Bible in the Mishnah*, p. 26.

thirsty earth, a virgin vine as Isaiah said, which is pressed by a spear *p. 55 in the wine-press of the cross [19]. Then* your eyes which are darkened by error will be opened, and your soul which is sick in the infirmity of the law will be revived. And when the veil which covers your face has been lifted [20] and you have seen the light of the splendour of Christ, then you will say, "The Lord Christ is my strength and my glory, and he has become my helper. And I will give thanks to him and say, 'I give thanks to you that you have answered me and become my Saviour. For you have resued my soul from the death which is ignorance, and my feet from the slippery ways of sin' ". **9**. Know that as the bitter waters of Marah were changed into sweetness by the tree which Moses cast into them [21], so the world has been changed through the tree of the cross from the bitterness of ignorance to the sweetness of true knowledge. Everything which was worn out has been changed and become something (new). Thus instead of the heathen pictures of the pagan gods, behold the pious and dignified pictures of the servants of the most high Godhead. And instead of the images of idolatry which proclaimed the vile and abominable deeds of shame which their gods did in their lifetimes, behold, the icons of these proclaim the victory and the bloody martyrdoms [22] which they showed forth in their lives within the pagan communities. Yet the fulness of sin did not prevail over them. **10**. If you are willing, accept (it); but if not, behold, you have free will. And I am innocent of your blood as it is written by Ezekiel: *If you warn the sinner and he does not repent, you shall save yourself. But if you have not* *p. 56 *warned him, the sinner shall die in his sins, and I will require his blood* at your hands* [23]. **11**. If you could have profited from a multitude of

[19] Cf. Gen. 49.11f, Num. 13.23, Is. 5.1-7,7.14,65.8, IV Ezra 5.5 (Barnabas, xii.1), Jn. 15,19.34. For the imagery, which appears to have a Jewish Christian background, cf. Daniélou, *Theology*, p. 104f, *Études*, pp. 100-7, and Aphraates, *Demonstrations*, II,40, where the cluster = the people of Israel, and the blessing hidden in the cluster is the King Messiah = Christ. Here in the Disputation the cluster seems to have the narrower meaning (Christ), though the overtones of the wider meaning are present with the reference to Isaiah.

[20] Cf. II Cor. 3.14ff.

[21] Cf. Ex. 15.25, Ephraem, *Commentary on Genesis and Exodus*, tx., p.146, Aphraates, *Demonstrations*, I, 960.

[22] PS, *Thes.*, col.2342f gives for ܢܚܫܝܪ̈ܐ the meanings 'Hunters, slaughters, hunts', while Br, p. 424, adds the meaning 'wild animals'. So Sergius is probably referring to the martyrdoms in the arena where the saints were hunted and slaughtered like wild animals.

[23] Ezek. 3.17-21,33.8f.

words, there would have been many things to say to you. But if, on account of these (which I have said) , you do not repent even a l.ttle and you are not persuaded, then it is certain that these among the many (which I could have said) are not sufficient. First you asked me about the Messiah, and I invoked the prophets and they came and bore witness, but you did not accept (it). And you asked me about the bones of the righteous, and Moses, Elisha, and others, bore witness, but you were not persuaded. And again, I startled you with regard to the pictures and icons of the saints. But because your foot has slipped from the way of Christ's truth, behold, you seize and hold on to arguments in which you think you may stand firm. But you do not know that even they will utterly overthrow you so that you will not stand firm. **12**. However, let us leave the many (which I could have said) alone and let us bring in one (subject) to the debate and discussion, and let us seek the truth that it may stand in the midst and settle the dispute between you and me, which is this — whether the Messish has come or not. If he has come, behold, all that Chistians hold is the truth, and you are clothed in error as with a cloak. Now it is certain that he came to his native land [24]. And if you do not believe the things which have been said until now by the prophets, perhaps you have other prophets who teach you otherwise. Go, and like a madman who is insane and gone out of his mind who though many speak reason to him persists in his madness, search in them, and sit (and) wait for him until he comes. **13**. But concerning this about which we were talking I will add one saying, the conclusion of all these words. David said : *Precious in the sight of the Lord is the death of the righteous* [25]. If their death is precious in his sight, it is certain that also the bones of the righteous are precious in his sight. Then he agrees with * Christians who honour him whom *p. 57
God honours. And Solomon said : *The souls of the righteous* [26] *are in the hands of God* [27]; and so also are their bones. And Christ, our Lord, said to us : *He who receives you receives me, and he who receives me receives him who sent me* [28]. Then we Christians, whenever we kiss the pictures of the righteous, it is as though we are embracing their bones. And when

[24] Cf. perhaps Jn. 1.11. There may be a word play in the Syriac between mā'ṭā (native land) and 'eṯā (he came).

[25] Ps. 116.15.

[26] ܕܙܕܝ̈ܩܐ (of the righteous) added in margin by S. scr.

[27] Wis. 3.1.

[28] Mt. 10.40; cf. Jn. 13.20, Mk. 9.37, Lk. 9.48.

we honour their bones, we praise and acknowledge their Lord in them [29], to whom be praise, and honour, and dominion, and worship, with his Father and his life-giving [30] holy Spirit, for ever and ever, Amen.

XVIII.1. The Jew (said) [1]: I myself know that you have too much to say, and everything which I ask you, you refute with idle talk. For the doctrine of the son of Mary [2] is like this — a subtle contrivance of words. However, I want you to tell me why you eat the pig which is the most defiled and unclean among the animals, (and) which the law also declares more unclean and defiled than all animals. And also its appearance is abominable to look upon. For its food is every unclean thing on the face of the earth, and the scripture treats it as equal to the insects, vermin, and mice. For it said : *And the eaters of pigs' flesh, vermin, and mice, shall come to an end together, says the Lord* [3]. And now, say whatever you wish, and I shall be pleased to listen.

2. Sergius (said) : Explain to me in what way the pig is more unclean than the rest of the animals and the birds which the law declares unclean. For it says : *You shall regard as clean the animal which is cloven-*
*p. 58 *footed and chews the cud*; *eat it. But you shall regard as unclean * the pig which is cloven-footed but does not chew the cud. And again, you shall regard as unclean the camel which chews the cud but is not cloven-footed* [4]. Tell me now, in what way does the uncleanness of the pig exceed that of the camel and the ass of which you make use, or (that of) the horse and the mule which are utterly unclean according to the law. For they are not cloven-footed and they do not chew the cud, but you make use of them and think nothing of it ; only the pig is abominable to you. Tell me why you do this.

3. The Jew (said) : I have told you that it is made a grave for every unclean thing of the earth, for there is no limit and no measure to its

[29] Cf. ch. xiii.12.
[30] Or : 'living'; cf. ch. xxii.18.

[1] For a discussion similar to that which follows cf. APHRAATES, *Demonstration*, XV.
[2] Cf. ch. xviii.6. It is possible that behind the use of this title lie Jewish allegations that Jesus was illegitimate; cf. the *Jewish Encyclopaedia*, VII, p. 170, and the references there. But contrast *JACOB OF SARUG, Against the Jews*, III, 1.307, where the Christian author uses the title with no apparent overtones.
[3] Is. 66.17.
[4] Lev. 11.3-7; cf. Dt. 14.6-8.

uncleanness. For it is made a grave, as I have said, for all the filth of the earth.

4. Sergius (said) : I also have said that if (it is unclean) because it eats defiled filth, behold, the mule, the wild ass, the horse, and the camel, are clean and pure, since [5] they do not eat any filth, but their food is hay and grass [6]. Then eat these and grow fat like them, but do not eat of a bird, the cock, whose brother is the pig. If its food is pronounced unclean — for it eats everything it can and swallows up both reptile and vermin — do not eat it [7]. Behold the peacock which is beautiful and does not eat any filth ! Eat the peacock and the pelican [8], and the rest — any (animal) whose food is clean, whether it be cattle, or a (wild) animal, or a bird, or an insect of the earth. But you have broken the law of Moses, and made for yourself a new law [9].

5. The Jew (said) : Now I know that you have completely mocked me [10].

6. Sergius (said) : Truly I have completely mocked you, because you know neither the scripture nor the power of God, as * Christ, whom *p. 59
you call the son of Mary, said to your fathers, the Sadducees [11].

7. The Jew (said) : But how ?

8. Sergius (said) : As I have told you, if because of its food the pig is unclean, so are the cock and the fish unclean like it, and the horse also, (all of) which you have regarded as clean and pure. And the argument has led to the conclusion that they [12] are unclean [13].

[5] Lit. : 'and'.

[6] Sergius is being ironic, the point being that the law declares them unclean although they do not eat any fiflth. So the Jew's criterion for the pigs' uncleanness is totally inadequate.

[7] Another example proving the inadequacy of the Jew's criterion for uncleanness. The cock, although its food is filth, is not pronounced unclean by the law.

[8] The reverse of the situation with the cock. The law declares the peacock and the pelican unclean (cf. Lev. 11.18f) although their food is clean.

[9] MS : 'they have broken the law of Moses, and I will make for yourself a new law'. The meaning according to the emended text (for which cf. text vol.) is that by setting up a new criterion of uncleanness, whereby an animal is unclean according to the food which it eats, the Jew must logically declare clean animals whom the law declares clean, and *vice versa*.

[10] Sergius seems to be using the Aph'el of ܓܪܐ in the sense usual to the Ethpa'al + ܒ.

[11] Cf. Mk. 12.24.

[12] i.e. the cock and the fish.

[13] Lit. : 'the argument produces uncleanness'.

But in vain the law has said concerning them [14] that they are unclean [15].

9. The Jew (said) : We cannot say that they are clean, although their food is not unclean.

10. Sergius (said) : So then, you cannot say that the pig is unclean because of its food, or that all who eat unclean things like it are unclean in the same way as it is, or that those who do not eat filth are clean while the law declares them unclean.

11. The Jew (said) : I cannot pronounce unclean the cock and the fish who swallow filth, whom the law pronounces clean. And I cannot pronounce clean the horse and the mule because their food is clean, as long as the law declares them unclean.

12. Sergius (said) : Behold then, you fight against God who created them, and against the law which declares them unclean, and against yourself because you do not know the sense in which the law is to be understood [16].

13. The Jew (said) : How do I not know the sense in which the law is to be understood [16] ?

14. Sergius (said) : Because you do not distinguish its intention. For if you had distinguished its intention, you would have understood what it teaches.

15. The Jew (said) : Show me its intention and explain to me what it teaches. For entirely for this purpose we have come to this (discussion) that we might arrive at the truth, and that it might be clearly known with whom the truth lies. For you take offence at us and we at you. But I, as one who loves the truth, have drawn near to you, al-
*p. 60 though nothing [17] but my (own) intentions * has compelled me, because I marvel at your (adopting an) ascetic way of life [18] on this column, by which action you have devoted yourself to the restraint of an ascetic

[14] i.e. the horse and the mule, etc.

[15] The text of this paragraph is probably disarranged. The words ܘܣܘܣܝܐ ܐܦ (and the horse also) seem to be out of place, for it is the cock and the fish, not the horse, which the Jew has regarded as clean and pure. The Jew's new criterion leads to the conclusion that they are unclean, whereas, judged by the food it eats, the horse must be clean. It is the last sentence of the paragraph which refers to the horse, mule, etc., for by applying the Jew's new criterion the law's decree that they are unclean is reversed.

[16] Lit. : 'the sense which the law declares'.

[17] Lit. : 'no-one'.

[18] Possibly a play on words : ḥušāḇay (my intentions), ḥᵉḇušyāḵ (your ascetic way of life).

way of life like this [19]. Therefore, let us diligently seek the truth without anyone concealing the truth from his fellow. Tell me then, how do I not understand the will of the Lord from the reading of the law?

16. Sergius (said): Know then even you, like a wise man, that I have not devoted myself to this restraint rashly or needlessly, and not for the sake of anything uncertain, but for the sake of the clear and certain truth. For it is hateful for a labourer not to know his reward, or for a hired servant not to recognize his master. Therefore I know the reward of my labour, and I recognize my master. And therefore I do not keep silent concerning the truth. For I am the servant of *him who wishes that all men should live and come to the knowledge of the truth* [20].

17. The Jew (said): I also pursue the knowledge of the truth [21], and I wish that if you know anything besides these things of which you have spoken, you will explain (them) clearly.

XIX.1. Sergius (said): Do you acknowledge that the creator of all is one?

2. The Jew (said): I acknowledge that the creator of all is one and not two or many.

3. Sergius (said): And did he create all the clean and unclean things which the law distinguishes?

4. The Jew (said): Yes, and no other.

5. Sergius (said): And is what Moses wrote true? — *God saw all that he had made, and behold, it was excellent and good* [1].

6. The Jew (said): Yes, it is true.

7. Sergius (said): But how then does that which you hold agree with this which you have testified is true? If the creator is one and all that he has made is very good, then there is nothing which is unclean in his creation [2]. If it is good, * then it is not unclean; and if it is unclean, it is *p. 61
not good. For it is impossible for anything to be both unclean and good at the same time. For uncleanness is not good.

[19] Cf. the Introduction, p. 2, 61.

[20] ܕܫܪܪܐ (of the truth) added above the line. The quotation is I Tim. 2.4. and agrees with the Greek text against P. Perhaps Sergius knew the familiar Greek rendering, living as he did in an area heavily influenced by Greek-speaking Christianity.

[21] ܕܫܪܪܐ (of the truth) added below the line.

[1] Gen. 1.31.

[2] Cf. Aphraates, *Demonstrations*, I,732, who starts his discussion of the Jewish food laws with this point.

8. The Jew (said) : But why then did he declare unclean and make distinctions ?

9. Sergius (said) : It is not for you to say to me, 'Why did he declare unclean and make distinctions ?' but it is for me to require at your hand why indeed he witnessed concerning everything that it is good, and afterwards said, 'Declare unclean and make distinctions' [3]. You then, like a teacher of the law [4], and like a Hebrew who boasts in the law, tell me how God saw that all which he had made was very good, and after many generations commanded you saying, 'You shall not eat such and such ; you shall regard it as unclean'.

10. The Jew (said) : From the beginning the clean and the unclean were distinguished, as God said to Noah : Bring with you into the ark two pairs from all the cattle, (wild) animals, and birds, and seven pairs from those which are clean [5]. Behold, the clean were distinguished from the unclean, and not recently did the law make known the clean and the unclean.

11. Sergius (said) : When they entered into the ark he called the clean by name, that is, the harmless, which are exploited for food both by men and those (animals) which are unclean, namely, the wild, rapacious, and bold, beasts, which even until today are inferior in fertility — the lions, the leopards, and the rest. And again, behold, we see that these which are food are fertile [6]. Even this pig, whose name is detestable in your sight, is not placed on the side of the unclean by Noah's action. For it is not reckoned with the wild beast but with the driven [7] and those which are eaten. And because it is exploited more than all animals, so God has increased its offspring and fertility. By (doing) this the creator has testified concerning it that it is not unclean for men's food, for those whose conscience accepts it. **12**. But that you may
*p. 62 confirm * (the truth of) the argument for yourself, let us bring for a witness to it the passage which Moses related concerning Noah : *And God blessed Noah and his sons and said to them, 'Be fruitful and multiply,*

[3] Or : 'afterwards said that it is unclean, and made distinctions'.

[4] Cf. ch. xvi.4 and the Introduction, p. 70.

[5] Cf. Gen. 6.19f, 7.2ff.

[6] Sergius seems to be attempting to prove (not very successfully) that the distinction between clean and unclean animals in the story of Noah's ark refers to the difference between domesticated, fertile animals used for food, and infertile, wild animals which are of no use to man.

[7] i.e. the domestic animal.

and fill the earth. The fear of you and the dread of you shall be [*upon*] *every animal of the earth, and upon every bird of heaven, and upon every creeping thing which the earth breeds, and* (*upon*) *all the fish of the sea; into your hands they shall be delivered. Every creeping thing that lives shall be food for you. Like the green plant I have given you everything. Only you shall not eat flesh with its life,* (*that is*), *its blood* [8]. And he said the same things to those of the house of Adam, and he regarded them [9] as a green plant [10]. **13.** Where then is [11] the uncleanness either of the pig or of anything (else)? In the beginning and the middle and the end of the times he forbids only blood. God said : *Like the green plant I have given you everything* [12]. But will you pronounce unclean after God, the creator, has pronounced clean, and will you declare defiled that (concerning) which he said then, in the beginning : Like the green plant I have given you everything [12]? He said at the end of the times : *There is nothing from outside which by entering a man can defile him*; *but that which comes out from his heart, that defiles the man* [13].

14. The Jew (said) : But if, as you say, he regarded them in the beginning like the green plant, and in the end said that they do not defile a man, why through Moses did he increase (the number of) unclean things and distinguish the clean? For he said to them : *You shall regard as unclean every animal which is not cloven-footed and does not chew the cud* [14]. He explained again his statement concerning that which is cloven-footed but does not chew the cud, and he said : *You shall regard as unclean the camel, which chews the cud but is not cloven-footed. And you shall regard as unclean the pig, which is cloven-footed but does not chew the cud* [15]. * If they were regarded as the green plant and there is no un- *p. 63
cleanness, why then did he increase the prohibition and the commandment concerning them? For the law and the commandment were not instituted in vain.

15. Sergius (said) : O free man, understand like a wise man, that

[8] Gen. 9.1-4. Cf. Aphraates, *Demonstrations*, I,736.

[9] i.e. all animals.

[10] Cf. Gen. 1.29.

[11] ܐܝܬܘܗܝ (is) added in margin by S. scr.

[12] Gen. 9.3.

[13] Mk. 7.15; cf. Mt.15.11, and Aphraates, *Demonstrations*, I,728.

[14] Cf. Lev. 11.3.

[15] Lev. 11.4,7. Both Sergius's quotations from Lev.11 and those of the Jew show a certain amount of confusion. Both ignore the item : 'parts the hoof', both never quote the text exactly, and in some cases they both quote only their inferences from it.

there are no unclean things, but distinctions between clean and unclean things provide mental bonds to bind man's soul to God [16]. Because God knew that man's will had an inclination to fall into the sin of paganism, on various occasions he set round about the fence of commandments [17], that you might remain free to (worship) him, and that you might not wander in the pathless desert of error away from the knowledge of his worship. Like a skilful doctor who anticipates the illness with herbs and mixtures, incisions and cauterizations, that it may not spread in the body and result in destruction, so also God, wise in everything, was anxious that the race of men should not lose (sight of) him. **16.** He gave a commandment to every generation like that herb which is useful for its sickness : to Adam, that he should not eat from the tree of knowledge [18]; to Noah, that they should not eat blood [19] and (the covenant of) the rainbow [20]; to Abraham, the covenant of circumcision [21]; and because the ulcers and sores in the body of the world had increased, so to Moses God increased the commandments and the precepts as remedies for the healing of that generation, because it was full of a multitude of evils and of paganism [22]. **17.** But know this also, that for the just whose knowledge is sure in the love of God, nothing is defiled or unclean. Tell me, was Samson who ate honey from the skeleton of a lion [23] defiled ? Or was he who drank water from an ass's jaw-bone [24] unclean ? Or was Elijah who ate bread and meat from the mouth of unclean [25] ravens [26] unclean ? Were they condemned, or what accusation was laid against them [27] ? For, through the faith of our Lord Jesus
*p. 64 Christ, he who split * the jaw of the ass and caused water to come out for the Nazarite's thirst and sent the ravens to serve the prophet, proclaims

[16] Lit. : 'but (they are) the cause of the mental bonds of man's soul to God'.

[17] Cf. *Mishnah, Aboth*, I.1, III.4.

[18] Cf. Gen. 3.3.

[19] Cf. Gen. 9.4.

[20] Cf. Gen. 9.12f.

[21] Cf. Gen. 17.

[22] For the theory of successive covenants, each one granted to meet changing circumstances cf. Aphraates, *Demonstrations*, I,473f,497f, Jacob of Sarug, *Against the Jews*, III, ll.109ff, and Kazan, *Isaac of Antiach's Homily*, OC, 49, p. 73.

[23] Cf. Jud. 14.9, and Aphraates, *Demonstrations*, I,744f.

[24] Cf. Jud. 15.19.

[25] Cf. Lev. 11.15.

[26] Cf. I Kings 17.6, and Ephraem, *Hymns on Unleavened Bread*, XIX.15, Aphraates, *Demonstrations*, I,745.

[27] Lit. : 'followed them'.

clean all the foods in the mouth of those who believe in him, whether the pig or any other. **18.** Nothing can defile the heart in which God dwells and which is inflamed with love for him, as nothing which enters a fire can defile it, but it changes to its form everything which falls into it. For it is written : *The righteous* [28] *shall live by faith* [29]. And again, as nothing can defile him who fears God, so nothing is clean to the wicked and him who provokes God (to anger), but all the things which are clean in the law become polluted in the mouth of the wicked, as everything which falls into a trough of slime becomes unclean. Are these things true, or do they not seem to you to be true ?

XX.1. The Jew (said) : They are true and I cannot say that they are not true. For the truth which is in them compels me to say that they are true. But what shall we do about that which is written : *The eaters of pigs' flesh, vermin, and mice, shall come to and end together, said the Lord* [1] ?

2. Sergius (said) : I compare you very much to a foolish child, lacking in knowledge, who when someone shows him pure gold and precious pearls continues in his childish state, and does not desire any of them but nuts and things to which his childish state is accustomed. For you use the passage [2] like an infant and not like a discreet man who discerns the meaning of scripture. Now it is necessary for us to bring the passage forward that it may stand on its own, (and) that it may not through ignorance be wrongly treated. **3.** It is right that you should know that the prophet Isaiah* completely exposes your sins, those which were *p. 65
done in secret and in darkness, and (those done) openly and before the eye. You seemed to be like keepers of the law, and you boasted before strangers of being the sons of Abraham. Then the Lord saw that your deeds and words did not agree with each other, and he rebuked you through the prophet, and said : *But you, draw near hither, sons of the afflicted woman, seed of the adulterer and the fornicator. Of whom have you made sport, and against whom have you opened your mouth and stuck out your tongue ? Behold, you are the offspring of iniquity and a deceitful seed, who are comforted by idols under every tree of the forest. And you have slain children in the valleys under the clefts of rock. Your portion and in-*

[28] Cf. Text vol.
[29] Hab. 2.4, Gal. 3.11; cf. Rom. 1.17.

[1] Is. 66.17.
[2] i.e. Is. 66.17.

heritance is with the portion of the valleys, and also upon them you have poured out drink-offerings and offered up oblations[3]. *Upon the high and lofty mountains you have made your bed, and also thither you went up to offer sacrifices. And behind the doors upon the door-posts you have inscribed your memorial*[4]. **4.** (With) many things like these he reproaches your synagogue in the person of a harlot who, when she has hated her husband and loved others, devises against him all sorts of evil things[5]. So you also have not only eaten pigs' flesh but have not even kept one of the commandments, inasmuch as you have turned away from that commandment : *Love the Lord your God with all your heart*[6]. And it is clear from that (passage) that you have sacrificed children to demons[7], (concerning) which he said to you through Jeremiah : *It never entered my mind*[8]. In the same way that you utterly provoked God to jealousy, you have eaten pigs and slain children. And if there was anything else more evil than these, you did (it). This (about) which you asked was said concerning you, not concerning us Christians. **5.** Hear these things
*p. 66 * which Isaiah repeated concerning you, when he said: *I have spread out my hands all the day to a disobedient people, who walk according to their own opinions in a way which is not good; a people who continually provoke me to anger, sacrificing in gardens, and burning incense upon bricks, and sitting in graves, and spending the night in caves, and eating pigs' flesh, and polluting their vessels with dead bodies — to break the law and to defile the holy covenant that they might provoke the Lord to anger*[9]. *And they say, 'Go far away, do not*[10] *come near me, for I am set apart'. These were smoke in my wrath and a fire that burns all day. Behold, it is written before me : I will not keep silent until I repay them twofold into their bosom their sins and the sins of their fathers*[11]. **6.** Again, when he threatened punishment for your sins, he said : *And those slain by the Lord shall be many. Those who sanctify and purify themselves one after another in the midst, and eat pigs' flesh, vermin, and mice, shall come to an end together,*

[3] The MS omits ܥܠ ܗܠܝܢ ܐܬܒܝܐ (shall I be consoled with these things ?) by a scribal error (homoeoarcton); cf. Is. 57.6 P.

[4] Is. 57.3-8.

[5] Lit. : 'all evils'.

[6] Dt. 6.5.

[7] Cf. ch. v.6, and n.17 to ch. v.

[8] Jer. 19.5,32.35.

[9] For this addition cf. DIETTRICH, *Pešitto zum Propheten Jesaia*, p. 213.

[10] ܠܐ (not) added above the line by S. scr.

[11] Is. 65.2-7. Cf. DBS, *Against the Jews*, vii.11, APHRAATES, *Demonstrations*, I, 572

says the Lord. And I shall know your deeds and thoughts when I have come to gather all nations and tongues. And they shall come and see my glory, and I will set a sign among them. And from them I will send survivors to the nations, to Tarshish, and to Pul, and to Lud [12]*, and to Tubal, and to Javan, and to the distant islands, that have not heard my name or seen my glory. And they shall declare my glory among the nations, and they shall bring all your brethren from all the nations as an offering to the Lord, upon horses, and in carriages, and in chariots, to my holy mountain Jerusalem, says the Lord, as the Israelites bring the meal offering in clean vessels to the house of the Lord. Also some of them I will take for priests and Levites, says the Lord. As the new heavens and * the new earth which I will make,* *p. 67
they will remain before me, says the Lord [13]. **7**. Behold these things! You have compelled me to speak again about your ignorance, that I might show you that for us Christians everything is clean through the love of our Lord Jesus Christ. We have nothing which is defiled, just as you have nothing which is clean. For by the 'survivors' whom he sent to us, who are the holy apostles, he pronounced everything clean to us, and he chose us for himself to be priests and Levites, as he said. And behold, we serve him in purity and holiness, in celibacy and abstinence, and in poverty [14]. And he who eats, eats [15] in purity and gives thanks to God who has pronounced all (foods) clean. **8**. Behold, the perfect priesthood is ours and you *'have been left like a booth in a vineyard'* [16], which is plucked and remains without fruit. You are deprived of priesthood, prophecy, and kingdom [17]. And you make out the house of the nations [18] to be a shameful and derisery thing, and you are enemies even in the sight of those who are strangers to Christ. But we

[12] Faint marginal note below line may be rectifying the omission of ܕܢܓܕܝܢ ܩܫܬܐ (who draw the bow) from Is. 66.18 P.

13. Is. 66.16-22. The translation of the last sentence of this quotation depends on Sergius's interpretation given in the next paragraph, whereby the 'they' who remain stands for the 'priests and Levites' who are the Christians, or more narrowly, clergy and ascetics. The quotation has been cut off in the middle of v.22 because its continuation : 'so shall your descendants and your name remain', hardly suits Sergius's argument. For the interpretation cf. LACTANTIUS, *Divine Institutes*, IV.11.

[14] These are the ideals and key concepts of the stylite movement; cf. DELEHAYE, *Les saints stylites*, pp. cxliv-clxxvi.

[15] Trans. based on a slight emendation; cf. text vol. The MS reads : 'that which is eaten (he) eats'. Cf. Rom. 14.6.

[16] Is.1.8. Cf. EPHRAAM, *Sermon c. Jews*, 211f,217.

[17] Cf. Hos. 3.4, and ch. viii.5.

[18] i.e. the Church.

are truly honoured in the sight of all nations, as Isaiah said concerning us : *All who see you shall acknowledge that you are the seed which the Lord has blessed* [19].

9. The Jew (said) : He did not speak at all concerning you, but concerning us, the seed of Abraham, as he said to him : *I will bless you* [20], *and I will multiply you exceedingly* [21]. Why then do you take what is ours and make it your own ?

10. Sergius (said) : How is it fulfilled in your case [22] that 'all who see you acknowledge you' ? For it is not fulfilled with regard to you that all who see you by the sight of the eye shall know you. But everyone who sees us Christians [23] by the sight of the eye acknowledges us to be Christians [24] — that is, '*the seed which the Lord has blessed*'. **11**. Let the prophecy of Isaiah come (forward) : *Lift up an ensign to the nations. The Lord has proclaimed to the ends of the earth* : *Say to the daughter of Zion, 'Behold, your deliverer comes*; *behold, his reward is with him, and his wealth before*
*p. 68 *him'*. * *And they shall be called the holy people, the redeemed of the Lord* [25].
12. Again (he said) : *And I will bring forth a seed from Jacob, and from Judah an inheritor of my mountain*; *and my chosen shall inherit it, and my servants shall dwell there. But you who have forsaken the Lord, and forgotten his holy mountain, and filled tables for Fortune, and mixed for them bowls of wine, I will smite you* [26] *with the sword, and all of you shall bow down to the slaughter*; *because I called you, and you did not answer, and I spoke, but you did not listen, but you did what is evil before me, and you chose that which I do not desire. Therefore thus said the Lord* : *Behold, my servants shall eat, but you shall be hungry*; *behold, my servants shall drink, but you shall be thirsty*; *behold, my servants shall rejoice, but you shall weep*; *behold, my servants shall sing praises from the gladness of their heart* [27], *but you shall cry from the pain of your heart and from the crushing of your spirit. You shall leave your name to my chosen for curses* [28], *and the Lord God will kill you*; *but he will call his servants by another name* [29].

[19] Is. 61.9.

[20] Gen. 12.2. Cf. Jacob of Sarug, J, fol. 204r-v.

[21] Gen. 17.2.

[22] Lit. : 'with you'.

[23] The native Syriac word.

[24] The Greek loan word : χριστιανόι.

[25] Is. 62.10-12.

[26] Cf. Diettrich, *Pešitto zum Propheten Jesaia*, p. 214.

[27] Lit. : 'from the good things of their heart'.

[28] i.e. you will exchange your name for curses.

[29] Cf. ch. xi.11.

For behold, I create new heavens and a new earth; and the former things shall not be remembered, nor come into mind. But they shall rejoice for ever in that which I create[30]. And there are many things like these without my reciting all the scripture. **13**. You have persuaded me that we should come to the school of Isaiah, and I have acquired much profit. I have seen many things by faith, things which I cannot bring (forward now)[31]. Because you asked one (question)[32], as it were, against my position), so this one[33] has turned out to be against yours. However, I have two things to say to you that you may be convinced by them if you wish, one at the beginning of his prophecy and one at its end, although I am omitting many things in between. At the beginning he says :[*Hear*][34], *O heavens, and give ear, O earth : sons have I reared and brought up,* * *but they have rebelled against me*[35]. And again, at the end he *p. 69
says : *And you shall go forth and see the dead bodies of the men who have rebelled against me, whose worm shall not die, and whose fire shall not be quenched. And they shall be a spectacle to all flesh*[36].

XXI.1. The Jew (said) : I know that we have rebelled against the Lord our God from when our fathers sold Joseph, and in Egypt, and in the land of Canaan; as David said concerning us : *We have sinned with our fathers, and we have gone astray and done evil*[1]. If again, as you say, the sin of (killing) the son of Mary was added to us, behold, a double evil! Then woe to us! What has happened to us[2] that, instead of being the heirs and sons of Abraham, we are strangers and enemies?

2. Sergius (said) : Tell me, what good have you experienced[3] after the crucifixion of the son of Mary? Have you been aware that God has helped you to your advantage or to your disadvantage?[4]

30 Is. 65.9, 11-15,17f.

31 i.e. the many other testimonies he could have cited from the book of Isaiah.

32 i.e. concerning the quotation from Is. 66.17; cf. ch. xviii.1, xx.1.

33 i.e. the quotation from Is. 65.9ff.

34 An illegible marginal note is probably making this correction to Is. 1.2 P.

35 Is. 1.2. Cf. DBS, *Against the Jews*, iii.5,ix.4, APHRAATES, *Demonstrations*, I,774,789.

36 Is. 66.24; cf. ch. iii.4, and the Introduction, p. 14.

1 Ps. 106.6.

2 Possibly an echo of the Old Syriac rendering of Lk. 23.48; cf. also the *Descensus Christi ad Inferos*, XI.

3 Lit. : 'seen'.

4 Cf. DBS, *Against the Jews*, iii.23, and JACOB OF SARUG, H, fol. 41r-v.

3. The Jew (said) : If I say that we have profited, reality [5] refutes me. And if I say that we have suffered loss, again our dispersion and wandering in all regions testifies to our humiliation and adversities.

4. Sergius (said) : Come then, let us investigate diligently the real state of affairs until the truth manifests itself to us also in this as in all things [6]. Hear what Josephus, the wise man of the Jews [7], wrote, who related the destruction of Jerusalem after the crucifixion of the son of Mary. **5**. And Christ prophesied these things concerning it when he entered it on Palm Sunday [8]. It is written : *He wept over it*, and said to it, '*Behold, the days are coming when your enemies will surround you, and hem you in on every side*; *and they will overthrow you and your children within you, because you did not know the time of your visitation* [9]. *There will be wrath upon this people, and they will be delivered to the edge of the*
*p. 70 *sword, and be led away captive to every place*' [10]. * And again (he said): *But woe to those who are pregnant and to those who give suck in those days* ! *For there shall be tribulation the like of which there been has not from the beginning of the creation which God created until now, and never shall be, And if the Lord had not shortened these days, no human being would have been saved. But for the sake of the elect those days will be shortened* [11]. And when he was going out to be crucified, he said to the women who were mourning for him and to the crowds : *Daughters of Jerusalem, do not weep for me, but for your husbands and your children. For behold, the days are coming in which they will say to the mountains, 'Fall upon us', and to the hills, 'Cover us'* [12]. **6**. Come, hear now the chronicle of the wise Josephus, (concerning) what happened in the reign of the Caesars Vespasian and Titus. For God in his mercy gave you an opportunity for repentance for thirty-nine years [13], but instead of repenting you shed much blood of the saints in these years [14]. When your presumption again became apparent in your evil deeds, then vengeful justice was

[5] Or : 'the real state of affairs'.

[6] Or more literally : 'in all them', perhaps refering to all that has previously been discussed.

[7] Or : 'the Jewish scholar'; for the epithet cf. Bar Hebraeus, *Chronicle*, p. 48.

[8] For what follows cf. Eusebius, *Ecclesiastical History*, 3.7, and the Introduction, p.

[9] Lk. 19.41, 43f.

[10] Lk. 21.23f.

[11] Mk. 13.17,19f, Mt. 24.21f.

[12] Lk. 23.28,30.

[13] ܒܬܪ ܙܩܝܦܘܬܐ (after the crucifixion) added above line by S. scr.

[14] See the Introduction, p. 47f, 50, and *Descensus Christi ad Inferos*, XI.

executed [15] upon you in severe wrath, because of the rebellion which you declared against the Romans. **7.** For thus Josephus said : I think that all the tribulations and adversities of old are much less in comparison with those which have happened to the Jews [16] in Jerusalem [17]. For because the Jews have sinned against their creator, (their) good fortune has transferred to the Romans [18]. And this is the evil thing — that God darkened the mind of the Jews because of their wickedness [19]. And Josephus [20] said to the Jews, 'But you, which of the things blessed by the law-giver [21] have you done, or what that he has cursed have you left undone ? [22] Now as * it seems to me, even the Shechinah of God has *p. 71 departed from the sanctuary. And if a good man flees from an unclean house, and hates those who are within it, how much more shall God abandon an unclean people ! [23] No other city has endured such things as these, neither has any other generation from of old brought forth evil things like these [24]. It is God who has condemned the people of the Jews, and turned their every way of escape to destruction [25]. And from one gate of the city the dead went out — one hundred and fifteen thousand ; and six hundred thousand in number were cast out from the city wall [26]. **8.** Now I think that if the Romans had delayed attacking the city, either it would have been swallowed up in the abyss [27], or submersed in the waters [28], or it would have received the affliction of Sodom [29]. God bore with a more godless generation than these [30]. For

[15] Lit. : 'revealed'.

[16] ܠܝܗܘܕܝܐ (to the Jews) added in margin by S. scr.

[17] *B.J.*, I.12 ; cf. the Introduction, p. 41f.

[18] *B.J.*, III.354 ; cf. the Introduction, p. 42.

[19] The marks in the margin of the MS (for which cf. text vol., p. x) indicate that this is a quotation from *B.J.*, but if so, I have been unable to trace it. The quotation marks may be a scribal error.

[20] Lit. : 'he'.

[21] i.e. Moses.

[22] *B.J.*, V. 401.

[23] *B.J.*, V. 442.

[23] *B.J.*, V. 412f ; cf. the Introduction, p. 42f.

[24] *B.J.*, V. 442.

[25] *B.J.*, V. 559.

[26] *B.J.*, V. 567,569 ; cf. the Introduction, p. 45.

[27] A reference to the fate of Korah etc., Num. 16.32.

[28] A reference to Noah's generation.

[29] Cf. Gen. 19.24ff.

[30] *B.J.*, V. 566 ; cf. the Introduction, p. 43-5.

in this siege, out of immeasurable distress, even women descended [31] to inhuman cruelty in that they ate their children [32]. When the city [33] had been subjected to Titus Caesar, he said, 'Let God blot out the men who eat their children; and let him not leave under the sun a city in which mothers have eaten the fruit of their wombs. Yet (such food) befits fathers who, after this bitter suffering of hunger, (still) stand armed before the temple' [34]. **9**. Consider now that it has not been heard concerning any other people under heaven except you that it ate its children. But you do not eat the pig, yet you reproach us on account of it [35]. Can you say that God did these things to you unjustly?

10. The Jew (said): God forbid that I should say that God did wrong, *p. 72 * for it is written: *You are righteous, O Lord, and your judgements are exceedingly upright* [36]. And again (it is written): *The Lord is righteous in all his ways* [37].

11. Sergius (said): If the Lord is righteous in all his ways and you, as you say, do not go astray, why has your people, your city, and your temple which was unique in the world, received wrath like this? [38] **12**. Hear then the things which Eleazar the Jew said, who also was one of those who endured the tribulation. For Eleazar said: The people of the Jews, which from of old was the friend of God, has been committed to destruction. For if God had made peace with us or been only a little angry with us, he would not have averted his eyes from a destruction like this of all these men. For he has brought upon his holy city the fire of destruction from (her) enemies [39]. **13**. These are they who died in the famine — one million, one hundred thousand; and those who were killed and those who were sold — one hundred and sixty thousand [40]. These things Josephus, your wise man, related concerning the recompense which the God of your fathers gave to you because you crucified 'the deceiver of your people', as you said: *He deceives our*

[31] Lit.: 'came to'.

[32] Cf. *B.J.*, VI. 201-13.

[33] Lit.: 'it'.

[34] *B.J.* VI. 217f; cf. the Introduction, p. 37f.

[35] Lit.: 'the pig'.

[36] Ps. 119.137.

[37] Ps. 145.17.

[38] Or.: 'why has your people, your city, and your temple, received wrath like this, of which there has never been (anything) like it in the world'.

[39] Eleazar of Machaerus in *B.J.*, VII. 327f; cf. the Introduction, p. 45.

[40] See the Introduction, p. 49.

people, when he began from Galilee even to here [41]. But this is your recompense — the destruction of your city, (and) the burning of your temple, as he who does not lie spoke to you the truth: *Behold, your house is left to you desolate* [42]. And again, he added to you hunger, pestilence, persecution, dispersion, captivity, and the sword which lays waste after you, as Ezekiel said [43]. These things you have received in this world as a foretaste until he who is to come comes, that by him justice might be avenged upon you, as your crimes deserve. For not even yet have you been satisfied with error, and with the evil will which you have acquired towards God and his Messiah, (as it is written): *They took counsel together against * the Lord and against his Messiah* [44]. *p. 73

14. But let us continue with Josephus, and let us see the rest of these things. The judgement of God proclaimed long ago the burning of the temple [45]. And it was not burnt by the will of Caesar [46]. One false prophet deceived the people saying, 'The Lord says that all the people should assemble at the temple' [47]. See how you incline after error and after lying spirits of falsehood who like dogs and vultures smell the scent of an unclean thing! Thus you also are enticed after worthlessness. **15**. Let us follow again the rest of these things. The Jews more than the Romans set the city on fire [48]. All these evil things which she endured in this siege are more than the good things which were in her from the day that her foundations were laid. And doubtless, no other deserved a retribution like this except this generation which she also bore [49]. And when Titus Caesar entered and saw the great buildings, he was amazed at their fortifications. And he said, 'The power of God has fought, and it is God who has thrust down the Jews from these safe high places' [50]. But neither her pre-eminence [51], nor her wealth, nor her fame in all the world, nor her glory and her worship, was able [52] (to pre-

[41] Lk. 23.2,5; cf. Jn. 7.12.
[42] Mt. 23.38, Lk. 13.35.
[43] Cf. Ezek. 5.2,12.
[44] Ps. 2.2; cf. ch. xv.15, and n.29 to ch.xv.
[45] *B.J.*, VI. 250; cf. the Introduction, p. 39.
[46] *B.J.*, VI. 266.
[47] Cf. *B.J.*, VI. 285.
[48] *B.J.*, VI. 251; cf. the Introduction, p. 39.
[49] *B.J.*, VI. 408; cf. the Introduction, p. 39f.
[50] *B.J.*, VI. 409,411; cf. the Introduction, p. 40.
[51] Or: 'her great age'.
[52] Emending to the past tense by adding ܗܘܐ (was); cf. the Introduction, p. 41.

vent)[53] the destruction which came upon her. This is the end of the destruction of Jerusalem[54].

XXII.1. The Jew said : Then, when I approached you, I approached inadvisedly, for I was unaware that you[1] (Christians) had all this knowledge. But now I am amazed how, after knowing (all) this, there are among you some Christians who associate with us in the synagogue,
*p. 74 * and who bring offerings and alms and oil[2], and at the time of the Passover send unleavened bread (and), doubtless, other things also[3]. They are not entirely Christians, and some of our men have said that, if they were truly Christians, they would not associate with us in our synagogue and in our law. And now, because of this, we are all the more scandalized.

2. Sergius (said) : Understand now, like a wise man, that in every religion which exists weak and feeble (adherents) are found, and therefore a wise man ought not to be scandalized. However, the learned man is not scandalized, and the discerning does not stray, because milestones are placed on the king's highway, and it is plain and clear to those who see. If anyone goes astray and departs from it, he makes it clear about himself that he has strayed of his own accord or that he has gone out of his mind. **3.** So, let the way of Christ be laid for you as the highway of the great king; and like true guides the prophets stand upon it, and declare to everyone that the king has come. As it is written in Isaiah : *And you shall hear a word from behind you, saying, 'This is the way, walk in it'*[4]. For as long as a man walks in the straight way there is no need for another to call out to him from behind him and turn him back. But Isaiah, as one who sees hidden things, predicted your error to you, (namely), that after Christ (had come) you would go astray; and behold, you do go astray. Behold, Isaiah and the prophets cry to you always : *This is the way, walk in it*[4]. But you do not cleave either to the prophets or to reality[5]. And they[6] appear before your eyes. **4.** For it would

[53] The Syriac translates the Greek so literally that this needs to be added in the English translation to bring out the implied meaning.

[54] *B.J.*, VI. 442; cf. the Introduction, p. 40f.

[1] Pl.

[2] Emending ܡܫܝܚܐ (Messiah) to ܡܫܚܐ (oil).

[3] See the Introduction, pp. 63, 74-77.

[4] Is. 30.21.

[5] If the pl. ܠܫܘܪ̈ܪܐ is read (cf. text vol.), we could translate : 'or to the facts'

[6] i.e. the events predicted by the prophets.

have been right for you, as sons of Abraham and sons of the prophets, to be the nations' guides towards Christ, as are * the prophecies of the *p. 75 prophets. But because your foundation is moving away [7] from the faith which is in God and his Messiah, it is a trifling thing for you to seek to fall like a tottering wall and an abandoned fence [8]. That is what David foretold concerning you, that, on account of Christ, you would run into treachery [9]. And also you plotted to thrust him out from his honour, if it was within your power [10]. **5.** For you are no different from your fathers [11], who saw the miracles of Moses, but, during the forty days that he remained with God, a calf was implanted in their heart instead of him. So also you, wicked sons of impious fathers, have failed to wonder and be amazed at the signs of Jesus, and you have seized on a pretext in weak Christians who, doubtless, are the children of heathen and their mind has not yet been cleansed from the fear of their fathers' idols. Or they are the children of Hebrews, and the former custom still prevails [12] over them [13]. **6.** For a thousand thousands, and ten thousand ten thousands of times, God has called out to you with terrifying miracles which he performed before your eyes : *I am the Lord your God who brought you up from the land of Egypt* [14]. But in the twinkling of an eye you returned to the paganism which you loved. So also now, in the same way, you have left out (of consideration) [15] the prophecies of the prophets concerning Christ, and the time of the weeks of years [16] which they fixed for his coming, and the miracles * and mighty works which *p. 76 he performed among your people and among you, and the trials and

[7] If the addition ܗܘܬ is made (cf. text vol.) the trans. would be : 'because your foundation moved...' Or, leaving the text as it stands, we could paraphrase ܡܢ and translate : 'because your foundation is unstable (lacking) the faith...' There is a confusing alternation in this section between past and present tenses designed, no doubt, to emphasize the solidarity between past and present Jews in apostasy from God.

[8] Cf. perhaps Ezek. 13.9-16.

[9] Cf. Ps. 2.2.

[10] Lit. : 'if it came into your hands'.

[11] Lit. : 'you are not strangers to your fathers'.

[12] This meaning of ܢܓܦ is recorded only in the lexica of Bar-Ali and Bar-Bahlul (see PS, *Thes.*, col. 2441) ; normally it means 'hiss, rage', so the use of the word here confirms the meaning recorded in the lexica.

[13] Cf. the Introduction, p. 74-7.

[14] Ex. 20.2, Dt. 5.6.

[15] For the rendering of ܫܒܩ by 'leave out (of consideration) cf. the extract from Ephraem translated by Burkitt in *Evangelion da-Mepharreshe*, II, p. 139.

[16] Cf. Dn. 9.25ff.

evil things which came upon you after you crucified him; and you have seized on a pretext in some Christians who, in some respects, honour your synagogue. **7.** But perhaps you have lied about them, and you do these things because you love apostasy from the true God. For he, Christ, said to you: *If you believed Moses, you would also believe me; Moses wrote about me* [17]. For besides the symbols and types with which Moses depicted him, he wrote on that (subject): *A prophet like me the Lord will raise up for you from your brethren* [18]. Here clearly he shows him forth. But you, in your stubborn unbelief, interpret it of Joshua, the son of Nun [19]. However, if it had been written before Joshua, the son of Nun, arose and before Moses ordained him, there would, perhaps, have been a place for your argument. But if it is apparent that after he showed him to all the people, and ordained him, and filled him with spirit and power as the Lord commanded, and afterwards said, '*The Lord will raise up for you a prophet like me*' [18], it has been made clear that he did not speak about Joshua, the son of Nun, but about Jesus Christ, the Son of God. **8.** But let the book of Moses come..... [20] and let it testify concerning the truth. *And the Lord spoke with Moses and said to him,' [Go up] to this mountain of Abarim, and see the land of Canaan which I have given to [the children of] Israel. And see it, and [you] also be gathered to [your] people [as] Aaron your brother [was gathered], because you made bitter the word of my mouth in the wilderness of Zin in the strife [of the congregation], and you did not sanctify me at the waters before their eyes'. And Moses spoke before the Lord and said, 'Let the Lord,*
*p. 77 *the God of the spirits of all* flesh, appoint a man over the congregation, who shall go out* [21] *before them and come in (before them), and who shall lead them out and bring them in; that the congregation of the Lord may not be as sheep which have no shepherd'. And the Lord said to Moses, 'Take to yourself Joshua the son of Nun, a man in whom is the spirit, and lay your hand upon him. and make him stand before Eleazar the priest and before all the congregation. And commission him before their eyes, and bestow upon him some of your honour, and all the congregation of the Israelites*

[17] Jn. 5.46.

[18] Dt. 18.15,18, but following the text of Acts 3.22. Cf. ch. xvii.7, xxii.9,18, and Dbs, *Against the Jews*, vi.20, Jacob of Sarug, *Against the Jews*, I, 1,177, Silvester, *Discussion*, p. 85.

[19] So the Jews with whom Dbs debated — see *Against the Jews* vi.21

[20] A four or five letter word has become illegible in the MS.

[21] Or.: 'that he may go out...'

shall obey him [22]. **9**. These things are written in the book of Numbers which is the fourth. [But[[23] in the book which is called 'The Second Law', it is written thus : *Be perfect before the Lord your God. For these nations, which you are about to dispossess* [24], *give heed to diviners and soothsayers : but the Lord your God has not allowed you (to do) so. The Lord your God will raise up for you a prophet like me from among you, from your brethren; give heed to him. And the Lord said to me, 'I will raise up for them a prophet like you from among their brethren; and I will put my words in his mouth, and he shall speak to them everything which I command him. And the man who does not give heed to my words which he speaks in my name, I myself will require it of him'* [25]. **10**. What then do you want that is clearer than these ? How do these things fit the servant of Moses ? For the Lord and Moses said that the prophet who was to arise would be like Moses. And in what respect did the disciple, Hoshea [26] the son of Nun, resemble, and (in what respect) was he like, his master Moses ? What laws did he lay down ? [27] Or did he make and deliver a covenant to the world ? But God [28] taught him not to turn aside from the law of his master, neither to the right nor to the left, and that he should meditate on it night and day [29]. Again the scripture testifies * and says: *And there has never again arisen in Israel* *p. 78
a prophet like Moses, whom the Lord knew face to face [30]. **11**. But Jesus Christ is not only like Moses, but his glory is many times greater than that of Moses. For Moses was only called the son of a virgin [31] when he was not the son of a virgin; but Christ was truly the son of a virgin. For the reality is greater than the type, and the substance than the shadow. Moses is the type, and Christ is the anti-type [32] and the truth [33].

22 Num. 27.12-20.

23 Part of this word may be visible in the MS.

24 Lit. : 'inherit'.

25 Dt. 18.13-15,17f.

26 Sergius uses this form of Joshua's name here to emphasize the difference between him and Jesus Christ. 'Joshua' and 'Jesus' are identical names in Syriac — ܝܫܘܥ.

27 Cf. DBS, *Against the Jews*, vi.21.

28 Lit. : 'he'.

29 Cf. Josh. 1.7f.

30 Dt. 34.10.

31 Referring to the adoption of Moses by Pharaoh's daughter — Ex. 2.10. For this comparison between Pharaoh's daughter and Mary cf. JACOB OF SARUG, *Against the Jews*, I,ll. 181-5.

32 Or : 'original, prototype'.

33 Cf. APHRAATES, *Demonstrations*, I, 524,957ff.

For as the child of a virgin is greater than the name 'the son of a virgin', so when the dispensation of Moses [34] and that of Christ are compared with each other, the dispensation of Christ [35] and his signs are more glorious than of Moses. **12.** But you have left out (of consideration) the miracles, the mighty deeds, and the wonders, and behold, you are scandalized by some Christians who give oil or bring unleavened bread to your provocative [36] synagogue. For it is not a house of prayer as you in your error think, but your synagogue is a house of wrath and anger, as it is written concerning you : *Their prayer shall be sin* [37]. And in Isaiah it is written : *When you spread forth your hands, I will avert my eyes from you*; *and even though you multiply prayer, I will not listen, for your hands are full of blood* [38]. **13.** Now then, you think that the blood of which Isaiah says your hands are full, is the blood of bulls and sheep. The prophet contended with your fathers whose hands were full of the blood of the prophets and the righteous, but he intended the prophecy for you, the children of sinners on whose hands the blood of Christ is spotted. As it is written : *You shall place a spot upon them, and you shall set your preparation* — that is, your wrath — *against their faces* [39]. For
*p. 79 whenever your fingers are stretched forth * in prayer, not only is your prayer not heard, but also the wrath of the God is aroused against you. For as your wrath is all the more aroused against a man if he kills your son, and, (with) his body and his hands sprinkled [40] with gifts, and when he draws near to you, you see the blood of your beloved on his fingers; so also you, by your prayer and your sacrifices, arouse the wrath of God against you and against him who associates with you. **14.** And as again, if a man comes with the murderer of your son to make supplication to you wishing to please the murderer; and you, because you see the blood on the murderer's hands, treat with contempt the gifts which they offer to you, and look upon them both with one threatening glance full of wrath and indignation; so every Christian who offers anything in your synagogue is regarded before God. **15.** This man in

[34] Lit. : 'that of Moses'.

[35] i.e. the whole period from Christ's conception to his ascension; cf. ch.x.6 and DBS, *Against the Jews*, vii.16.

[36] i.e. which provokes God to anger.

[37] Ps. 109.7.

[38] Is. 1.15; cf. APHRAATES, *Demonstrations*, I,182.

[39] Ps. 21.12.

[40] Or : 'defiled'.

his madness is undecided with regard to them both, and in his folly he thinks thus : If Christianity is good, behold, I am baptised as a Christian. But if Judaism is also useful, behold, I will associate partly with Judaism that I might hold on to the sabbath. This is how his mind has been working. Or perhaps he does these things because he stands in awe of men. In his madness he has forgotten * (*p. 80) that which is written: *The Lord is* (*a God*) [41] *of knowledge, and crafty devices do not stand firm before him* [42]. And (he has forgotten) this : *God will scatter the bones of those who please men* [43]. **16**. For your fathers were not disheartened by all the signs which God performed through Moses in Egypt, and in the sea, and in the desert, and until he went up Mount Sinai. Yet they would set them [44] aside (by) following the calf which they had forged, and they would say, '*This is your god, O Israel, who brought you up from the land of Egypt*' [45]. And you, just like your fathers, when you saw the signs of Jesus — the sick who were healed, the lepers who were cleansed, the lame who walked, the withered who were restored, the blind (whose eyes) were opened, the paralysed who were made straight, the demons who were driven away, the elements which were changed, (and) the dead who rose — you dared to say, '*This man does not cast out demons except by Beelzebub, the prince of the devils*' [46]. After all these miracles and wonders you, the sons of 'the sons of vipers' [47], say now, 'Christians scandalize us'. **17**. Therefore he will name you sons of darkness and the very sons of those who are disobedient to God. *You loved curses and you did not delight in blessings* [48], and it is a trifling thing for you to seek to depart from God. And you were clothed with curses like armour [49], as David said concerning you. And behold, we see that like water and oil that curse has entered into your bones. And it is to you like a cloak for the body, and like a girdle, all the time [50]. David [51] explained and said : *This is the work of those who malign the Lord* [52]. For

[41] P omits the אֵל of Mt; hence the hiatus in the sense.

[42] I Sam. 2.3.

[43] Ps. 53.5.

[44] i.e. the signs performed by Moses.

[45] Ex. 32.4, Neh. 9.18. Cf. Ephraem, *Sermon c. Jews*, 216, dbs, *Against the Jews*, iv.22.

[46] Mt. 12.24.

[47] Cf. Mt. 3.7.

[48] Ps. 109.17.

[49] Cf. Ps. 109.18.

[50] Cf. Ps. 109.18f.

[51] Lit. : 'he'.

[52] Ps. 109.20.

you are the ones who maligned the Lord Christ. **18**. But because you boast in Moses, let us return to Moses, and as [53] we began from him [54], so let us end with him. *The Lord will raise up for you a prophet like me*
*p. 81 *from * your brethren* [55]. *And I will put my words in his mouth, and every person who does not give heed to that prophet who speaks in my name shall perish* [56]. And also Christ said to you : *I have come in the name of my Father, and you do not receive me; if another should come in his own name, you would receive him* [57]. Here he indicated the false and deceiving Messiah whom you in your error are expecting. David said : *Blessed is he who comes in the name of the Lord* [58], to whom be glory, and honour, and dominion, with his Father and his life-giving holy Spirit [59], for ever and ever Amen.

19. The Disputation which was composed by Sergius the Stylite, who (lived) in Gousit, against a Jew who disputed with him, is finished. Let everyone who reads pray for the sinner, Romanus the abbot, who copied (it) out for...... [60].

[53] The MS reads ܐܝܟܐ ܕ which means 'where', but the context requires the meaning 'as'; perhaps it is an error for ܐܝܟ ܕ.

[54] Cf. ch. i.2.

[55] Dt. 18.15, but following the text of Acts 3.22; cf. n. 18 above.

[56] Dt. 18.18f.

[57] Jn. 5.43.

[58] Ps. 118.26. Cf. DBS, *Against the Jews*, v.16.

[59] Or : 'living holy Spirit'.

[60] The colophon is incomplete; see the Introduction to the Text vol., p. XI. We can only guess the meaning of ܠܪܫ, especially as there is no diacritical point on the ܪ. Reading ܠܕܫ would give the trans.: 'who wrote (this) treatise)'. Any of the numerous compounds of ܪܫ could be read; e.g. ܠܪܫ ܕܝܪܐ (for the abbot), or : ܠܪܫ ܐܒ̈ܗܘܬܐ (for the bishop).

INDEX OF BIBLICAL REFERENCES

INDEX OF LITERARY WORKS

INDEX OF SUBJECTS AND PROPER NAMES

CONTENTS